John Adams Vinton

Vinton Book: Africa, Asia, Papal Lands

John Adams Vinton

Vinton Book: Africa, Asia, Papal Lands

ISBN/EAN: 9783743308732

Manufactured in Europe, USA, Canada, Australia, Japa

Cover: Foto ©Andreas Hilbeck / pixelio.de

Manufactured and distributed by brebook publishing software (www.brebook.com)

John Adams Vinton

Vinton Book: Africa, Asia, Papal Lands

V I N T O N   B O O K   C O P Y

VOLUME I

Reverend John A. Vinton, then of South Boston, later of Winchester, Massachusetts, compiled in 1869 brief biographies of missionaries of the American Board from the beginning of the Board's history till 1869, writing them in longhand in a blank book.

Mr. Vinton died November 13, 1877

The biographies were brought down to 1878 by Dr. Alfred O. Treat. From 1878 to 1886 the notices were prepared by Miss A.M. Chapin. In copying the Vinton Book, we have divided it into four volumes.

Volume 1 covers the Missions in:-

AFRICA
ASIA: Eastern, China, Japan
ASIA: Southern, India and Ceylon
PAPAL LANDS: Austria, Italy, Spain, Mexico

Addenda pages (17A and 19A) supplied by Dr. Ross Shiels
164 Hamilton St. (#508)
Pretoria 0083
South Africa

Name	Page
Abbott, Amos	121
Abbott, Mrs. Amos (Anstress)	122
Abbott, Justin E.	134
Abbott, Mrs. J. E. (Camilla)	135
Abeel, David	27, 34, 74
Abraham, Andrew	16
Abraham, Mrs. A. (Sarah)	16
Adams, Arthur H., M.D.	90
Adams, Mrs. A. H.	90
Adams, Edwin A.	100
Adams, Mrs. E. A.	100
Adams, Henry M.	5
Adams, Newton, M.D.	13
Adams, Mrs. N. (Sarah)	13
AFRICA: EAST CENTRAL	25
AFRICA: SOUTH AFRICA MISSION	11
AFRICA: WEST CENTRAL AFRICA	8
AFRICA: WESTERN	1
Agnew, Eliza	159
Aiken, Edwin E.	67
Aiken, Mrs. E. E. (Maud)	67
Aiken, Mrs. E. E. (Rose)	67
Aitchison, Wm.	50
Alexander, Walter S.	101, 102
Alexander, Mrs. W. S.	101, 102
Alexy, Gustave	111
Allchin, George	88
Allchin, Mrs. George	89
Allen, David O.	118
Allen, Mrs. D. O. (Myra)	118
Allen, Mrs. D. O. (Orpah)	118
Allen, Mrs. D. O. (Azubah)	119
Ament, William S.	63
Ament, Mrs. W. S.	63
AMOY MISSION	34
Anderson, Martha A.	138
Andrews, Mary E.	58
Apthorp, George H.	146
Apthorp, Mrs. G. H. (Mary)	146
ARCOT MISSION	137
Ashley, Harriet S.	138
Ashley, Sarah W.	180
Atkinson, John L.	82
Atkinson, Mrs. J. L.	83
Atkinson, William H.	130
Atkinson, Mrs. W. H. (Calista)	130
Atwood, Iraeaual., M.D.	67, 69
Atwood, Mrs. I. J.	67, 69
AUSTRIA: MISSION TO	99
Bagster, Walter W.	8
Baldwin, Caleb C.	39
Baldwin, Mrs. C. C.	39
Ball, Dyer, M.D.	29, 77C
Ball, Mrs. Dyer (Isabella)	30, 77C
Ball, Mrs. Dyer (Lucy)	30
Ballantine, Henry	122
Ballantine, Mrs. Henry (Elizabeth)	122
Ballantine, Henry W.	129
Ballantine, Mrs. H. W. (Mary)	130
Ballantine, William O., M.D.	138
Ballantine, Mrs. W. O. (Alice)	139
Ballantine, Mrs. W. O. (Josephine)	139
Bardwell, Horatio	116
Bardwell, Mrs. H. (Rachel)	116
Barker, William P.	127
Barker, Mrs. W. P.	128
Barrows, Martha J.	93
Bates, James A.	155
Bates, Mrs. J. A. (Sarah)	155
Beach, Harlan P.	65
Beach, Mrs. H. P.	65
Benham, Nathan S.	75
Benham, Mrs. N. S.	76
Berry, John C., M.D.	90
Berry, Mrs. J. C.	90
Best, Jacob	4
Best, Mrs. J. (Gertrude)	4
Beveridge, John	103
Bissell, Arthur D.	135
Bissell, Mrs. A. D. (Ellen)	135
Bissell, Edwin C.	101
Bissell, Mrs. E. C.	101
Bissell, Henry M.	109
Bissell, Mrs. H. M.	109
Bissell, Lemuel	127
Bissell, Mrs. L. (Mary)	127
Blake, Hannah	112
Blakely, Josiah B.	44
Blakely, Mrs. J. B.	44
Blodget, Henry	49
Blodget, Mrs. H.	50
Boggs, George W.	121
Boggs, Mrs. G. W. (Isabella)	121
Bonney, Samuel W.	30
Bonney, Mrs. S. W.	30
Bowen, George	127
Bradley, Dan B., M.D.	75
Bradley, Mrs. D. B.	75
Brewster, Frederick H.	32
Brewster, Mrs. F. H.	32
Bridgman, Elijah C.	27, 48
Bridgman, Mrs. E. C. (Eliza)	49
Bridgman, Henry M.	19
Bridgman, Mrs. H. M. (Laura)	19
Bridgman, James G.	30
Brown, Emily M.	95
Brown, Sarah F.	159
Bruce, Henry J.	129
Bruce, Mrs. H. J.	129

Bryant, James C.	13		CHINA: CANTON MISSION	27
Bryant, Mrs. J. C. (Dolly)	14		Clapp, Dwight H.	71
Burgess, Ebenezer	123		Clapp, Mrs. D. H.	71
Burgess, Mrs. E. (Mary)	123		Clapp, Sarah B.	
Burgess, Mrs. E. (Abigail)	123		See Goodrich, Chauncey	
Burnell, Alfred H.	178		Clark, Albert W.	99
Burnell, Mrs. A.H.(Abbie)	178		Clark, Mrs. A. W. (Nellie)	100
Burnell, Thomas S.	159,171		Clark, Mrs. A. W. (Ruth)	100
Burnell, Mrs. T. S.(Martha)	159,171		Clark, Walter H.	6
			Clarkson, Virginia(See Mrs.C.M.Cady)	
Bushnell, Albert	3		Colby, Abbie May	94
Bushnell, Mrs. A. (Lydia)	3		Cope, Edward	149,165
Bushnell, Mrs. A. (Lucina)	3		Cope, Mrs. Edward (Emily)	149
Butler, John Q. A.	20		Crane, Nathaniel M.	165
Butler, Mrs. J.Q.A. (Anna)	20		Crane, Mrs. N. M. (Julia)	165
			Crawford, Matthew A.	108
Cady, Chauncey M.	70,89		Crawford, Mrs. M. A.	108
Cady, Mrs. C. M.	90,94		Cummings, Seneca	38
Campbell, John M.	2		Cummings, Mrs. Seneca	39
CANTON MISSION	27		Curtis, William W.	86
Capell, Mary A.	159,165		Curtis, Mrs. W.W. (Delia)	86
CAPE PALMAS MISSION	1		Curtis, Mrs. W.W. (Lydia)	86
Capron, William B.	171			
Capron, Mrs. W. B. (Sarah)	172		Daughaday, Mary A.	95
Cary, Otis	87		Davis, Anna Young	94
Cary, Mrs. Otis	87		Davis, Jerome D.	80
Case, Alden Buel	105		Davis, Mrs. J.D.(Frances)	81,95,97
Case, Mrs. A. B.	106		Davis, Mrs. J.D.(Sophia)	80
Caswell, Jesse	76		Davis, Robert H.	88,97
Caswell, Mrs. Jesse	76		Davis, Mrs. R. H.	88,97
CEYLON MISSION	141		Day, Laura A.	20
Champion, George	12		Dean, Samuel C.	128
Champion, Mrs. (Susan)	12		Dean, Mrs. S. C. (Elizabeth)	128
Chandler, Gertrude A.	182		DeForest, John K. H.	84
Chandler, John E.	169		DeForest, Mrs. J. K. H.	85
Chandler, Mrs. J.E.(Charlotte)	169		DeRiemer, William E.	155
			DeRiemer, Mrs. Wm. E.(Emily)	156
Chandler, John S.	175		Dexter, Granville M.	83
Chandler, Mrs. J.S. (Jane)	175		Dexter, Mrs. G. M.	83
Chandler, Mrs. J.S. (Henrietta)	176,182		Dickinson, James T.	77A
			Diament, Naomi	80
Chandler, Henrietta S.	181		Diver, William B., M.D.	32
Chapin, Franklin M.	64		Doane, Edward T.	85
Chapin, Mrs. F. M.	64		Doane, Mrs. E. T.	85
Chapin, Jane E.	60		Dohne, Jacob L.	17
Chapin, Lyman D.	51		Dohne, Mrs. J.L.(Caroline)	17
Chapin, Mrs. L. D.	51		Doolittle, Justus	40
Chapin, William W.	130		Doolittle, Mrs. J. (Louisa)	40
Chapin, Mrs. W. W.(Catharine)	130		Doolittle, Mrs. J. (Lucy)	40
Cherry, Henry	164		Doolittle, Mrs. J. (Sophia)	40
Cherry, Mrs. Henry(Charlotte)	164		Doty, Elihu	35
Cherry, Mrs. Henry(Henrietta)	164		Doty, Mrs. E. (Clarissa)	35
Cherry, Mrs. Henry(Jane)	159,164		Doty, Mrs. E. (Eleanor)	35
Chester, Edward, M.D.	172		Dudley, Julia E.	92
Chester, Mrs. E. (Sophia)	172		Dulles, John W.	165

Dutton, George A.	105	Green, Samuel F., M.D.	158
Dwight, Robert O.	164	Green, Mrs. S. F.(Margaret)	158
Dwight, Mrs. R. O. (Mary)	164,183	Greene, Daniel C.	72
		Greene, Mrs. D. C.	73
EASTERN ASIA	27	Griswold, Benjamin	2
Eaton, James D.	105	Griswold, Mrs. B. (Mary)	2
Eaton, Mrs. J. D.	105	Grout, Aldin	12
Eckard, James R.	148,163	Grout, Mrs. A.(Hannah)	13
Eckard, Mrs. J. R.(Margaret)	148	Grout, Mrs. A.II(Charlotte)	13
Edwards, John	108	Grout, Lewis	14
Edwards, Mrs. John	108	Grout, Mrs. Lewis (Lydia)	14
Edwards, Mrs. Mary Kelley	20	Gulick, John T.	52,88
Evans, Jane G.	60	Gulick, Mrs. J. T. (Emily)	52
		Gulick, Mrs. J. T. (Frances)	52,88,93
Fairbank, Samuel B.	125		
Fairbank, Mrs. S. B. (Abbie)	125	Gulick, Julia A. E.	92,98
Fairbank, Mrs. S. B. (Mary)	125	Gulick, Luther H., M.D.	102,110
Farrar, Cynthia	138	Gulick, Mrs. L. H.	102,110
Fay, William E.	9	Gulick, Orramel H.	80,97
Fay, Mrs. W. E. (Annie)	9	Gulick, Mrs. O. H.	80,97
Fletcher, Adin H.	150	Gulick, Thomas L.	111
Fletcher, Mrs. A. H.	151	Gulick, Mrs. T. L.	111
FOOCHOW MISSION	37	Gulick, William H.	110
Ford, George	169	Gulick, Mrs. W. H.	110
Ford, Mrs. George (Ann)	169	Gunnison, Effie B.	96
Ford, Henry A., M.D.	6	Gutterson, George H.	177
Ford, Mrs. H. A. (Olivia)	6	Gutterson, Mrs. G. H. (Emma)	177
French, Henry S. G.	76		
French, Mrs. H.S.G.	76	Hager, Charles R., M.D.	73
French, Ozro	123	Hager, Mrs. C. R. (Lizzie)	73
French, Mrs. Ozro (Jane)	123	Hager, Mrs. C. R. (Marie)	73
Frost, Edmund	117	Hale, Flora J. See Isaac Pierson	
Frost, Mrs. E.(Clarissa)	118,146	Hall, Alanson C.	163
		Hall, Mrs. A. C.	163
Gaines, Marshall R.	89	Hall, Gordon	115
Gaines, Mrs. M. R.	89	Hall, Mrs. Gordon	115
Gardner, Fannie A.	94	Hance, Gertrude R.	20
Garretson, Elsie M.	47	Harding, Charles	128
Garrett, James	135	Harding, Mrs. Charles (Julia)	128
Garrett, Mrs. James	136	Harding, Mrs. C. (Elizabeth)	129
Gates, Lorin S.	133	Harding, Ruby E.	140
Gates, Mrs. L.S.(Frances)	134	Harris, Alice B.	48
Goodenough, Herbert D.	23	Hartley, Carrie	161
Goodenough, Mrs. Herbert(Caroline)	23	Hartwell, Charles	40
		Hartwell, Mrs. C. (Hannah)	41
Goodrich, Chauncey	52	Hartwell, Mrs. C. (Lucy)	41
Goodrich, Mrs. C. (Abbie)	52	Hartwell, Emily	46
Goodrich, Mrs. C. (Justine)	53,93	Haskins, Isabel M.	109
Goodrich, Mrs. C. (Sarah)	53,66	Hastings, Eurotas P.	152
Gordon, Marquis L.,M.D.	82	Hastings, Mrs. E. P. (Anna)	152
Gordon, Mrs. M. L.	82	Hastings, Katherine E.	161
Gouldy, Mary E.	92	Hastings, Richard C.	157
Graves, Allen	117	Hastings, Mrs. R. C.(Minnie)	157
Graves, Mrs. A. (Mary)	117	Haven, Ada	66
Green, Helen W.	7	Hazen, Allen	125

Name	Page
Hazen, Mrs. Allen (Martha)	126
Hazen, Hervey C.	174
Hazen, Mrs. H. C. (Hattie)	175,179
Hazen, Mrs. H.C. (Ida)	174
Hemenway, Asa	76
Hemenway, Mrs. Asa	77
Herrick, Edward P.	103
Herrick, Mrs. E. P.	103
Herrick, Hubert P.	5
Herrick, Mrs. H.P. (Julia)	5
Herrick, James	167
Herrick, Mrs. J. (Elizabeth)	167
Hervey, William	119
Hervey, Mrs. William (Elizabeth)	120
Hillis, Hester A.	160
Hitchcock, Milan H.	154
Hitchcock, Mrs. M.H. (Lucy)	154
Hoisington, Henry R.	146,163
Hoisington, Mrs. H.R. (Nancy)	147
Holbrook, Charles W.	24
Holbrook, Mrs. C.W. (Sarah)	24
Holbrook, Mary A., M.D.	86,91
Holcombe, Chester	54
Holcombe, Mrs. Chester	54
Holcombe, Gilbert T.	60
HONG KONG MISSION	73
Hooper, Frances See Mrs. J. C. Davis	
Hope, Matthew B., M.D.	77B
Howland, John	109
Howland, Mrs. John	109
Howland, Samuel W.	156
Howland, Mrs. S.W. (Mary)	157
Howland, Mrs. S.W. (Ella)	157
Howland, Susan R.	160
Howland, William S.	175
Howland, Mrs. W.S. (Mary)	175
Howland, William W.	151
Howland, Mrs. W.W. (Susan)	151
Hubbard, George H.	45
Hubbard, Mrs. G. H.	45
Hubbard, George W.	136
Hubbard, Mrs. G.W. (Emma)	136
Hume, Edward S.	133
Hume, Mrs. E.S. (Charlotte)	133
Hume, Robert A.	132
Hume, Mrs. R. A. (Abbie)	132
Hume, Mrs. R. A. (Katie)	133,139
Hume, Robert W.	124
Hume, Mrs. R.W. (Hannah)	124
Hunt, Myron W.	61
Hunt, Mrs. M. W.	61
Hunt, Phineas R.	59,186
Hunt, Mrs. P.R. (Abigail)	59,136
Hurd, Isaac N.	136
Hurd, Mrs. I. N. (Mary)	136
Hutchings, Samuel	147,185
Hutchings, Mrs. S. (Elizabeth)	147
Ireland, William	15
Ireland, Mrs. W. (Jane)	15
Ireland, Mrs. W. (Relief)	15
ITALY, MISSION TO	102
Jack, Andrew D.	5
Jack, Mrs. A.D. (Mercy)	5
James, Benjamin V.	6
James, Mrs. B.V. (Elizabeth)	7
JAPAN, MISSION TO	78
JAPAN: NORTHERN JAPAN	
Jencks, DeWitt Clinton	91
Jencks, Mrs. D. C.	91
Johnson, Stephen	37,78 75
Johnson, Mrs. S. (Caroline)	38
Johnson, Mrs. S. (Hannah)	37
Johnson, Mrs. S. (Mary)	38
Jones, John P.	177
Jones, Mrs. J.P. (Sarah)	177
Joralmon, John S.	36
Joralmon, Mrs. J. S.	36
Judson, Adoniram	113
Judson, Mrs. A. (Ann)	114
Kellogg, Emilie L.	95
Kilbon, Charles W.	21
Kilbon, Mrs. C.W. (Mary)	21
Kilbourn, James K.	103,108
Kilbourn, Mrs. J. K.	104,108
Lathrop, Jane E.	150,164
Lawrence, John J.	163
Lawrence, Mrs. J.J. (Mary)	163
Learned, Dwight W.	85
Learned, Mrs. D.W.	86
Leavitt, Horace H.	83
Leavitt, Mrs. H. H.	83
Leitch, George W.	160
Leitch, Margaret W.	161
Leitch, Mary	160
Lindley, Daniel	11
Lindley, Mrs. (Lucy)	11
Lindley, Martha J.	22
Little, Charles	170
Little, Mrs. C. (Amelia)	170
Little, Mrs. C. (Susan)	170
Lloyd, Charles H.	19
Lloyd, Mrs. C. H. (Catharine)	19
Lord, Nathan L., M.D.	153,171
Lord, Mrs. N.L. (Laura)	154

Macy, William A.	31,48	Nott, Samuel	116
MADRAS MISSION	183	Nott, Mrs. S. (Roxana)	116
MADURA MISSION	162	Noyes, Joseph T.	170
MAHRATTAS, MISSION TO	115	Noyes, Mrs. J.T. (Elizabeth)	170
March, Samuel D.	14	Noyes, Mrs. J.T. (Martha)	171
March, Mrs. S.D. (Mary)	15		
Meigs, Benjamin C.	142	Ogden, Emma K., M.D.	139
Meigs, Mrs. B.C.(Sarah)	143	Osborne, Daniel E., M.D.	71
Mellen, William	18	Osborne, Mrs. D.E.	72
Mellen, Mrs. W. (Lauranna)	18	Osgood, Dauphin W., M.D.	42
Merritt, Mrs. C.P.W.	68	Osgood, Mrs. D. W.	42
Merritt, Charles W., M.D.	68	Ousley, Benjamin F.	26
MEXICO: NORTHERN MEXICO, MISSION TO	103	Ousley, Mrs. B. F.(Henrietta)	26
MEXICO: WESTERN MEXICO	107	Palmer, Henry K., M.D.	179, 179A
Miller, Samuel T.	10	Palmer, Mrs. H.K. (Flora)	179
Mills, Cyrus T. and Mrs.	152	PAPAL LANDS	99
Minor, Eastman S.	158	Park, Charles W.	131
Minor, Mrs. E.S. (Judith)	158,182	Park, Mrs. C.W. (Anna)	132
Minor, Mrs. E. S. (Lucy)	158	Parker, Peter, M.D.	28
Morgan, G.F.G.	107	Parker, Mrs. Peter (Harriet)	30
Morris, Fannie M.	22	Parmelee, Harriet F.	94
Munger, Sendol B.	121	Payson, Adelia	43
Munger, Mrs. S.B. (Maria)	121	Peck, Albert P., M.D.	68
Munger, Mrs. S.B. (Mary)	121	Peck, Mrs. A. P.	68
Munger, Mrs. S.B. (Sarah)	121	Peck, Marshall R.	176
Murdock, Virginia C., M.D.	66	Peck, Mrs. M. R.	176
Muzzy, Clarendon F.	165	Peet, Jennie	43
Muzzy, Mrs. C. F. (Mary)	159,165	Peet, Lyman B.	38
Muzzy, Mrs. C. F. (Semantha)	165	Peet, Mrs. L.B. (Hannah)	38
		Peet, Mrs. L.B.(Rebecca)	38
McCoy, Daniel C.	56	Penfield, Thornton B.	174
McCoy, Mrs. D. C.	56	Penfield, Mrs. T.B.(Charlotte)	174
McFarland, Elisabeth	94		
McKinney, Silas	14	Perkins, James C.	179
McKinney, Mrs. S. (Fanny)	14	Perkins, Mrs.J.C.(Charlotte)	179
McMillan, George M.	168	Perkins, Mrs. J.C. (Lucy)	179
McMillan, Mrs. G.M.(Rebecca)	169	Perkins, Henry P.	64
		Perkins, Mrs. H.P., M.D.	65
Neesima, Joseph	91	Perry, John M.	143
Newell, Samuel	115	Perry, Mrs. J.M.(Harriet)	149
Newell, Mrs. S. (Harriet)	115	Pettee, James H.	87
Newell, Mrs. Samuel(Philomela)	116	Pettee, Mrs. J. H.	88
Newton, Ella J.	44	Phelps, Fidelia	22
Nichols, Francis O., M.D.	10	Pierce, Epaminondas	5
Nichols, Mrs. F.O. (Mary)	10	Pierce, Mrs. E.(Susan)	5
Nichols, John	117	Pierce, Mary E.	77
Nichols, Mrs. J. (Elizabeth)	117	Pierson, Isaac	56
Noble, Willis C., M.D.	65	Pierson, Mrs. I. (Flora)	57,66
Noble, Mrs. W. C.	65	Pierson, Mrs. I. (Sarah)	56
Norris, Sarah F., M.D.	138	Pinkerton, Mary E.	22
North, Alfred	77C,180	Pinkerton, Miron W.	21
North, Mrs. Alfred	77C,180	Pinkerton, Mrs.M.W.P.(Louisa)	21
NORTH CHINA MISSION	48	Pixley, Stephen C.	18
		Pixley, Mrs. S.C. (Louisa)	18

Pohlman, William J.	35
Pohlman, Mrs. W. J.	36
Pollock, Sarah	181
Poor, Daniel	143,163
Poor, Mrs. D. (Ann)	143
Poor, Mrs. D. (Susan)	143
Porter, Henry D., M.D.	61
Porter, Mrs. H. D.	61
Porter, Mary H.	59
Porter, Rollin	4
Porter, Mrs. R. P. (Nancy)	4
Preston, Ira M.	3
Preston, Mrs. I. (Jane)	3
Price, Francis M.	70
Price, Mrs. F. P.	70
Price, Martha E.	22
Quick, James	154
Quick, Mrs. James (Maria)	155
Ramsey, William	120
Ramsey, Mrs. W. (Mary)	120
Rankin, Melinda	103
Read, Hollis	120
Read, Mrs. H. (Caroline)	120
Rendall, Henrietta S.	
See Chandler, Mrs. J. S.	
Rendall, John	168
Rendall, Mrs. J. (Jane)	168
Rendall, Mary E.	181
Rentlinger, Mrs. Louis	7
Rice, Luther	114
Richards, Erwin H.	25,25A
Richards, Mrs. E.H. (Mittie)	25
Richards, James	141
Richards, Mrs. J. (Sarah)	141
Richards, Susie F.	112
Richards, William L.	39
Roberts, James H.	62
Roberts, Mrs. J. H.	63
Robbins, Elijah	19
Robbins, Mrs. E. (Adeline)	19
Robbins, Samuel	75
Robbins, Mrs. S. R.	75
Robinson, Charles	74
Robinson, Mrs. Charles	74
Rood, David	15
Rood, Mrs. David (Alzina)	15
Root, M. Pauline, M.D.	182
Rounds, Frances	
See Mrs. R.H. Davis	88,97
Saint John, Monis L., M.D.	6
Saint John, Mrs. (Sarah)	6
Sampson, William C.	136

Sampson, Mrs. W. C. (Mary)	136
Sanders, Marshall D.	152
Sanders, Mrs. M.D.(Georgiana)	152
Sanders, Mrs. M.D.(Caroline)	152
Sanders, William H.	8
Sanders, Mrs. W. H. (Mary)	8
Sanders, Mrs. W. H.II(Sarah)	8
Schauffler, Henry A.	99
Schauffler, Mrs. H. A.	99
Scudder, Catherine S.	98
Scudder, David C.	173
Scudder, Mrs. D. C.(Harriet)	174
Scudder, Doremus, M.D.	97
Scudder, Mrs. Doremus	97
Scudder, Ezekiel C.	189
Scudder, Mrs. E. C.(Sarah)	189
Scudder, Henry M.	186,187
Scudder, Mrs. H. M. (Fanny)	187
Scudder, Jared W., M.D.	189
Scudder, Mrs. J. W. (Julia)	189
Scudder, John, M.D.	148,184
Scudder, Mrs. J. (Harriet)	185
Scudder, Joseph	188
Scudder, Mrs. J. (Sarah)	188
Scudder, Louisa	189
Scudder, William W.	151,187
Scudder, Mrs. W.W.(Catharine)	151,188
Scudder, Mrs. W.W.(Elizabeth)	188
Searle, Susan A.	95
SHANGHAI MISSION	48
SHANSI MISSION	69
Shaw, William H.	64
Shaw, Mrs. W. H.	64
Sheffield, Devello Z.	55
Sheffield, Mrs. D. Z.	55
Shelton, Charles S., M.D.	178
Shelton, Mrs. C.S.(Henrietta)	178
SIAM, MISSION TO	74
SINGAPORE, MISSION TO	77A
Sisson, Elizabeth	181
Smith, Arthur H.	57
Smith, Mrs. A. H.	57
Smith, James	134
Smith, Mrs. J. (Maud)	134
Smith, John C.	149
Smith, Mrs. J. C. (Eunice)	150
Smith, Mrs. J. C. (Mary)	150,178
Smith, Rosella A.	150
Smith, Thomas S.	156
Smith, Mrs. T. S. (Emily)	156
SOUTHERN ASIA	113
SPAIN, MISSION TO	110
Spaulding, Levi	144
Spaulding, Mrs. Levi (Mary)	144

Name	Page
Sprague, William P.	62
Sprague, Mrs. W.P. (Margaret)	62
Sprague, Mrs. W.P. (Viette)	62
Stanley, Charles A.	50
Stanley, Mrs. C.A.	51
Starkweather, Alice J.	93
Steele, John, M.D.	178
Steele, Mrs. John (Mary)	150, 178
Stephens, John L.	107
Stevens, Edwin	28
Stinson, Martin L.	69
Stinson, Mrs. M. L.	69
Stone, Cyrus	119
Stone, Mrs. C. (Abigail)	119
Stone, Mrs. C. (Atossa)	119
Stone, Seth B.	17
Stone, Mrs. S.B. (Catharine)	18
Stover, Wesley M.	9
Stover, Mrs. M. (Bertha)	9
Strong, Carrie M.	104
Swift, Eva M.	182
Talcott, Eliza	92
Talmage, John VanNest	36
Talmage, Mrs. J.V.N.	36
Taylor, Horace S.	166
Taylor, Mrs. H.S. (Martha)	167
Taylor, Martha S.	180
Taylor, Wallace, M.D.	84
Taylor, Mrs. Wallace	84
Tenney, Charles D.	70
Tenney, Mrs. C.D.	70
Thompson, James Brettle	71
Thompson, Mrs. J. B.	71
Thompson, Thomas W.	53
Thompson, Mary A.	80
Todd, William	162
Todd, Mrs. William (Clarissa)	162
Todd, Mrs. Wm. (Lucy)	162
Townshend, Harriet E.	159
Tracy, Ira	29, 77A
Tracy, Mrs. Ira	77A
Tracy, James E.	178
Tracy, Mrs. J.E. (Fannie)	178
Tracy, Stephen, M.D.	77
Tracy, Mrs. Stephen	77
Tracy, William	166
Tracy, Mrs. Wm. (Emily)	167
Travelli, Joseph S.	77B
Travelli, Mrs. J. S.	77B
Treat, Alfred O., M.D.	57
Tyler, Josiah	17
Tyler, Mrs. J. (Susan)	17
Van Allen, Jane Ann	7
Venable, Henry I.	11
Venable, Mrs. H. I. (Martha)	12
Vrooman, Daniel	31
Vrooman, Mrs. D (Elizabeth)	31
Vrooman, Mrs. D. (Maria)	31
Walker, Joseph E.	41
Walker, Mrs. Joseph E.	42
Walker, William	2
Walker, Mrs. W. (Catherine)	2
Walker, Mrs. W. (Lorinah)	2
Walker, Mrs. W. (Prudence)	2
Walter, Frederick A.T.	10
Walter, Mrs. F.A. (Margaret)	10
Ward, Ferdinand D.	166, 165
Ward, Mrs. F.D. (Jane)	168
Ward, Nathan, M.D.	147
Ward, Mrs. Nathan (Hannah)	148
Warren, Edward	142
Washburn, George T.	173
Washburn, Mrs. G.T. (Eliza)	173
Watkins, David F.	107
Watkins, Mrs. D. F.	107
Webster, Elijah A.	136
Webb, Edward	167
Webb, Mrs. E. (Nancy)	168
Webster, Mrs. E. A.	136
Webster, Maggie	159
Wells, Spencer R.	120
Wells, Mrs. S. R.	121
Wheeler, William T.	4
White, Charles T.	172
White, Mrs. C.T. (Anna)	172
White, David	1
White, Mrs. D. (Helen)	1
Whiting, Joseph L.	54
Whiting, Mrs. J. L.	54
Whitney, Henry T., M.D.	43
Whitney, Mrs. H. T.	44
Whittlesey, Samuel G.	149
Whittlesey, Mrs. S.G. (Anna)	149
Wilcox, William C.	24, 25
Wilcox, Mrs. W. C. (Ida)	24, 25
Wilder, George A.	23, 26
Wilder, Mrs. G. A.	23, 26
Wilder, Hyman A.	16
Wilder, Mrs. H. A. (Abby)	16
Williams, Mark	53
Williams, Mrs. Mark	53
Williams, S. Wells	32
Williams, Mrs. S. W.	33
Wilson, Alexander E., M.D.	1
Wilson, Mrs.A.E. (M. Hardcastle)	1
Wilson, Mrs. A.E. (M.Smithey)	12
Wilson, John L.	1
Wilson, Mrs. J. (Jane Bayard)	1

Wilson, Julia 93
Winslow, Miron 144,183
Winslow, Mrs. M. (Anne) 184
Winslow, Mrs. M. (Catharine) 184
Winslow, Mrs. M. (Ellen) 184
Winslow, Mrs. M. (Harriet) 183
Winslow, Mrs. M. (Mary)
  See Dwight, Mrs. R. O.
Winsor, Richard 131
Winsor, Mrs. R. (Mary) 131
Wood, George W. 77C
Wood, William 126
Wood, Mrs. Wm. (Lucy) 126
Wood, Mrs. Wm. (Eliza) 126
Wood, Mrs. Wm. (Elizabeth) 126
Woodhull, Kate C., M.D. 46
Woodhull, Hannah C. 46
Woodin, Simeon F. 41
Woodin, Mrs. Simeon 41
Woodward, Henry 144
Woodward, Mrs. H. (Clarissa)
  118,146
Woodward, Mrs. H. (Lydia) 146
Wyman, Robert 150
Wyman, Mrs. R. (Martha) 150

Addenda:

Dohne, Jacob Ludwig 17A
Lindley, Newton Adams 19A
Lloyd, Mrs. Charles H. 19A
  (Katherine)

WESTERN AFRICA

MISSION AT CAPE PALMAS: AFTERWARD AT GABOON

Commenced at Cape Palmas, 1834; removed to Gaboon, 1842

MISSIONARIES

John Leighton Wilson, born at Mount Clio, S. C. March 25, 1809; graduated Union Coll. 1829; Southern Sem. 1833; ordained Philadelphia, Sept. 22, 1833; embarked at Baltimore, Nov. 28, 1833; visited Cape Palmas; returned March 9, 1834; re-embarked at New York, Nov. 5, 1834; arrived Cape Palmas, Dec. 25, 1834; removed to Gaboon 1842; visited the United States, June 21, 1847; re-embarked at Providence, June 14, 1848; returned U. S. 1852; released, July 19, 1853. 1878, in Baltimore, Md. Gen. Sec'y South. Pres. Bd. For. Mis. Died Mayesville, S. C. July 13, 1886.

Mrs. Wilson (Jane E. Bayard) Savannah, Ga. born, Jan. 8, 1809; mar. May 20, 1834; released, July 19, 1853. 1878, living in Baltimore. Died Mayesville, S. C. 1885.

David White, born Pittsfield, Mass. March 27, 1807; prof. rel. 1827; grad. Union Coll. 1831; Princeton Sem. 1836; ord. Pittsfield, 1836; emb. Baltimore, Oct. 31, 1836; ar. Cape Palmas, Dec. 25, 1836; died Cape Palmas, Jan. 23, 1837.

Mrs. White (Helen Maria Wells) Newburgh, N. Y.; born Cambridge, Washington Co., N. Y. Nov. 24, 1813; mar. Oct. 12, 1836; died Cape Palmas, Jan. 27, 1837.

Alexander Erwin Wilson, M.D., born Mecklenburg County, N. C., Dec. 11, 1803; prof. rel. 1824; grad. Univ. of N. C. 1823; Union Theol. Sem, Va. 1834; ord. 1834; emb. Boston, Dec. 3, 1834; ar. Cape Town, South Africa, Feb. 5, 1835; a member of that mission till 1838; arrived at Mosika, June 16, 1836; at Port Natal, July 27, 1837; at Port Elisabeth, March 20, 1838; returned U. S. June 1838; re-emb. New York for Cape Palmas, July 27, 1839; arr. Cape Palmas Oct. 4, 1839; died Oct. 13, 1841 of dysentery. (Mr. Wilson's first wife was not connected with this mission.)

June 21, 1815; mar. Rev. Benjamin Griswold, below. Died Jan. 1849

William Walker, born Vershire, Vt. Oct. 3, 1808; prof. rel. Troy, Vt. Jan. 1832 1832; grad. Amh. Coll. 1838; Andover Sem. 1841; ord. Greensboro, Vt. Nov. 4, 1841; emb. Boston, Dec. 6, 1841; with Mrs. Griswold; arr. at Cape Palmas, Feb. 3, 1842; removed to Gaboon, Nov. 7, 1842; visited U. S. May 1845; re-emb. Sept. 1846; arr. at Gaboon, Dec. 24, 1846; vis. U. S. again 1850; re-emb. New York, Oct. 2, 1851; vis. U. S. a third time Dec. 16, 1858; sailed from New York for the Gaboon, July 31, 1860. Jan. 1878 at Milton, Wis. At the Gaboon, March 1883, returned and at Milton, Wis. July 1883. Died in Milton, Wis., Dec. 8, 1896.

Mrs. Walker (Prudence Richardson) born Dracut, Mass. April 21, 1809; prof. rel. April 1828; grad. Mt. Holyoke College; mar. Nov. 30, 1841; arr. at Cape Palmas, Feb. 3, 1842; died there, three months afterward, May 3, 1842. Obituary, Herald, vol. 39, p.30.

Mrs. Walker (Lerinah L. Shumway) born Oxford, Mass. Dec. 12, 1817. Grad. Mt. Holyoke Sem.; mar. Oct. 20, 1845; died at Gaboon, April 23, 1848.

Mrs. Walker (Catharine H. Hardcastle) New York City; born there Sept. 15, 1817; appointed Aug. 30, 1851; mar. Sept. 30, 1851; emb. New York, Oct. 2, 1851. Died Oct. 27, 1877, at Milton, Wis.

Benjamin Griswold, born Randolph, Vt., Aug. 13, 1811; prof. rel. 1833; grad. Dart. Coll. 1837; New Haven Sem. 1840; ord. Randolph, Vt. Oct. 2, 1841; emb. Boston, with Mr. Walker, Dec. 6, 1841; arr. Cape Palmas, Feb. 3, 1842; removed to Gaboon, Jan. 1843; died there July 14, 1844.

Mrs. Griswold (Mary(Hardcastle)Wilson) formerly wife of Rev. A. E. Wilson, above; mar. Mr. Griswold, Aug. 23, 1843; after his death vis. U. S. May 1845; re-emb. Providence, June 14, 1848 for Gaboon; died Jan. 1849.

John Milton Campbell, of Scotch descent; Georgetown, Brown Co., O.; born in Fleming Co., Ky.; Oct. 15, 1812; converted in childhood; grad. Miami Univ.

1840; Lane Sem. 1843; ord. Ripley, Brown Co., O. 1843; emb. Boston Jan. 1, 1844; arr. Cape Palmas, March 9, 1844; died Cape Palmas, April 19, 1844.

Albert Bushnell, Cincinnati, O.; born Rome, New York Feb. 9, 1818; prof. rel. Feb. 1831; educated at no college; grad. Lane Sem. 1843; ord. Cincinnati, Nov. 5, 1843; emb. Boston, Jan. 1, 1844; visited U. S. April 1846; re-emb. June 14, 1848; vis. U. S. again, 1852; re-emb. Dec. 10, 1853; arr. Gaboon, Jan. 29, 1854; vis. U. S. a third time, 1857; re-emb. June ?, 1858; vis. U. S. a fourth time, Nov. 3, 1861; re-emb. New York, April 11, 1863; arr. Gaboon, Aug. 22, 1863. 1877 at Gaboon. Died at Sierra Leone, Dec. 2, 1879. (See Herald Feb. 1880.)

Mrs. Bushnell (Lydia Ann Beers) born North Salem, Westchester Co., N. Y. Jan. 20, 1811; (emb. for Africa as a teacher under the patronage of Meth. Episc. Miss. Soc. June 16, 1837; mar. Rev. W. Stoker of that Soc. at Liberia March 13, 1839; he died July 25, 1839;) app. to the Gaboon 1842; mar. Mr. Bushnell at the Gaboon, March 12, 1845; returned to the U. S. with him, April 1846; re-emb. with him at Providence for Africa June 14, 1848; died at Gaboon Feb. 25, 1850.

Mrs. Bushnell (Lucina Jeannette Boughton) born Schodack, Rensselaer Co., N.Y. April 8, 1830; prof. rel. Feb. 1848; studied at Oberlin Sem., Ohio; mar. Sept. 12, 1853; emb. New York Dec. 10, 1853. 1877 at Gaboon. 1887 at Nassau, N. Y.

Ira Mills Preston, born Danvers, Mass. April 21, 1818; prof. rel. Marietta, O., Sept. 1839; grad. Marietta Coll. 1845; Lane Sem. 1848; ord. May 4, 1848; emb. at Providence, R. I. for Africa with Walker, Bushnell and others, June 14, 1848; arr. Gaboon, Aug. 1848; vis. U. S. Dec. 1850; re-emb. New York Oct. 2, 1851; vis. U. S. again, 1856; re-emb. Philadelphia, May 10, 1859; returned to U. S. June 13, 1867; released Dec. 24, 1867. 1878, instructor in Marietta Coll., Ohio. Ditto 1886.

Mrs. Preston (Jane Sophie Woodruff) born Westfield, Chautauqua Co., N. Y.;

April 27, 1826; prof. rel. at nine years of age, 1837; studied Marietta Female Sem.; mar. Marietta, May 29, 1848; emb. for Africa, June 14, 1848; returned to U. S. May 12, 1864; returned to U. S. Oct. 24, 1866; 1878 at Marietta, Ohio. Ditto 1886. Died at Marietta, Oct. 4, 1890.

William Thompson Wheeler, Terre Haute, Ind.; born Bowdoin, Me., Dec. 21, 1812; prof. rel. Terre Haute 1842; studied Lane Theol. Sem.; ord. Terre Haute, Oct. 1847; emb. with Walker, Bushnell, Preston etc. Providence, June 14, 1848; arr. Gaboon Aug. 1848; returned to U. S. 1849; released Oct. 9, 1849. Died 1851 in Ill. or Iowa.

Jacob Best, Stuyvesant, N. Y.; born Livingston, Columbia Co., N. Y., Feb. 3, 1823; prof. rel. Williamstown, Mass. 1842; grad. Williams Coll. 1844; Union Theol. Sem. N. Y. 1848; ord. New York City, Dec. 1848; emb. New York, Nov. 3, 1849; ar. Gaboon, Jan. 30, 1850; vis. U. S. July 3, 1853; re-emb. New York Dec. 10, 1853; ar. Gaboon, Jan. 29, 1854; again vis. U. S. 1856; re-emb. June 16, 1857; ar. Gaboon, Aug. 20, 1857; returned to U. S. 1861; released April 5, 1864. 1875 Pres. Ch. Waymart, Pa.; 1877 P. Brooklyn, Pa., ditto 1884.

Mrs. Best (Gertrude Nevins) born Ovid, N. Y. Dec. 17, 1822; mar. Dec. 1, 1853; appointed Dec. 6, 1853; emb. at New York Dec. 10, 1853; arr. at New York from Gaboon, May 18, 1855; re-emb. June 16, 1857; returned to U. S. 1861; rel. 1864. 1877 at Brooklyn, Pa. Ditto 1884.

Rollin Porter, Somersville, Ct.; born Lysander, Onondaga Co., N. Y. Feb. 12, 1822; prof. rel. Baldwinsville, N. Y. March 1841; studied Ellington School, Ct.; grad. Lane Theol. Sem. 1850; ord. Somers, Ct.; Aug. 18, 1850; emb. New York March 25, 1851; ar. Gaboon, June 6, 1851; died Gaboon, July 6, 1852.

Mrs. Porter (Nancy Ann Sikes) Somersville, Ct.; born Somers, Ct., June 21, 1825; prof. rel. March 1847; mar. at Somers, Feb. 16, 1851; died at Gaboon July 16, 1852.

Epaminondas James Pierce, born Philadelphia, Oct. 24, 1823; grad. Dart. Coll. 1845; Union Sem. N. Y. 1850; ord. Philadelphia, 1851; emb. New York Nov. 30, 1853; arr. Gaboon, Feb. 16, 1854; arr. at New York, on his return to U. S. Dec. 16, 1858. His name struck from the list of missionaries July 18, 1865. 1875 p. Pres. Ch. Farmingdale, N. J. 1877 still there. Ditto 1884. Died Farmingdale, N. J. March 13, 1892.

Mrs. Pierce (Susan Savory) born Bangor, Me. (Portland - her husband says - Nov. 5, 1824.) mar. about Nov. 25, 1853; died at Gaboon, Feb. 24, 1855.

Hubert Pierre Herrick, Macdonough, N. Y.: born there Dec. 26, 1827; grad. Amh. Coll. 1849; Auburn Sem. 1853; ord. prob. in Nov. 1853; emb. New York with Mr. Pierce, Nov. 30, 1853; arr. Gaboon, Feb. 16, 1854; vis. U.S. 1856; re-emb. June 16, 1857; ar. Gaboon, Aug. 20, 1857; died at Gaboon Dec. 20, 1857.

Mrs. Herrick (Julia Bushnell) Granville, O.; born there Feb. 16, 1827; mar. Nov. 1, 1853; emb. Nov. 30, 1853; returned to U. S. 1856. 1878, living in Oregon; m. Horatio V. Johnson.

Henry Martyn Adams, born Enosburgh, Vt., Nov. 20, 1823; prof. rel. Feb. 1839; grad. Amherst Coll. 1851; East Windsor Sem. 1854; ord. Enosburgh, Aug. 31, 1854; emb. New York, Sept. 29, 1854; arr. at Gaboon, early in 1855; died triumphantly Aug. 13, 1856. (See obituary in Herald, vol. 52: pp. 371-374)

Andrew Donnell Jack, Wabash, Ind.; born Kingston, Decatur Co., Ind. July 19, 1829; prof. rel. March 12, 1849; grad. Wabash Coll. 1854; Lane Sem. 1857; ord. Crawfordsville, Ind. July 12, 1857; emb. New York, Oct. 6, 1857; arr. Gaboon Jan. 18, 1858; returned to U. S. 1859; released 1864. 1875, p. Pres. Ch. Eureka, Pa. 1877, still there. 1884 Lawrence, Kan. 1887 Eureka, Pa.

Mrs. Jack (Mercy Elisabeth Tidball) Shiloah, Ind.; born Millersburgh, Homes Co., O. Nov. 28, 1829; prof'l rel. June 27, 1847; mar. Aug. 20, 1857; emb. Oct. 1857; returned to U. S. 1859.

Monis Lawrence Saint John, M.D. Marietta, O.; born Aurelius, Washington Co., O. July 15, 1831; prof. rel. Nov. 12, 1854; studied at Lane Theol. Sem.; emb. New York, Sept. 27, 1859; arr. at Gaboon, Jan. 27, 1860; returned to U. S. 1861; released July 9, 1861. Died 1862 or '63.

Mrs. Saint John (Sarah Ann Gutwood) born near Wellsburg, Brooke Co., West Virginia, July 14, 1836; prof. rel. May 1858; mar. Aurelius, Ohio, June 7, 1858; emb. New York Sept. 27, 1859; arr. Gaboon, Jan. 27, 1860; returned to U. S. 1861; released 1861.

Walter Halsey Clark, born Milton, Ulster Co., N. Y., July 2, 1832; prof. rel. Williamstown, Mass. June 1852; grad. Williams Coll. 1854; Union Sem., N. Y. 1859; ord. Milton, N. Y. June 30, 1859; emb. New York, Sept. 27, 1859; arr. Gaboon, Jan. 27, 1860; then unmarried; mar. Jan. 1, 1861, Maria M. Jackson, and was released May 7, 1861 to labor in the Presbyterian Mission on Corisco Island. 1875, a p. Pres. Ch. Ponca, Neb. 1877, a p. Silver Ridge, Neb. Ditto 1884. 1891 in Parkville, Mo.

MISSIONARY PHYSICIAN.

Henry A. Ford, M.D. Hudson, N. Y.   emb. Boston, June 20, 1850; arr. Gaboon, Oct. 7, 1850; vis. U. S. 1855-1856; died at Gaboon, Feb. 2, 1858.

Mrs. Ford (Olivia Smith) Oswego, N. Y.; born Lafayette, N. Y. Jan. 1830; emb. Unmarried, New York, Nov. 30, 1853; arr. Gaboon, Feb. 16, 1854; marr. 1855; returned to U. S. 1855.

ASSISTANT MISSIONARIES

Benjamin Van Rensselaer James, a colored man, and printer; born Elisabethtown, N. Y. April 21, 1814; prof. rel. Granville, N. Y. 1833; emb. Baltimore Oct. 31, 1836; arr. Fair Hope, Cape Palmas, Dec. 25, 1836; removed to Gaboon, 1844; vis. U. S. May 1845; released 1846; and joined the colony at Liberia. He died at

Mrs. James (Margaret Elisabeth Strobel) born Savannah, Ga. Jan. 10, 1804; prof. rel. June 1, 1828; mar. Fair Hope, Nov. 28, 1838. Died at Monrovia, about 1870 or '71.

Jane Ann Van Allen, Dorset, Vt.; born Amsterdam, Montgomery Co., N. Y. May 2, 1829; prof. rel. Jan. 1850; emb. at New York with Mr. Jack, Oct. 6, 1857; arr. Gaboon, Jan. 18, 1858; returned to U. S. 1862.

Helen M. Green
emb. New York, April 11, 1863; arr. Gaboon, Aug. 22, 1863; returned to U. S. May 12, 1864. Mar. a Mr. Merwin. 1876, living in Plainfield, N. J.

Mrs. Louise Rentlinger, teacher at Gaboon, 1869-70.
1877 at Corisco, under Pres. Bd. Ditto 1887. This mission was transferred to the Presbyterian Board in 1870

WEST CENTRAL AFRICA MISSION.

This Mission was commenced at Bailundu in 1880.

MISSIONARIES.

Walter Weldon Bagster, born London, Middlesex, Eng. Oct. 20, 1847; prof. rel. London, July 28, 1869; two years in Pacific Theol. Sem., Oakland, Cal.; ord. 1st Cong'l Ch., Oakland, Cal., June 9, 1880; emb. N. Y., Aug. 7, 1880; arr. Benguela, Nov. 13, 1880. Died at Bailundu Feb. 22, 1882. (See Herald June 1882)

William Henry Sanders, born Tillipally, Jaffna, Ceylon, Mar. 2, 1856 ; son of Rev. Marshall D. Sanders formerly missionary to Ceylon; prof. rel. July 1868; Williamstown, Mass.; grad. Williams Coll. 1877; Theol. Inst. of Conn. May 1880; ord. Williamstown, Mass. June 8, 1880; emb. N. Y. Aug. 7, 1880; arr. Benguela Nov. 13, 1880; Oct. 1885 at Bailundu. Vis. U. S. arr. N. Y. April 26, 1892; re-emb. N. Y. Apr. 15, 1893; arr. Benguella July 17. Vis. U. S. arr; Boston, Aug. 20, 1903; re-emb. Boston April 25, 1905; arr. at Benguella June 21, 1905. Left field June 1911; DD 1912 Williams Col.; emb. Aug. 1912; arrived field Oct. 1912; left field Apr. 1918; emb. July 1919; arrived field Oct. 1919; emb. March 1925; arrived field Apr. 1925; arrived home July 24, 1930. Retired July 25, 1931. Died May 30, 1947 at Wilmington,

Mrs. Sanders (Mary Jane Mawhir) born Belfast, Ireland, April 4, 1855; prof. rel. Oct. 1870; studied at Oberlin; emb. March 9, 1882; arr. Benguela, June 7; mar. at Bailundu Sept. 12, 1882; Oct. 1885 at Bailundu. Died at Kamandongo, Bihe, Aug. 8, 1891. (See Nov. Herald 1891, p. 442)

Mrs. Sanders (Sarah Bell) (See vol. 11, p. 29) born Radrum, Ireland, July 10, 1862, arrived mar. Benguella, Oct. 17, 1893; vis.U. S. arr. Boston Aug. 20, 1903; re-emb. Boston Apr. 25, 1905. Arr. Benguella June 26, 1905; arr. home Aug. 20, 1911; sailed Aug. 31, 1912; arr. home Nov. 3, 1918; sailed July 24, 1919; ar. home July 6, 1924; sailed Mar. 14, 1925. arr. home July 24, 1930. Retired July 25,

William Edwards Fay, born Louisville, Ky., Nov. 8, 1855; prof. rel. Marietta, O., 1867; grad. Marietta Coll. in 1878 and Oberlin Theol. Sem. 1881; ord. Springfield, O., July 28, 1881; emb. Boston, March 9, 1882; arr. Benguela, June 7, 1882; robbed and driven away from the mission by the natives July 4, 1884. Messrs Fay and Stover visited the U. S. for conference, arr. N. Y. Oct. 12,1884; re-emb. Boston, April 3, 1886; vis. U. S. arr. N. Y., Sept. 20, 1890; re-emb. Boston May 16, 1891; arr. Benguella, July 23, 1891; vis. U. S. arr. Boston, Nov. 3, 1900; re-emb. Boston Apr. 19, 1902; vis. U. S. on account of ill health arr. N. Y. Mar. 5, 1907. Died at Oberlin, Ohio, October 13, 1907. (See Herald p.586)

Mrs. Fay (Annie M. Kimball) born Flatbush, N. Y. Nov. 26, 1860; prof. rel. Watertown, May 1877; studied Watertown High Sch. and Kindergarten Normal Class; mar. March 10, 1886; emb. Boston, Apr. 3, 1886; arr. N. Y. Sept. 20, 1890; re-emb. Boston, May 16, 1891; arr. Benguella, July 23, 1891. Vis. U. S. arr. Boston, Nov. 3, 1900; re-emb. Boston Apr. 19, 1902; vis. U. S. arr. N. Y. Mar. 5, 1907. Died in Milford, Ohio Feb 23, 1952. Buried in Marietta, Ohio.

Wesley Meyers Stover, born York, York Co., Pa., Nov. 28, 1850; prof. rel. Mar. 1870; grad. Oberlin Coll., June 12, 1878 and Oberlin Theol. Sem. June 25, 1881; ord. at Oberlin, June 21, 1881; emb. Boston, March 9, 1882; arr. Benguela, June 7, 1882; visited U. S. with Mr. Fay (see above) arr. N. Y. Oct. 12, 1884; re-emb. Boston June 6, 1885. Oct. 1885 at Bailundu; vis. U. S. arr. N. Y. Dec. 28, 1895; re-emb. N. Y. July 10, 1897; arr. Benguella, Sept.; arr. Eng. May 8, 1908. Died in Claremont, Calif. on July 8, 1922. (Miss'y Herald page 345) D.D. 1909; sailed from Eng. Feb. 1, 1910; arrived home 1914(?); sailed 1915(?); arr. home June 17, 1920. Died in Claremont July 8, 1922.

Mrs. Stover (Bertha Bennett Dodge) born Milton, DuPage Co., Ill., Feb. 4, 1853; prof. rel. Mar. 13, 1871, Wheaton, Ill.; mar. at Milton, Ill. June 12, 1880; emb. Boston, Mar. 9, 1882; arr. Benguella June 7, 1882; visited U. S. Oct. 12, 1884; re-emb. Boston June 6, 1885. Oct. 1885 at Bailundu;

U. S. arr. Boston, Oct. 6, 1904; re-emb. Boston, May 5, 1908; arr. field Sept. 3, 1909; arr. home 1915; left field Jan. 31,1920; arr. home June 17, 1920. Died in Claremont, Calif. October 17, 1957.

MISSIONARY PHYSICIANS

Francis Oliver Nichols, M.D., born West Amesbury, Mass. Mar. 20, 1855: prof. rel. Haverhill, Mass. 1873: educated at Colby University and Medical School of Maine, Bowdoin Coll.; emb. N. Y. Aug. 6, 1881: arr. Benguela Oct. 8, 1881: returned to U. S., arriving at Boston Oct. 23, 1883: released June 5, 1883.

Mrs. Nichols (Mary Frances Burnham) born Plaistow, Rockingham Co., N. H. May 9, 1856; prof. rel. June 1876; educated Atkinson Academy; mar. Aug. 3, 1881; emb. N. Y. Aug. 6, 1881; arr. Benguela Oct. 8, 1881; returned to U.S. arriving at Boston, Oct. 23, 1883; released June 5, 1883.

ASSISTANT MISSIONARIES

Samuel Taylor Miller, was the first colored man sent to this mission: born Burkeville, Nottoway Co., Va., Feb. 22, 1855; prof. rel. Burkeville; educated at Hampton, Va.; emb. with Messrs Bagster and Sanders from N. Y. Aug. 7, 1880; returned with Messrs Fay and Stover, arriving N. Y. Dec. 14, 1884; released March 10, 1885. (Benj. V. James was sent to Cape Palmas 1836 - a colored man.)

Frederick Amandus Theodore Walter, born Hamburg, Germany, Nov. 19, 1856; prof. rel. Jan. 1876; emb. N. Y. April 7, 1881; arr. Benguela Sept. 5, 1881; Oct. 1885 at Benguela. Vis. U. S. arr. N. Y. July 1, 1888; released Jan. 25, 1889. Died Philadelphia, Mar. 17, 1903. (See May 1903 Herald, p. 227)

Mrs. Walter (Margaret Drysdale Wardlaw) born Benton, Dunbartonshire, Scotland, April 23, 1847; prof. rel. June 1864; mar. March 28, 1881; emb. N. Y. April 7, 1881; arr. Benguela Sept. 5, 1881 Oct. 1885 at Benguela. Vis. U. S. arr. N.Y.

Mission to the Zulus, established in 1835
Near Port Natal.

Daniel Lindley, son of Rev. Jacob Lindley of Athens, Ohio; Waterford, O.; born Washington Co., Pa., Aug. 24, 1801; prof. rel. Athens, O., 1821; grad. Ohio Univ. 1824; Union Theol. Sem., Va. 1831; ord. Nov. 7, 1834; emb. with Champion, Grout and others, Boston, Dec. 3, 1834; arr. Cape Town, Feb. 5, 1835; travelled by land thence one thousand miles in wagons drawn each by twelve yoke of oxen; arr. Griqua Town, May 16, 1835; and there commenced their missionary work; remained there five months; arr. Mosika, in Moselekatsi's country, June 16, 1836; the mission here broken up by a war between him and the Dutch Boers, Jan. 17, 1837; the mission re-established among the maritime Zulus, near Port Natal, July 27, 1837; the mission again broken up in Feb. 1838. Mr. Lindley and others leave Natal May 11, 1838; and arr. at Delagoa Bay, May 20; thence to Port Elizabeth; returned to Port Natal, June 12, 1839; from that time till 1847, Mr. Lindley labored chiefly among the Dutch colonists, or Boers, receiving from them his support, but retaining his connection with the Board; established in 1847 at Inanda among the Zulus; arr. at Boston on a visit to U. S. Sept. 15, 1859; re-emb. at Boston with wife and six children Oct. 28, 1862. Returned to U. S. 1873; sailed from Africa Apr. 26, 1873. Jan. 1878 living in New York City. Died Sept. 3, 1880. (See obituary in Herald, Nov. 1880, p. 458)

Mrs. Lindley (Lucy Allen) Buffalo, N. Y.; born Chatham, Columbia Co., N. Y. April 16, 1810; prof. rel. 1830; mar. Hartford, Ct., Nov. 20, 1834; emb. Boston Dec. 3, 1834; vis. U. S. Sept. 15, 1859 to Oct. 28, 1862. Returned to U. S. 1873. Died New York City Nov. 22, 1877. (Obituary Herald Jan. 1878)

Henry Isaac Venable, born Shelby Co., Ky. June 20, 1811; grad. Clinton Coll., Ky. 1830; Union Theol. Sem. 1834; ord. Danville, Ky. Oct. 9, 1834; emb. with Mr. Lindley and others Boston, Dec. 3, 1834; arr. Cape Town, Feb. 5, 1835; arr. Griqua Town, May 16, 1835; arr. Mosika June 16, 1836; compelled to abandon that station Jan. 17, 1837; proceeded across the country 1300 miles to Dingaan's

SOUTHERN AFRICA

Mission to the Zulus, established in 1835
Near Port Natal.

Daniel Lindley, son of Rev. Jacob Lindley of Athens, Ohio; Waterford, O.; born
.... rel. Athens, O., 1821; grad. Ohio
.... ord. Nov. 7, 1834; emb. with Champion,
.... arr. Cape Town, Feb. 5, 1835; travelled
.... ons drawn each by twelve yoke of oxen;
.... commenced their missionary work; re-
.... in Moselekatsi's country, June 16,
.... r between him and the Dutch Boers,
.... among the maritime Zulus, near Port
.... broken up in Feb. 1838. Mr. Lindley
.... arr. at Delagoa Bay, May 20; thence
.... l, June 12, 1839; from that time till
.... the Dutch colonists, or Boers, receiv-
.... his connection with the Board; estab-
.... ; arr. at Boston on a visit to U. S.
.... ife and six children Oct. 28, 1862.
.... ca Apr. 26, 1873. Jan. 1878 living in
.... e obituary in Herald, Nov. 1880, p. 458)

"The memory of Daniel Lindley, the pioneer missionary at Inanda, was honored last December (1967) when a new bridge in Pietermaritzburg was named the Daniel Lindley Bridge. I had the very happy experience of going to the ceremony with our American Consul-General and his wife, Mr. and Mrs. Duggan, as Mr. Duggan had been asked to do the formal opening of the bridge — 'in honour of one of Maritzburg's distinguished early citizens, who was also an American missionary.'"

(From Dr. Lavinia Scott's general letter dated April 27, 1968. She is principal of Inanda Seminary.)

Mrs. Lindley (Lucy Allen) Buffalo, N. Y.; born Chatham, Columbia Co., N. Y. April 16, 1810; prof. rel. 1830; mar. Hartford, Ct., Nov. 20, 1834; emb. Boston Dec. 3, 1834; vis. U. S. Sept. 15, 1859 to Oct. 28, 1862. Returned to U. S. 1873. Died New York City Nov. 22, 1877. (Obituary Herald Jan. 1878)

Henry Isaac Venable, born Shelby Co., Ky. June 20, 1811; grad. Clinton Coll., Ky. 1830; Union Theol. Sem. 1834; ord. Danville, Ky. Oct. 9, 1834; emb. with Mr. Lindley and others Boston, Dec. 3, 1834; arr. Cape Town, Feb. 5, 1835; arr. Griqua Town, May 16, 1835; arr. Mosika June 16, 1836; compelled to abandon that station Jan. 17, 1837; proceeded across the country 1300 miles to ......

SOUTHERN AFRICA

Mission to the Zulus, established in 1835
Near Port Natal.

Daniel Lindley, son of Rev. Jacob Lindley of Athens, Ohio; Waterford, O.; born Washington Co., Pa., Aug. 24, 1801; prof. rel. Athens, O., 1821; grad. Ohio Univ. 1824; Union Theol. Sem., Va. 1831; ord. Nov. 7, 1834; emb. with Champion, Grout and others, Boston, Dec. 3, 1834; arr. Cape Town, Feb. 5, 1835; travelled by land thence one thousand miles in wagons drawn each by twelve yoke of oxen; arr. Griqua Town, May 16, 1835; and there commenced their missionary work; remained there five months; arr. Mosika, in Moselekatsi's country, June 16, 1836; the mission here broken up by a war between him and the Dutch Boers, Jan. 17, 1837; the mission re-established among the maritime Zulus, near Port Natal, July 27, 1837; the mission again broken up in Feb. 1838. Mr. Lindley and others leave Natal May 11, 1838; and arr. at Delagoa Bay, May 20; thence to Port Elisabeth; returned to Port Natal, June 12, 1839; from that time till 1847, Mr. Lindley labored chiefly among the Dutch colonists, or Boers, receiving from them his support, but retaining his connection with the Board; established in 1847 at Inanda among the Zulus; arr. at Boston on a visit to U. S. Sept. 15, 1859; re-emb. at Boston with wife and six children Oct. 28, 1862. Returned to U. S. 1873; sailed from Africa Apr. 26, 1873. Jan. 1878 living in New York City. Died Sept. 3, 1880. (See obituary in Herald, Nov. 1880, p. 458)

Mrs. Lindley (Lucy Allen) Buffalo, N. Y.; born Chatham, Columbia Co., N. Y. April 16, 1810; prof. rel. 1830; mar. Hartford, Ct., Nov. 20, 1834; emb. Boston Dec. 3, 1834; vis. U. S. Sept. 15, 1859 to Oct. 28, 1862. Returned to U. S. 1873. Died New York City Nov. 22, 1877. (Obituary Herald Jan. 1878)

Henry Isaac Venable, born Shelby Co., Ky. June 20, 1811; grad. Clinton Coll., Ky. 1830; Union Theol. Sem. 1834; ord. Danville, Ky. Oct. 9, 1834; emb. with Mr. Lindley and others Boston, Dec. 3, 1834; arr. Cape Town, Feb. 5, 1835; arr. Griqua Town, May 16, 1835; arr. Mosika June 16, 1836; compelled to abandon that station Jan. 17, 1837; proceeded across the country 1300 miles to Dingan's

country, and arr. Port Natal, on their way, July 27, 1837; visited Dingaan, Sept. 1, 1837; compelled to quit the Zulu country, Feb. 1838; arr. Port. Elisabeth, March 30, 1838; soon after went to Cape Town; returned to U. S.. Sailed for Cape Town Jan. 9, 1839; arr. Boston, March 2, 1839; released July 2, 1839. 1878, residing in Paris, Ill. Died there, May 22, 1878.

Mrs. Venable (Martha Aliciana Martin) born Paris, Bourbon Co., Ky., June 13, 1813; mar. South Hanover, Ind. Oct. 21, 1834; emb. Boston Dec. 3, 1834; returned to U. S. March 2, 1839. 1878 in Paris, Ill.

Alexander Erwin Wilson, M.D. See Western Africa, page 5.

Mrs. Wilson (Mary Jane Smithey) born Richmond, Va. Nov. 30, 1813; emb. Boston, Dec. 3, 1834; accompanied her husband and the other missionaries in the toilsome journey across the country; ar. Mosika, June 16, 1836; died at Mosika, Sept. 18, 1836.

George Champion, born Colchester, Ct., June 3, 1810; prof. rel. Aug. 1825; grad. Yale Coll. 1831; Andover Sem. 1834; ord. Colchester Nov. 13, 1834; emb. Boston with Lindley and others, Dec. 3, 1834; arr. Cape Town, Feb. 5, 1835; sailed thence July 23, 1835; ar. Algoa Bay, Aug. 6; at Port Natal, Dec. 20, 1835; visited Dingaan, Jan. 17, 1836; commenced a station at Ginani in his country., Sept. 26, 1836; compelled to abandon the country, Feb. 1838; at Port Elisabeth, April 1838; emb. Cape Town for U. S. Feb. 3, 1839; arr. Boston April 9, 1839; died at Santa Cruz, Dec. 17, 1841.

Mrs. Champion (Susan Larned) Webster, Mass.; born Oxford, Mass. March 30, 1808; prof. rel. Aug. 1822; mar. Nov. 14, 1834; Died, July 5, 1876, in her 73. Buried in Oxford, Mass.

Aldin Grout, born Pelham, Mass. Sept. 2, 1803; prof. rel. Nov. 1824; grad. Amh. Coll. 1831; Andover Sem. 1834; ord. Holden, Mass. Nov. 13, 1834; emb. with Lindley and others, Boston, Dec. 3, 1834; arr. Cape Town, Feb. 5, 1835;

mission broken up, Feb. 1838; visited U. S. May 1838; re-emb. Boston, March 7,
1840; arr. Cape Town, May 12, 1840; arr. Port Natal, June 30, 1840; commenced
a station among the Zulus, May 1841; visited U. S. arr. Boston, Sept. 1, 1857;
re-emb. Oct. 28, 1858; returned to U. S.   1870; sailed from Natal, Feb.
13, 1870. Jan. 1878 residing in Springfield, Mass. Ditto 1886. Died in
Springfield Feb. 12, 1894. (See April Herald, 1894, page 149)

Mrs. Grout (Hannah Davis) sister of the wife of James F. Clarke of the
Western Turkey Mission; born Holden, Mass. Feb. 6, 1805; prof. rel. Oct. 1817;
mar. Nov. 17, 1834; died at Bethelsdorp, S. Africa, Feb. 24, 1836.

Mrs. Grout (Charlotte Bailey) born Holden, Mass. June 21, 1811; mar. Holden,
Nov. 23, 1838; emb. Boston, March 7, 1840. Returned to U. S. 1870. Jan. 1878
in Springfield. Ditto 1886, where she died Dec. 26, 1896.

Newton Adams, M.D., born East Bloomfield, Ontario Co., N. Y. Aug. 4, 1804;
prof. rel. March 1832; emb. with Lindley and others, Boston, Dec. 3, 1834; arr.
Cape Town, Feb. 5, 1835; visited Dingaan Jan. 17, 1836; arr. Port Natal, May
21, 1836; commenced a station there; mission broken up Feb. 1838; returned to
Natal, June 12, 1839; ord. Cape Town, Dec. 10, 1844; died at Umlazi, S. Africa,
Dec. 16, 1851. (See Miss'y Herald Apr. 1852 p. 120)

Mrs. Adams (Sarah Carpenter VanTine) Cleveland, Ohio; born Pittstown, N. Y.,
1800
April 2, 1802; prof. rel. Auburn, N. Y. Feb. 1821; mar. Nov. 2, 1834; emb.
Boston, Dec. 3, 1834; returned from ill health to U. S. 1855. She died at
Cleveland, Ohio, Nov. 1, 1870. (See obituary notice in Herald for Jan. 1871
p. 28)

James Churchill Bryant, Littleton, Mass.; born Easton, Mass. April 8, 1812;
prof. rel. Mount Vernon, N. H. Jan. 1829; grad. Amh. Coll. 1836; Andover Sem.
1840; ord. pastor, Littleton, Mass. Oct. 28, 1840; pastor at Littleton 5½
years; emb. Boston, April 15, 1846; arr. Port Natal, Aug. 15, 1846; died at
Inanda, S. Africa, Dec. 23, 1850. (See obituary, Herald, vol. 47, pp. 143-201)

14.

Mrs. Bryant (Dolly F. Bursiel) born Bedford, N. H. Jan. 7, 1812; mar. Nelson, N. H. Oct. 22, 1840; emb. Boston, April 15, 1846; returned U. S. 1851. 1862, married Mr. Rufus Patten, farmer, Westford, Mass. Died in Littleton, Mass., Jan. 13, 1904.

Lewis Grout, West Brattleboro, Vt., born Newfane, Vt., Jan. 28, 1815; prof. rel. 1836; grad. Yale Coll. 1842; Andover Sem. 1846; ordained Springfield, Vt. Oct. 8, 1846; emb. Boston, Oct. 10, 1846; ar. Umlazi, Feb. 14, 1847; vis. U. S. 1862; released, Aug. 12, 1862. 1878, in W. Brattleboro, Vt. Ditto 1886. Died W. Brattleboro, Vt., Mar. 12, 1905. (See May 1905, Herald) (New agent Am. Miss. Assoc. W. Brattleboro, Vt.)

Mrs. Grout (Lydia Bates) born Springfield, Vt. Aug. 16, 1816; prof. rel. Nov. 24, 1834; grad. Mt. Holyoke Sem.; mar. Oct. 8, 1846; vis. U. S. 1862; released Aug. 1862. Died in West Brattleboro, Vt. Apr. 27, 1897.

Silas McKinney, born Binghamton, Broome Co., N. Y., Nov. 2, 1818; prof. rel. 1833; grad. Union Coll. 1842; Auburn Sem. 1846; ord. Binghamton, Sept. 1846; emb. Boston, April 29, 1847; arr. Umlazi, July 31, 1847; vis. U. S. July 6, 1853; re-emb. Boston, Sept. 12, 1856; arr. Natal, Jan. 20, 1857; vis. U. S. April 5, 1863; rel. April 3, 1866. 1877, a p. Tuscarora, N. Y. 1886, Fairport, N. Y. 1887, 11 Jefferson St., Auburn, N. Y. Died Auburn, N. Y. April 28, 1888.

Mrs. McKinney (Fanny M. Nelson) Cortlandville, Cortland Co., N. Y.; born Amherst, Mass. Oct. 7, 1817; prof. rel. Homer, N. Y. 1831; mar. Cortlandville, Feb. 24, 1847; emb. Boston, April 1847; died at Boston Saw Mills, 30 miles from Pietermaritzberg Nov. 26, 1861.

Samuel Dexter Marsh, born Ware, Mass. Nov. 28, 1817; prof. rel. 1836; grad. Yale Coll. 1844; New Haven Sem. 1847; ord. Ware Village, Sept. 9, 1847; emb. Boston, Oct. 28, 1847; arr. Natal Bay, Jan. 20, 1848; died Dec. 11, 1853. (Obituary, Herald, vol. 50; pp. 156, 199, 370)

Mrs. Marsh (Mary Sherman Skinner) born New Haven, Ct., Jan. 2, 1826; prof. rel. July 5, 1840; mar. Fairfield, Ct., Aug. 31, 1847; returned to U. S. May 13, 1854. 1856, in New Haven, Conn.

David Rood, Plainfield, Mass.; born Buckland, Mass. April 25, 1818; prof. rel. Plainfield, 1838; grad. Williams Coll. 1844; East Windsor Sem. 1847; ord. Plainfield, Oct. 6, 1847; emb. Boston, Oct. 28, 1847; arr. Natal Bay, Jan. 20, 1848; vis. U. S. Aug. 1860; re-emb. Boston, May 10, 1862; arr. Natal, Aug. 23, 1862. Jan, 1878, in Africa; station, Umvobi; ditto 1886. Vis. U. S. arr. N. Y., July 6, 1888; died in Covert , Mich. Apr. 8, 1891.

Mrs. Rood (Alzina V. Pixley) born Plainfield, Mass. Aug. 19, 1822; prof. rel. July 3, 1842; Grad. Mt. Holyoke Sem.; mar. Oct. 3, 1847; vis. U. S. 1860; re-emb. May 10, 1862; arr. N. Y. July 6, 1888. Jan. 1878 at Umvobi, ditto 1886. Died Lakewood, N. J. March 10, 1901.

William Ireland, Quincy, Ill.; born near Oswestry, Shropshire, England, Dec. 20, 1821; prof. rel. Greenwich, Ct., May 1830; grad. Illinois Coll. 1845; Andover Sem. 1848; ord. New Ipswich, N. H. Sept. 22, 1848; emb. Boston, Oct. 14, 1848; arr. Port Natal, Feb. 13, 1849; visited U. S. July 22, 1863; re-emb. Boston, Jan. 2, 1865. Vis. U. S. 1875. Sailed N. Y. May 13, 1876. Ar. Natal, July 24, 1876. Jan. 1878 in Africa; station, Amanzimtobe. 1886 at Adams. Returned to U. S. arr. June 1888. Died at Mass. Gen'l Hospital, Boston, Oct. 12, 1888.

Mrs. Ireland (Jane Wilson) born New Ipswich, N. H. Jan. 18, 1820; prof. rel. Sept. 3, 1837; mar. at New Ipswich, Sept. 28, 1848; emb. Oct. 1848; died Jan. 25, 1862.

Mrs. Ireland (Relief Oriana Grout) dau. of Rev. Aldin Grout of the Zulu Mission, born Bethelsdorp, Cape Colony, S. Africa, Dec. 9, 1835. Educated at Monson and Mt. Holyoke. Mar. Kenosha, Wis. June 1864. Sailed Boston, Jan. 2, 1865. Jan. 1878, at Amanzimtote, Vis. U. S. arr. Boston, Aug. 25, 1883; re-emb. Aug. 15,

1884; arr. Durban Oct. 4, 1884. 1886 in Adams; returned to U. S. arr. Boston, Oct. 25, 1897. Died West Groton, N. Y. March 3, 1902. (See Herald April 1902, p. 153)

Andrew Abraham, born Florida, Montgomery Co., N. Y. Oct. 12, 1818; prof. rel. Durensburgh, Schenectady Co., N. Y. 1840; studied at Union Coll.; Union Theol. Sem. 1848; ord. New York City, Oct. 13, 1848; emb. Boston, April 7, 1849; arr. Cape Town, June 13, 1849; arr. Port Natal, July 16, 1849; vis. U. S. 1873. Sailed N. Y. July 11, 1875. Ar. Durban (Natal) Sept. 22, 1875. Jan. 1878, at Mapumulo. Died Mapumulo, Sept. 13, 1878. (See Herald, Dec. 1878)

Mrs. Abraham (Sarah Lydia Biddle) daughter of Rev. William Biddle of Brookfield, Ct.; born in Hartfordshire, Eng. Nov. 12, 1822; prof. rel. April 1834; mar. Brookfield, Ct., Feb. 6, 1849; emb. April 1849. Vis. U. S. 1873. Ret'd. as above, Jan. 1878, at Mapumulo. Died in Natal Oct. 30, 1878. (See Herald Feb. 1879)

Hyman Augustine Wilder, Olivet, Eaton Co., Michigan; born Cornwall, Vt., Feb. 17, 1822; prof. rel. Moriah, Essex Co., N. Y. 1836; grad. Williams Coll. 1845; East Windsor Sem. 1848; ord. South Adams, Mass. Feb. 28, 1849; emb. Boston, April 7, 1849; arr. Cape Town, June 13, 1849; arr. Port Natal, July 16, 1849; vis. U. S. July 16, 1868. Sailed with wife from New York for Liverpool, returning to his field July 6, 1870; arr. at Durban, S. Africa, Sept. 17, 1870. Ret. to U. S. Jan. 30, 1877. Died Sept. 7, 1877 at Hartford, Conn.

Mrs. Wilder (Abby Temperance Linsley) Millville, Orleans Co., N. Y.; born Cornwall, Vt., Aug. 23, 1822; prof. rel. 1835; studied Mount Holyoke Sem.; a teacher some years; mar. Feb. 21, 1849; sailed etc. as above. (Mrs. Wilder is sister to the wife of Rev. Alvin B. Goodale, missionary in Turkey.) Ret. U. S. Jan. 30, 1877. They left Africa, Nov. 1876. With her son Rev. Geo. A. Wilder, re-emb. Boston Sept. , 1881. Oct. 1885 still at Umtwalumi; returned to U. S. arr. N. Y. June 18, 1889. Died at Winchester, Mass. Mar. 27, 1912.

U.S. arr. N.Y. June 18, 1889. d of d of Manchester, Mass.
(See Miss. Herald May 1912, p. 224) March 27, 1912.

Josiah Tyler, son of Rev. Bennet Tyler, DD. formerly President of Dartmouth College and of East Windsor Theol. Sem.; East Windsor, Ct.; born Hanover, N. H. July 9, 1823; prof. rel. Amherst 1842; grad. Amh. Coll. 1845; East Windsor Sem. 1848; ord. East Windsor, Ct. in Chapel of Theol. Inst. Feb. 23, 1849; emb. with Mr. Wilder, Boston, April 7, 1849; arr. Cape Town June 13, 1849; arr. Port Natal, July 16, 1849; vis. U. S. 1871; re-emb. May 10, 1873; ar. Natal Sept. 17, 1873. Jan. 1878, still in the field - Station Umsunduzi. Visited America in summer of 1881 in feeble health, reembarked from N. Y. 1881, Oct. 15; arr. Durban, Dec. 22, Oct. 1885 still in the field. Vis. U. S. a r. Boston, Sept. 1, 1889; died Asheville, N. C. Dec. 20, 1895. (See Feb. 1896 Herald p, 53)

Mrs. Tyler (Susan W. Clark) Northampton, Mass.; born March 22, 1828; prof. rel. Oct. 1840; mar. Feb. 27, 1849. Vis. U. S. 1871. Sailed as above - ar. Natal July 16, 1873. Jan. 1878, still in the field, Station, Umsunduzi. Died Nov. 17, 1887 at Umsunduzi.

Jacob Ludwig Döhne, a native of Germany; left that country in 1836, as a missionary to South Africa, under the direction of the Berlin Miss. Soc.; after their mission in Caffraria was broken up by war in 1846, was for some time acting pastor of a Reformed Dutch Church, Petermaritzburg, S. Africa; appointed a missionary of the A.B.C.F.M. Dec. 10, 1850; released from its service Aug. 20, 1861. Died in Natal, So. Africa, June 1, 1879. (See Herald Oct. 1879)

Mrs. Dohne (Caroline   ) probably a native of Germany.

Seth Bradley Stone, born Madison, Ct., Sept. 30, 1817; grad. Yale Coll. 1842; Union Sem., N. Y. 1850; ord. 1850; emb. Boston, Oct. 14, 1850; ar. Port Natal

17A'

Addenda to Vinton Book
Volume I

Jacob Ludwig DOHNE born on 9 November 1811
at Zierbergen, Hesse, Germany
died on 2 June 1879
at Fort Pine, Natal, southern Africa

married 1. Bertha GÖHLER
died on 23 Feb 1840
near Shilohheim, Cape Colony
2. Auguste KEMBLY
died on 23 Sept 1846
at Bethanie, Orange Free State
3. Caroline Elizabeth Wilhelmine
WATERMEYER
born 2 Nov 1817
died 13 March 1888
at Paddock, Natal Colony

1832 joined the Berlin Missionary Society
1836 sent to southern Africa; soon located in Transkei
1838/9 married Bertha Gohler who came from Germany
1844 → occupied in the translation of the Bible into Xhosa.
1846-47 Seventh Frontier War

Jacob Ludwig DÖHNE continued

1847 appointed (by British Government) Minister to the Boers in Pietermaritzburg

1847 resigned from Berlin Missionary Society

1849 accepted into service of the American Board of Commissioners for Foreign Missions (A.B.C.F.M.) and began a mission station at Table Mountain near Pietermaritzburg

1858 published a Zulu-English Dictionary in Cape Town, Cape Colony

1861 returned to employ of Berlin Missionary Society with the intention of working full-time on the translation of the Bible into Zulu
settled between Christianenburg (New Germany) and Durban, Natal; new missionaries arriving in Natal learned Zulu from him. The translation of the Bible did not progress well

1871 resigned from Berlin Missionary Society, partly because of differences with other missionaries

1871 → moved to Utrecht, Natal and then to Biggarsberg, Glencoe, Natal

1879 during the Zulu War he was forced to flee to Fort Pine, Natal

1879 died at Fort Pine; buried on the farm Kirkland, Dundee district, Natal

Bertha Amalia Christina — 15 Nov 1844
Joseph Ludwig — 29 July 1845
Caroline Wilhelmina Anna — 3 June 1848
Lucy Johanna — 23 Dec 1849
John George — 27 May 1851
Gottfried Andreas — 22 Feb 1853
Emelia Sophia — 10 Aug 1855
Frederick Watermeyer — 28 July 1857
Louis Jakob — 22 Feb 1859
Augusta Henrietta Maria } twins b. 23 March 1860
Beatrice Charlotte Louranno

reference: Zöllner L and Heese J A. "The Berlin Missionaries in South Africa and their descendants". Human Sciences Research Council, Pretoria, 1984.

July 16. Ret. to U. S. 1875. Died, New York City, Jan. 27, 1877.

Mrs. Stone (Catharine Matilda Stone) Williamsburgh, L. I.; born New York City, June 16, 1825; prof. rel. 1848; mar.   1850; emb. Oct. 14, 1850; vis. U. S. Aug. 21, 1862; re-emb. Boston Oct. 10, 1863. Vis. U. S. 1871. Sailed N. Y. May 17, 1873. Ret. U. S. 1875. 1887 Staten Island, N. Y. 1896, 11 Central Ave., New Brighton. Died New Brighton, N. Y. Jan. 20, 1902.

William Mellen; born Temple, N. H. Feb. 16, 1817; prof. rel. Templeton, Mass. 1834; studied at the Mission Institute, Quincy, Ill. and New Haven Sem. 1849; ord. 1850, July 20; emb. Boston, June 23, 1851; arr. Port Natal, Sept. 10, 1851. Returned to U. S. 1875. Released, 1876. 1886 at Oberlin, O. Died at Oberlin Feb. 12, 1892.

Mrs. Mellen (Laurana W. Fairbank) born Oakham, Mass. July 12, 1829; mar. June 21, 1851. Sailed as above. Ar. Natal, Sept. 10, 1851. Returned U. S. 1874. Released 1876. 1886 at Oberlin, O. Ditto 1892. Died at Oberlin, O. July 23, 1892. (See Sept. Herald, p. 379, 1892)

Stephen C. Pixley, born Plainfield, Mass. June 23, 1829; grad. Williams Coll. 1852; East Windsor Sem. 1855; ordained Plainfield, Sept. 25, 1855; emb. Boston, Oct. 25, 1855; arr. Cape Town, Dec. 22, 1855. Jan. 1878, in Africa, Station, Inanda. Vis. U. S. arr. at Quebec June 8, 1881; re-emb. Boston Oct. 20, 1883; arr. Durban, Dec. 13, 1883; Oct. 1885 still at Lindley. Vis. U. S. arr. N.Y. May 6, 1898; re-emb. Boston Oct. 21, 1899. Died Feb. 21, 1914 at Durban. (See Miss. Herald May 1914, p.235 - June 14, p. 258)

Mrs. Pixley (Louisa Healey) Northampton, Mass.; born Chesterfield, Mass. March 16, 1833; grad. Mt. Holyoke Sem.; mar. Oct. 18, 1855. Jan. 1878 in Africa; at Inanda. Vis. U. S. arr. U. S. June 8, 1881; re-emb. Boston, Oct. 20, 1883; arr. Durban, Dec.13, 1883. Oct. 1885 still at Lindley. Vis. U. S. arr. N.Y. May 6, 1898; re-emb. Boston, Oct. 21, 1899. Died at Lindley, Natal, Sept. 30,

Elijah Robbins, born Thompson, Ct. March 12, 1828; prof. rel. July 4, 1852; grad. Yale Coll. 1856; East Windsor Sem. 1859; ord. East Hartford, Ct., Aug. 3, 1859; emb. Boston, Sept. 29, 1859; arr. Natal, Dec. 1859; vis. U. S. 1872. Sailed New York, June 9, 1874. Jan. 1878 at Amanzintote. 1886 at Adams. Died at Adams, June 30, 1889. (See obit. notice Herald, Oct. 1889, pp. 402)

Mrs. Robbins (Adeline Bissell) Rockville, Ct.; born Schoharie, N. Y. Jan. 19, 1834; prof. rel. 1852; mar. Aug. 17, 1859. Vis. U. S. 1872. Ret. as above Jan. 1878 at Amanzimtote. 1886 Adams. Died at Adams, Oct. 20, 1888.

Henry Martyn Bridgman, born Westhampton, Mass. Jan. 8, 1830; prof. rel. Sept. 1849; grad. Amh. Coll. 1857; East Windsor Sem. and Union Sem., N. Y. 1860; ord. Westhampton, June 27, 1860; emb. Boston, Sept. 1, 1860; arr. at Durban, Nov. 23, 1860; visited U. S. June 8, 1867; re-emb. New York, Nov. 14, 1868; ar. Port Natal, April[1] 1869. Jan. 1870 in Africa, Station Umzumbi. Vis. U. S. arr. June 20, 1885; re-emb. Sept. 5, 1885; arr. Umzumbi, Oct. 17. Died at Amanzimtote, Natal, Aug. 23, 1896. (See Dec. 1896 Herald)

Mrs. Bridgman (Laura Brainerd Nichols) born East Haddam, Ct. June 20, 1834; prof. rel. Sept. 1, 1853; grad. Mt. Holyoke Sem.(3 yrs); mar. Aug. 1, 1860. Sailed as above.Jan. 1870 at Umzumbi. Vis. U. S. arr. June 20, 1885; re-emb. July 2, 1886. Vis. U. S. arr. N. Y. Sept. 12, 1903; re-emb. Boston Oct. 12, 1904. Died June 13, 1923 at Umzumbi, Africa. (See Miss. Herald 1923, p.160)

Charles Hooker Lloyd, born New Haven, Ct., Feb. 21, 1833; prof. rel. New York, Jan. 1856; studied N. York Univ.; Princeton Theol. Sem. 1862; ord. New York April 29, 1862; emb. N. York, June 21, 1862; arr. Natal, Dec. 11, 1862; died Feb. 10, 1865.

Mrs. Lloyd (Catharine C. Parker) daughter of Willard Parker, M.D.; born

Addenda to Vinton Book

Volume I

Mrs. Charles H. Lloyd, born Katherine Caroline PARKER, daughter of Dr. Willard Parker } born on 28 June 1841

she married 2ndly Newton Adams Lindley
on 26 January 1870
near Inanda Mission Station, Natal
she died on 4 July 1879 in New York, U.S.A.

Newton Adams LINDLEY was born on 26 July 1841 in Pietermaritzburg, Natal, southern Africa. He was the son of Revd Daniel Lindley and Lucy (Allen) Lindley (ABCFM missionaries in Natal).
He qualified M.D. c 1868 after serving a preceptor-ship with Dr. Willard Parker of New York.
He worked in Inanda, Natal then in Newcastle, Natal (c 1870-1872), New York city, Florida (Jacksonville).
He died on 28 September 1878 in Staten Island, N.Y.

ref: 1) marriage certificate of Newton Adams Lindley and Katherine Caroline Lloyd
2) E.W. Smith "The Life and Times of Daniel Lindley (1801-92)." London: Epworth Press, 1949

autumn, 1878, of yellow fever. Died in New York, July 23, 1879. (See Herald, Oct. 1879)

ASSISTANT MISSIONARIES

John Quincy Adams Butler, printer; Chelsea, Mass.; born Essex, Mass. Oct. 27, 1826; prof. rel. South Boston, 1844; emb. Boston, March 13, 1850; arr. Cape Town, May 20, 1850; returned to U. S. May 13, 1854; released Jan. 27, 1854. Jan. 1878, residing in Chelsea, Mass. Ditto 1886. Died in Worcester, Aug. 27, 1889.

Mrs. Butler (Anna Sophia Parker) Chelsea, Mass.; born Andover, Maine, Jan. 14, 1820; prof. rel. Boston, July 1839; mar. Feb. 28, 1850; ret. to U. S. 1854. Jan. 1878 in Chelsea. Ditto 1886. Ditto 1900. Died at Chelsea, Nov. 6, 1902.

Mrs. Mary Kelley Edwards (Mary Kelley) Troy, Ohio; born West Milton, Miami Co., Ohio, July 8, 1829; prof. rel. 1842; emb. Boston, Aug. 19, 1868; arr. Durban near Natal, Nov. 16, 1868; reached her station, Inanda, Nov. 18. Vis. U. S. 1874. (She is the widow of William N. Edwards, mar. West Milton, O. July 15, 1850.) Sailed, New York, May 13, 1876. Ar. Natal, July 24. Jan. 1878 at Inanda. 1886 Inanda. (Was released temporarily in 1875, for family reasons.) Retired to Honor Roll 1925. Died at Inanda, South Africa, Sept. 23, 1927.

Laura A. Day from Rockford, Illinois; born Essex, Chittenden Co., Vt., Nov. 1, 1832; prof. rel. same place winter 1853. Joined Meth. Ch. Grad. Oberlin O. Sailed with Rev. H. A. Wilder and wife of this mission from New York for Liverpool, on the way to this field, July 6, 1870; ar. Durban, Sept. 17, Jan. 1878 in Africa. Station, Amenzimtote. Vis. U. S. 1879; re-emb. N. Y. Oct. 7, 1880; Oct. 1885 at Adams. Vis. U. S. arr. N. Y. Sept. 20, 1889.

Gertrude R. Hance from Binghamton, N. Y.; born Brookdale, Susquehanna

Co. Pa.; Dec. 17, 1844. Prof. rel. Apr. 1865, Presb. Ch. Sailed with Rev. H. A. Wilder (see above) from New York for Liverpool on the way to this mission, July 6, 1870; ar. Durban, Sept. 17, 1870. Jan. 1878 in Africa. Station Umvoti; Vis. U. S. arr. New York Sept. 10, 1886; re-emb. N. Y. June 1, 1888; arr. Durban, July 20, 1889; vis. U. S. arr. N. Y. April 12, 1899.

Rev. Myron Winslow Pinkerton, from Waupun, Wisconsin; born Boscawen, N. H. July 18, 1843; prof. rel. 1857; grad. Ripon Coll., Wis. 1868; Chicago Theol. Sem. 1871; ord. Ripon, Wis. July 14, 1871; sailed from New York for Liverpool on the way to this mission, Aug. 9, 1871; ar. Durban, Oct. 9 and Umtwalumi, Oct. 18, 1871. Jan. 1878 still in the field, Station Indundumi. Visited U. S. and re-emb. May 22, 1880. Died of fever - en-route to Umzila's Kingdom 1880, Nov. 10. (See obit. in Herald March 1881, p. 88)

Mrs. Pinkerton (Louisa M. Byington) of Chicago, Ill.; born Madrid, St. Lawrence Co., N. Y. Sept. 24, 1849. Prof. rel. Chicago 1865. M. June 15, 1871 at Chicago. Sailed as above. Ar. Umtwalumi, Oct. 18, 1871. Jan. 1878, still in the field at Indundumi. Ret. 1879. Ret. 1881. 1886 at Oberlin, O. Died Feb. 20, 1921. (Miss. Herald 1921, page 152)

Rev. Charles W. Kilbon, born Springfield, Mass. July 27, 1844. Prof. rel. 1858, uniting with Olivet Ch., Springfield. Grad. Hartford Sem. 1872, and spent the following year there as a grad. student. Ord. Mar. 10, 1873 at Springfield. Sailed New York, May 10, 1873. Ar. Natal, July 16, 1873. Jan. 1878 still in the field. Station Umtwalumi. Vis. U. S. arr. Aug. 22, 1885; re-emb. N. Y. Nov. 10, 1887. Vis. U. S. arr. N. Y. Sept. 12, 1903; released Dec. 19, 1905. Died Oct. 6, 1916. (Miss'y Herald 1916, p. 574)

Mrs. Kilbon (Mary B. Knox) Manchester, Conn. Born June 4, 1843; m. Apr. 8 1873. Sailed as above. Jan. 1878 at Umtwalumi. Vis. U. S. arr. Aug. 22, 1885; re-emb. Boston C. 23, 1891. Died at Amanzimtote, Natal Nof. 20, 1901. (See Feb. 1902 Herald, page 44.)

22.

<u>Martha J   Lindley</u>, dau. of Rev. Daniel Lindley;

Vis. U. S. 1876.
No evidence of appointment.

<u>Mary E   Pinkerton</u>, dau. of Rev. David Pinkerton; born Elkhorn, Wis., Sept. 1, 1846. Prof. rel. 1859. Educated at Knox Coll., Ill., and Iowa Coll., Grinnell, Iowa. Teacher. Sailed N. Y. June 3, 1874. Ar. Jan. 1878 at Umzumbi; vis. U. S. arr. Quebec June 8, 1881; released Oct. 23, 1883. 1886 in Chicago.

<u>Fannie M   Morris</u>, born Trenton, N. J., June 15, 1851. Prof. rel. 1866. Sailed Boston, May 19, 1877. Ar.   Jan. 1878 at Inanda; returned to U. S. arr. Quebec, June 8, 1881; released April 18, 1882. 1886 at Boston.

<u>Martha Endora Price</u>, born Gilmanton, N. H., April 11, 1847; prof. rel. May 1865, Gilmanton, N. H. Educated at Gilmanton Acad. and Mt. Holyoke. Engaged in teaching and City Mission work. Sailed Boston, May 19, 1877. Ar. June, 1877, at Inanda Jan. 1878 at Inanda. Visited U. S. arr. N. Y. June 20, 1885; emb. Boston April 8, 1889; arr. Durban May 23, 1889; vis. U. S. arr. N. Y. Apr. 5, 1900; re-emb. N. Y. Aug. 7, 1901; vis. U. S. arr. N. Y. Sept. 13, 1908; re-emb. N.Y. Nov. 17, 1909. Vis. U. S. arrived N. Y. (?) June 18, 1916. Died Nov. 30, 1926 at Portsmouth, N. H.   (See Herald, Jan. 1927, page. 40)

<u>Fidelia Phelps</u>, born Strongsville, O., Aug. 16, 1855; prof. rel. Sept. 18'1; educated Westfield Normal School and Mt. Holyoke Sem.; sailed N. Y. Sept. 25, 1884; arr. Durban Nov. 4, 1884. Oct. 1885 at Lindley. Vis. U. S. arr. Boston, Aug. 22, 1890; re-emb. N. Y. Jan. 23, 1892; arr. Durban Mar. 5, 1892. Vis. U. S. arr. N. Y. May 11, 1901; re-emb. Boston, May 7, 1902; vis. U. S. arr. N. Y. Feb. 24, 1910; re-emb. N. Y. Jan. 28, 1911. Vis. U. S. arr. N.Y. (?) June 18, 1916; re-emb. New Orleans, La., Jan. 8, 1918; arr. Durban Feb.

6, 1918. Begun 5th term Feb. 10, 1918. Arr. home May 6, 1930. Retired to Roll of Honor May 7, 1930. Died at Claremont, Cal. on July 3, 1933.

George Albert Wilder, son of Rev. Hyman A. Wilder, formerly miss'y to the Zulu mission; born Amanzimtote, Natal, So. Africa, March 14, 1855; prof. rel. Umtwalumi, Dec. 8, 1867; educated Phillips Acad.,;Andover; Williams College, grad. 1877; and Hartford Theol. Inst.; ord. Hartford, Ct., May 16, 1880; emb. N. Y. Oct. 9, 1880; arr. Durban, Dec. 13, 1880. Oct. 1885 at Umtwalumi; vis. U. S. arr. Boston Aug. 22, 1890; re-emb. N. Y. Oct. 2, 1891; arr. Durban Dec. 15, 1891; transferred to E. C. African mission May 16, 1893. (See page   ) DD in 1902. Died at Glen Ridge, N. J. Dec. 28, 1935.

Mrs. Wilder (Alice Cort Scamman) born Biddeford, Maine May 20, 1857; prof. rel. May 3, 1874; educated Buffalo Fem. Acad.;Mar. May 27, 1880; emb. N. Y. Oct. 9, 1880; arr. Durban Dec. 13, 1880. Oct. 1885 at Umtwalumi. Vis. U. S. arr. Boston Aug. 22, 1890; re-emb. N. Y. Oct. 2, 1891; arr. Durban Dec. 15, 1891; vis. U. S. arr. N. Y. June 18, 1901; re-emb. Boston April 7, 1903; transferred to East Cent. Africa May 16, 1893. (See page   ) Died Oct. 6, 1929 Glen Ridge, N. J. See Mis. Her. Dec. 1929 - p. 478

Herbert Delos Goodenough, born Barton, Washington Co., Wis. May 22, 1852; prof. rel. West Bend, Wis. 1871; educated at Oberlin; grad. coll. 1877, Theol. Dept. 1881; ord. Oberlin June 26, 1881; emb. Boston Sept. 1, 1881; arr. Durban, Oct. 30, 1881. Oct. 1885 at Adams. Vis. U. S. arr. Boston July 1, 1888; re-emb. Boston June 29, 1889; arr. Durban Aug. 28, 1889; Vis. U. S. arr. N. Y. April 5, 1900; re-emb. N. Y. Aug. 7, 1901; Left field July 13, 1911; re-emb. Sept. 23, 1912. Resignation accepted Sept. 16, 1913, he remaining in the field. Died in Mattapoisett, Mass. August 24, 1927. (See Herald Dec. 1927, page 467)

Mrs. Goodenough (Caroline Louise Leonard) born Bridgewater, Mass. Dec. 31, 1856; prof. rel. Oberlin, Ohio, 1874; educated Bridgewater High School and

...rlin; mar. Aug. 22, 1878; emb. Boston Sept. 1, 1881; arr. Durban Oct. 30, 1881. Oct. 1885 at Adams. Vis. U. S. arr. Boston July 1, 1888; re-emb. Boston June 29, 1889; arr. Durban Aug. 29, 1889; Vis. U. S. arr. Boston July 7, 1898. Ret'd to field, arr. home Jan. 22, 1910. Resigned Sept. 10, 1912. Returned to Africa 1925. Died at Umkomaas, Natal, S. Africa, Jan. 10, 1942

Charles Werden Holbrook, born Abington, Plymouth Co., Mass. Oct. 25, 1856; prof. rel. Rockland, Mass. July 1869; grad. Amherst Coll. 1880; Andover Theol. Sem. 1883; ord. Rockland Aug. 28, 1883; emb. Boston Oct. 20, 1883; arr. Durban, Dec. 13, 1883. Oct. 1885 at Mapumulo. Vis. U. S. arr. Boston Sept. 3, 1892; released March 17, 1896. Died Dec. 19, 1933 in New York (City?).

Mrs. Holbrook (Sarah Elizabeth Lyman) born Easthampton, Hampshire Co., Mass. Sept. 23, 1856; prof. rel. Easthampton 1869; educated Mt. Holyoke Sem.; mar. Aug. 23, 1883; emb. Boston Oct. 20, 1883; arr. Durban, Dec. 13, 1883. Oct. 1885 at Mapumulo. Vis. U. S. arr. Boston, Sept. 3, 1892; released Mar. 17, 1896.

William Cullen Wilcox (Transferred from East Cent. Africa Sept. 20, 1892) (See page 25) Vis. U. S. arr. N. Y. Oct. 25, 1899; re-emb. New York Apr. 6, 1901. Vis. U. S. arr. N. Y. Oct. 10, 1908. Released Jan. 18, 1910. Died January 26, 1928, Bakersfield, Calif.

Mrs. Wilcox (Ida Belle Clary) Transferred from East Central Africa Sept. 20, 1892. (See page 25) Vis. U.S. arr. N. Y. Oct. 25, 1899; re-emb. New York April 6, 1901; vis. U. S. arr. N. Y. Oct. 10, 1908. Released Jan. 18, 1910.

This mission was commenced at Inhambane, July 1884.

MISSIONARIES

Erwin Hart Richards, born Orwell, O., May 4, 1851; prof. rel. Mecca, O. 1865; grad. Oberlin College 1877, Andover Theol. Sem. 1880; ord. Oberlin, Aug. 20, 1880; emb. N. Y. Oct. 9, 1880 to join the Zulu mission, with a view to ultimately going to Umzilas; arr. Durban Dec. 13, 1880; started for Umzilas Kingdom May 21, 1881: reached Umzilas Kraal, Oct. 10; after this he returned to Inenda where he remained till July 1884; during 1884 and '85 made two exploring expeditions into the interior. Oct. 1885 settled at Mongwe. Vis. U. S. arr. Boston Oct. 6, 1889; released July 1, 1890.

Mrs. Richards (Mittie Artemesia Bebout) born Savannah, Ashland Co., O., Sept. 9, 1854; prof. rel. May 1871; educated Savannah Academy and Oberlin Coll. mar. June 15, 1880; emb. N. Y. Oct. 9, 1880; arr. Durban Dec. 13, 1880; arr. Inhambane, July 1884; Oct. 1885 at Mongwe. Vis. U. S. arr. Boston Oct. 6, 1889; released July 1, 1890. Died of fever at Inhambane while on her way, with her husband, to commence a mission under Bishop Taylor on the Zambesi.

Willier Cullen Wilcox, born Richfield, O., Aug. 6, 1850; prof. rel. 1872; grad. Oberlin Coll. 1878, Oberlin Theol. Sem. 1881; studied nearly one year in Yale Sem.; ord. Oberlin July 26, 1881; emb. Boston, Sept. 1, 1881; arr. Durban Oct. 30; visited Inhambane Nov. 1883; returned to Inhambane June 1883. Oct. 1885 settled at Makodweni. Released May 3, 1887. 1888 Keene Valley, N. Y. Re-appt. Nov. 18, 1890; emb. N. Y. Jan. 14, 1891; arr. Inhambane April 20, 1891. Transferred to Zulu Miss. Sept. 20, 1892. (See page 24)

Mrs. Wilcox (Ida Belle Clary) born Northfield, Minn., Dec. 29, 1858; prof. rel. 1871; studied at Oberlin; mar. Northfield, Aug. 11, 1881; emb. Boston Sept. 1, 1881; arr. Durban Oct. 30; arr. Inhambane June 1883. Oct. 1885 at Makodweni   . Released May 3, 1887. 1888 Keene Valley, N. Y.

The Richards Collection

An ethnographic legacy from the Tonga and Zulu peoples of Southern Africa

by Jack Glazier
Assistant Professor of Sociology/Anthropology

Pausing before the ethnographic cases on the third floor of the King Building, the passer-by may examine the material culture of the Tonga and Zulu peoples of Southern Africa. For the past two years, display of the crafts of traditional Africa has caught the eyes of the Oberlin community. In setting up the current displays of artifacts used for food production and preparation, portage and warfare, anthropology students have made excellent use of a valuable collection procured by the Rev. Erwin Hart Richards (Oberlin class of 1877) during his latter 19th and early 20th century missionary endeavors. These artifacts now play an important and continuing role in the anthropology program at the College. The materials derive from the Rev. Mr. Richards' work among the Zulu of Natal, South Africa, and the Tonga of Mozambique. The department of Sociology-Anthropology now cares for this important array of Africana, and Oberlin alumni will be interested in the honor of this collection and its cultural significance.

Although we have no evidence concerning Mr. Richards' estimate of the long-term value of the items he collected, he obviously recognized their possible educational merit when he sent them to his alma mater. His early and continuing association with the College and town may explain how he came to contribute these artifacts to Oberlin.

Born in 1850 in Orwell, Ohio, Mr. Richards was the son of Samuel Newton Richards and Mary Jane Hart Richards. Several generations previously, the Richards and Harts had emigrated from Britain to Connecticut, and branches of each family finally settled in the Western Reserve. By the time he was six, young Richards had lost both of his parents to what his daughter identified as "galloping consumption." Relatives took him in, but ultimately foster parents reared him on their farm near Cortland, Ohio. Childless themselves, his foster parents looked to the time when Erwin would assume responsibility for the farm.

But his anticipated farming life was given up at the urging of his maternal aunt, Anna Hart. She had graduated from Oberlin in 1868, and she encouraged her nephew to take up Oberlin's life of learning and labor. As labor was necessary to pay his tuition and living expenses, his aunt assured Erwin that he might secure employment to support his studies. The new student arrived at the College in 1872 and he worked as a caretaker at the First Church, where he conveniently found living quarters. He entered school as a senior in the old preparatory department, then advanced to freshman status in 1873. Following a predictable curriculum, the young man graduated in 1877 and subsequently embarked on further study. In 1880, he received the A.M. from Oberlin, then the Bachelor of Sacred Theology from Andover Theological Seminary.

Following his education, he began his long career as a missionary in Africa. From 1880 to 1884, Mr. Richards and his wife, Mittie Bebout Richards who had been his classmate at Oberlin, held a post in Zululand in Natal. The Foreign Mission Board of the Congregational Church assigned them to this region, and during that period, Mr. Richards made excursions to Rhodesia to find additional mission stations. In 1884 he was reassigned to the vicinity of Inhambane. This town on the East African Coast is in the Portuguese territory of Mozambique, a colonial possession since the earliest voyages of discovery, but now a newly-independent nation. After some five years in Mozambique, the Richards and their young daughter returned to America for a leave in 1890. The young couple entrusted their daughter to the care of her maternal grandparents in Norwalk and returned to Mozambique in the same year. Mrs. Richards died of fever during this next period of service, and Mr. Richards returned home to undertake a lecture tour for the Mission Board during 1895-97. At the end of this period, he married Carrie Duncanson and they set out for East Africa. Their only child was born in Durban, South Africa, three years later. In 1902, the Richards departed for a trip home, but death claimed Carrie Richards en route, and she was buried at sea. Not wishing to leave his second daughter in America and hoping to return to Mozambique, Mr. Richards again contemplated marriage. His close friend and ministerial colleague, R. G. McClelland, arranged a union, offering his own daughter, Mary Jane McClelland, some 30 years younger than her prospective husband. The new family set out for Inhambane for Mr. Richards' final stint of missionary work, which concluded in 1908 with their return to Ohio. Eventually the family settled in Oberlin, making their home at 270 East College. For a number of years thereafter, Mr. Richards actively lectured around the country for the Mission Board of the Methodist Church, which he had joined some years

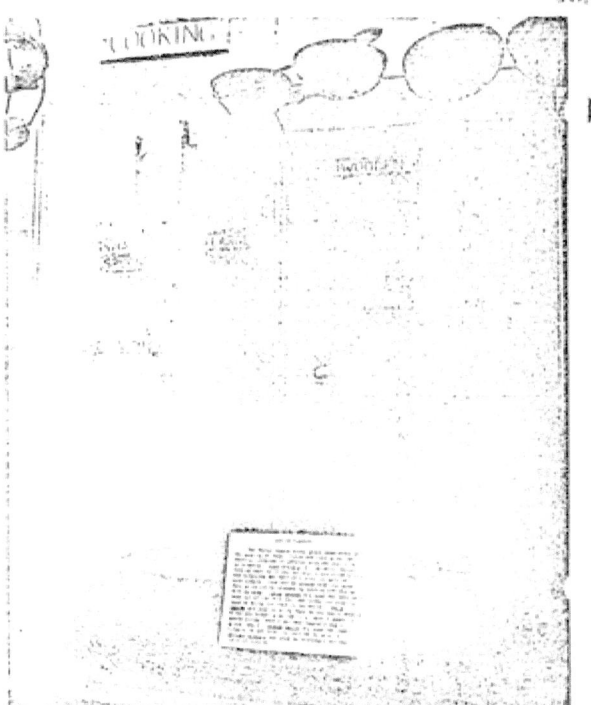

Part of the Richards Collection as displayed in the King Bldg.

before. Erwin Richards died at his Oberlin home early in 1928, only months after celebrating with friends the 50th anniversary of the class of 1877.

During his years in Africa, Mr. Richards periodically sent back to the College various anthropological and zoological specimens. Among the latter were skulls of predators such as lion and leopard, as well as those of ruminants such as kudu, eland and hartebeest, replete with horns. These striking remains gradually accumulated in the museum, and today might surprise an unwary visitor to the storage rooms adjoining King 306. Anthropological items in these early accessions include traditional weaponry and hunting paraphernalia such as bows and arrows, spears, knives, clubs and shields. Mr. Richards in the 1880's also forwarded cooking implements and musical instruments such as gourd rattles and xylophones, or timbila, composed of ten hardwood keys set atop gourd resonators. Also among the materials the College received were African pillows—those famous small, gracefully-crafted wooden head supports. Some African peoples use them to protect elaborate coiffures from contact with the ground. Many of these first acquisitions are from the Zulu but they constitute only a fraction of the total inventory.

The greater proportion of this anthropological legacy derives from Tongaland in the vicinity of the missionary's central work. Mr. Richards' intermittent shipments to the College established the collection, which was completed in 1932 by his widow, Mary Jane, who donated most of what constitutes the present Richards collection. Older Oberlinians may remember when the collection was stored and displayed in the Second Church, which stood on the site of the present Conservatory of Music. Yet, for many years, this important resource lay hidden and unused until its rediscovery in the late 1960's by Oberlin anthropologists. In the last two years, through donations from Mr. Richards' grandchildren and departmental funds, Oberlin anthropologists can utilize the Richards Collection in their study of African material culture.

Placing particular articles in displays, as pictured on the accompanying pages, the anthropologist represents fundamental aspects of Tonga and Zulu life. Such museum exhibits aim at establishing the cultural context, which can present as precisely as possible the nature and function of the articles displayed. Anthropology students working on the Richards collection have thus created exhibits which explain physical aspects of workmanship and technology used in producing the pieces, as they also examine the social dimension of specialization and division of labor associated with their production. Such information cannot emerge simply by inspection of the artifacts themselves. To appreciate the cultural relevance of the material, the anthropologist requires ethnographic information about the people who produced the article.

Although we know nothing about the circumstances under which Mr. Richards acquired the present collection, which could help in its interpretation, a useful and extensive ethnographic literature on the Zulu supports this endeavor. However, a similar volume of anthropological materials on the Mozambique Tonga does not exist. Inference about the Inhambane objects may be advanced by examining available accounts of other southern Bantu peoples akin to the Tonga. Most notably, Henri Junod's The Life of a South African Tribe (1927), despite some obvious biases and limitations, stands as

a landmark of ethnographic reporting and has proven of great value to a later generation of African-oriented anthropologists.

This two-volume study by Junod, a Swiss missionary, focuses on the Tsonga (or Thonga in Junod's now outmoded usage), a Bantu people of extensive distribution in Mozambique, Natal and the Transvaal. The Tsonga are more numerous and more dispersed than the Tonga of the relatively restricted region of the Inhambane coastal area. Although Junod distinguishes the Tonga and Tsonga primarily on linguistic grounds, the two groups are contiguous and share a common pool of technological and material expertise characteristic of the southern Bantu generally. From Junod's photographs, sketches and descriptions of Tsonga material culture, together with other sources, we attempt to interpret the significance of our own Tonga artifacts.

Further, we can place the Richards Collection in a broader context for comparative purpose since the Tsonga/Tonga peoples form one among four large subdivisions of the southern Bantu. A second group is the Nguni, including the Zulu, Swazi and Ndebele. The Sotho, including the Tswana, constitute a third group. The smallest in number of the four groupings is the Venda. Designating these peoples as Bantu relies essentially on a linguistic classification. All four groups speak mutually unintelligible languages which are nonetheless related structurally. Even more important for discovering historical relations between them is the lexical connection, for the languages share a high proportion of words deriving from the same roots. In studying the collection, we find these connections helpful since we are interested in the larger setting, pursuing as we do the fundamental anthropological goal of comparison.

Despite important cultural and social features differentiating these southern Bantu peoples, they all share patterns of traditional subsistence and technology. The Tsonga/Tonga, like other southern Bantu, lived on a mixed economy of stock-keeping and horticulture. They raised varieties of grain, mostly sorghum and maize, and kept cattle and goats. This mixed economy was maintained through a repertoire of material culture, using carved wood, pottery, leather and iron.

An important dimension of Tonga and Zulu life is shown in the weaponry of the Richards collection, with its shields, spears, clubs, bows and arrows, knives, and battle axes. Some of these pieces, such as axes, were also important for wood-working or other domestic tasks far removed from warfare. Numerous spears, on the other hand, suggest martial activity. In southern Africa, the spears are known as assagais (the name derives from a type of dogwood tree which often provides the wood); the weapons display carefully worked double-edged iron blades hafted to wooden shafts by means of thin iron wire, sinew or bark fiber. Warriors hurled the longer spears, with comparatively shorter blades, at enemies; they wielded the shorter spears, with blades relatively longer than those found on the throwing spears, in direct hand-to-hand combat.

Although the difference between these two types of spears may seem slight, the initial development and deployment of the shorter stabbing spear had profound consequences for the history of southern Africa. The technology underlying this history can be appreciated in the collection. Shaka, the famous early 19th century Zulu chief, introduced the shorter spear as he reorganized his military regiments, known as impis. Shaka created a full-time warrior force bivouacked throughout his domain. Once opponents released their conventional throwing spears, which were never particularly effective, Shaka's contingents could advance against their disarmed foes at close range with their longer-bladed spears in hand. Shaka's revolution in military tactics resulted in much bloodier conflict, and enabled him to consolidate the Zulu nation.

For whatever reasons, perhaps population pressures, warfare under Shaka had altered as it became an instrument for gaining land and extending political hegemony. Fundamental changes in the motives for war as well as in military organization had stimulated the "wars of wandering," or *Mfecane*, as they are known in Zulu. These wars are so designated because they triggered extensive population movements which fundamentally altered the political picture of southern Africa in the nineteenth century. Some Nguni survivors of the Zulu *Mfecane* adopted Zulu military tactics and organization, conquering peoples in Rhodesia, Malawi and Mozambique. Others copied Zulu techniques in an effort to withstand their expansion, and varieties of spear types of the sort represented in the Richards collection played no small role in these pivotal events.

In addition to these significant military pieces, one finds implements vital in Tonga food preparation in the current displays. As a people relying primarily on grain cultigens for their diet, the Tonga developed a material culture for preparing and serving the maize, millet and sorghum which form the grain staples of sub-Saharan Africa. Contemporary people at a rural market in Africa may purchase metal cups, plates and cooking pots, or even steel knives from Manchester. All of these might even be arrayed next to a case of Coca-Cola or nationally bottled European-style beer. The Richards collection reminds us of an earlier time when Western market items did not yet fully complement, much less supplant, indigenous crafts. The people Mr. Richards encountered clearly relied on their own highly functional traditional expertise. Men engaged in the manufacture of palm leaf baskets for winnowing and portage, wooden mortars and pestles for making meal, spoons, cups and bowls. Women used these implements and cooked the foods they prepared in clay pottery of their own manufacture. Without the use of a potter's wheel or coiling techniques, Tonga women produced pottery of fine shape and symmetry.

Tonga primarily directed food preparation toward the evening meal, consisting of a kind of porridge produced from prepared grains. The Tonga cook first husked, then winnowed and pounded the grain. She cooked the resulting ground meal in a clay pot, constantly stirring with a sort of four-bladed mixing stick. Sometimes she might steam the grain meal by sealing the normal crockery with ox dung. Tonga cuisine might be supplemented with beans and peas and en-

continued on page 57

I

New proposal for Westervelt

by Steven McQuillin '75

I am proposing a new plan for the use of Westervelt Hall in downtown Oberlin. Apartments for students and faculty would be created in a completely-renovated interior. The exterior would be restored to its former beauty.

The lawn in front of the building would be landscaped into a small park for the downtown area and the gothic steeple would be rebuilt. The cost of this project would be financed from the rents generated by the apartments. This proposal has been presented to the College administration for its consideration and this article is part of an effort to present the proposal to the Oberlin community in an attempt to gain support for the project.

Westervelt was built more than 100 years ago at a cost of only $37,000 and it served as the Union school and later as the high school for the town of Oberlin. In the 1920's it was purchased by E. C. Westervelt for use as a private trades school. Mr. Westervelt soon gave up his school and donated the building to Oberlin College which was then in need of classroom space because it had just torn down all the buildings in Tappan Square in order to qualify for funds from the estate of Charles Martin Hall.

The College spent $30,000 to renovate the interior and otherwise improve the building.

After the first part of the King building was opened in 1941, Westervelt Hall was abandoned and it has not been used since except for occasional storage. The building is of no real use to the College in its present state and the Board of Trustees has directed that the building be disposed of in a way that would benefit the town of Oberlin. Since the early 1960's there has been much discussion as to how the building, or its site, could best serve the community and the College.

When I came to Oberlin in the fall of 1971, the decision had just been made to preserve both Peters Hall and Warner Center (then called Warner Gym) by shifting the location of the then-proposed Seeley G. Mudd Learning Center. Then, with a strong spirit of preservation, the Space Utilization Committee was formed and I became a member. Richard P. Dober, a well-known and respected planner, was hired by the committee to study academic buildings and make proposals concerning the best utilization of the present facilities.

Dober suggested that Westervelt could become the town's library. This was quickly proved unfeasable because neither the funds for renovation nor for operation of a separate facility were within the means of the Oberlin Public Library.

In an effort to resolve the issue of Westervelt Hall at no cost to the College, the trustees authorized President Fuller in 1973 to offer to give the building to the City of Oberlin with the understanding that the city would use it for public or a combination of public-private purposes. The College administration also was authorized to negotiate a contract with the city which would provide a "significant return to the College" if the city should elect to sell the building.

The hope was, among people interested in saving the building, that Westervelt Hall would be renovated for use as a city hall. The city had preliminary plans drawn up and they compared very favorably to the cost of building a new city hall. However, there was no consensus on whether the issue of providing a new city hall was of prime importance and the funds necessary to do a complete renovation were not available.

Since 1973 the city has backed away from the issue of building any type of city hall and it now is spending funds allocated for this purpose on a new fire station. It is unrealistic, therefore, to hope that Westervelt will become Oberlin's city hall in the foreseeable future. Meantime, though City Council passed an emergency ordinance in April 1973 accepting Westervelt from the College, the deed still is held by the College because neither the city nor the College has been able to get together to discuss what a "significant return" would be if the city were to sell the property.

My feeling is that it would be a mistake to give the building to the town under any circumstances which permit the building to be torn down. I hope that my proposal will encourage the College to withdraw its 1973 offer.

Last year, Westervelt Hall was listed in the *National Register of Historic Buildings*, and, through the efforts of Assoc. Economics Prof. David Segal and former Administrative Vice President Bayley Mason, it was awarded a federal matching grant of $7,500 for restoration work. This money, although not a large amount, would

re-appt. Nov. 18, 1890; emb. N. Y. Jan. 14, 1891; arr. Inhambane Apr. 20, 1891; transferred to Zulu Miss. Sept. 20, 1892. Vis. U. S. arr. N. Y. Sept. 19, 1908.

Benjamin Forsyth Ousley, the first <u>ordained</u> colored missionary of the A.B.C. F.M. He was born a slave of the brother of Jefferson Davis, Warren, Miss. Oct. 1855 (?); prof. rel. Nashville, Tenn.; grad. Fisk Univ. 1881; Oberlin Theol. Sem. 1884; ord. Oberlin, June 22, 1884; emb. N. Y. Sept. 25, 1884; arr. Durban, Nov. 14, 1884; sailed Nov. 28 for Inhambane; Nov. 1885 at Kambini. Vis. U. S. arr. Boston May 27, 1890; re-emb. Boston July 25, 1891; arr. Durban, Sept. 5, 1891; returned to U. S. arr. N. Y. July 8, 1893. 1900 prof. in Alcorn College, Westside, Miss.

Mrs. Ousley (Henriette Bailey) born Washington Co., Miss. Oct. 4, 1852; prof. rel. 1875; educated Fisk Univ., Nashville, Tenn.; mar. Aug. 14, 1884; emb. N. Y. Sept. 25, 1884; arr. Durban, Nov. 14, 1884; sailed Nov. 28 for Inhambane; Nov. 1885 at Kambini. Vis. U. S. arr. Boston, May 27, 1890; re-emb. Boston July 25, 1891; arr. Durban, Sept. 5, 1891; returned to U. S. arr. N. Y. July 8, 1893.

George Albert Wilder. Transferred to this mission May 16, 1893 (see page 23) Vis. U. S. arr. N. Y. June 18, 1901; re-emb. Boston, April 7, 1903; vis. U.S. arr. N. Y. Sept. 24, 1910- sailed Sept. 2, 1913. Left field May 2, 1919; arr. home July 22, 1919; sailed Sept. 30, 1920; arr. Dec. 1920; left field Oct. 15, 1924; arr. home Jan. 6, 1925 Retired after 44 years of service, Dec. 8, 1925. Died Dec. 28, 1935 at Glen Ridge, N. J.

Mrs. Wilder (Alice Coit Seamman) Transferred from the Zulu mission May 16, 1893. (See page 23) Vis. U. S. arr. N. Y. June 18, 1901; re-emb. Boston, April 7, 1903; vis. U. S. arr. N. Y. Sept. 4, 1909. Sailed etc. as above. Died Glen Ridge, N. J. Oct. 6, 1929. *See M's. Her. Dec. 1929, p. 477.*

EASTERN ASIA

CANTON MISSION

The attention of the Board was called to China by the urgent representations of Rev. Robert Morrison, many years missionary of the London Missionary Society at Canton, and of D. W. C. Olyphant, Esq. an eminent Christian merchant in that place. Great difficulties were known to exist in the way of missions to that empire; but a beginning was at length made by sending Rev. Elijah C. Bridgman as a missionary to Canton. He sailed from New York in the ship Roman, Oct. 14, 1829. In the same ship went Rev. David Abeel, under a commission from the American Seaman's Friend Society, as a missionary to seamen at Canton and vicinity who might speak the English language, but with a conditional appointment from the Board to take effect at the end of one year. These missionaries went out unmarried, and arrived at Canton, Feb.19, 1830.

The death of Mr. Bonney, July 1864, and of Dr. Ball, March 1866, and the departure of their widows and of Mr. and Mrs. Vrooman, left the Board without a missionary there, and the Canton mission was discontinued in October 1866.

MISSIONARIES

Elijah Coleman Bridgman was the founder of this mission, and was a member of it till 1854, when he was transferred to Shanghai. For further notices of him, see North China Mission. Dr. Bridgman with wife went to Shanghai, June 23, '47, to rep. Canton, in Com' of Delegates for translation of New Testament. Remained until Feb. 3, 1852, when he and wife ret. to U.S. Ret. to Shanghai, May 3, '53. Died, Nov. 2, 1861.

David Abeel was appointed missionary to the Chinese in Oct. 1830. After spending some years in missionary labors elsewhere, he arr. at Canton, Feb. 20, 1839; removed to Amoy, 1842. See Amoy Mission. Died, Sept.4, 1846.

Edwin Stevens, born New Canaan, Ct. Aug. 1801; grad. Yale Coll. 1828; tutor there 1831; studied Theol. at New Haven till 1831; went out under the direction of the American Seamen's Friend Society, as chaplain to seamen at Canton, at which port he arrived in Nov. 1832; spent three years at Canton in that capacity. Agreeably to an understanding to the effect before he went out, he was appointed a missionary of the A.B.C.F.M. July 7, 1835, and made several exploring missionary voyages among the Chinese. While prosecuting one of these voyages, he was attacked with fever at Singapore, and died there, Jan. 5, 1837. He was unmarried.

Peter Parker, M.D. b. at Framingham, Mass, June 18, 1804; grad. Yale Coll. 1831; at Theol. Sem. New Haven 1834; studied at New Haven Medical School and received the degree of M.D. in 1834; ord. Philadelphia, May 16, 1834; emb. New York, unmarried, June 3, 1834; ar. Canton, Oct. 26, 1834; went to Singapore to acquire the Fuhkien dialect, returned to Canton Sept. 1835, opened a Dispensary in Canton and had 300 patients in Nov. 1835; embarked Canton (Macao) July 3, 1837, in ship Morrison, owned by Talbot, Olyphant & Co. in company with Mr. King, a partner in said house, Mrs. King and Mr. Samuel Wells Williams of the mission, with seven Japanese sailors on board, for Japan, to ascertain what openings there might be for commercial intercourse, and eventually for missionary labor among the people of that empire. The ship arrived in the Bay of Yedo, July 31, and in the Bay of Kagosima, Aug. 10; but was fired upon in both instances, and no communication permitted with the shore. The ship returned to Canton, Aug. 29. This was probably the first attempt to introduce Christianity into Japan, since the expulsion of the Jesuits two centuries before.

Dr. Parker ar. New York, Dec. 10, 1840; re-emb. with a wife, Boston, June 13, 1842; ar. Macao, Oct. 4, at Canton, Nov. 5, 1842. The Hospital under his care received more than 1600 patients in one year, making 16,000

Dr. Parker was released from his connection with the Board in 1847, having accepted the appointment of Secretary of Legation to the U.S. Embassy to China. He continued his labors in the Hospital as before. He was afterwards U. S. Commissioner to China. He returned to U.S. in 1857. 1858-1878 resident of Washington, D.C. Died Jan. 10, 1888 at Washington.

Mrs. Parker (Harriet Colby, dau. of John Ordway and Rebecca Guild (Sewell) Webster) born Gardner, Mo. May 16, 1818; mar. Mar. 29, 1841; emb. Boston, June 13, 1842; ar. Canton, Nov. 5. She was the first foreign lady who became a permanent resident in Canton. Released, 1847. 1878 in Washington, D.C.

Ira Tracy was a missionary at Canton from his arrival at that place, Oct.26, 1833, till his departure for Singapore, May 1834. For a further notice of him see Mission to Singapore. Died, Bloomington, Wis., Nov.10, 1875.

Dyer Ball, M.D. Charleston, S.C., b. West Boylston, Mass.; June 3,1796; prof. rel. Hadley, Mass., 1815; spent two years at Yale Coll., then engaged in teaching in South Carolina, and grad. Union Coll. 1826; pursued Theological studies at New Haven and Andover; licensed to preach 1828; ord. Shutesbury, 1831. After this, taught an academy in Charleston, S.C., pursued the study of medicine with reference to foreign missionary work, and received the degree of M.D. from the Medical Institution at Charleston. Relinquishing flattering financial prospects in S. Carolina, he came North to engage in the service of the A'B.C.F.M., but was detained a whole year by the commercial crisis of 1837. (Appt 1836) He sailed with four other missionaries and their wives from New York May 25, 1838; ar. Singapore, Sept.17, 1838. In June 1841, he went to Macao, for the benefit of Mrs. Ball's health; remained there till April 1843, when he removed to Hongkong. In 1845, he removed to Canton. He sailed for U.S. February 1854; re-emb. June 11, 1856; ar. Macao Canton, March 23, 1857. He died at Canton March 27, 1866, ae. 70, after a service of nearly 28 years. See Obituary in Herald, Vol. 62, pp 259-262.

Mrs. Ball (Lucy H. Mills) b. New Haven, Ct., Dec. 16, 1807; mar. 1827; emb. May 25, 1838; died, after a long illness at Hongkong, June 6, 1844.

Mrs. Ball (Isabella Robertson) born in Scotland in 1816; mar. at Canton, Feb. 26, 1846. After the death of Dr. Ball, she returned to her native land. 1878 residing in Hongkong, with her son. Died Sept. 25, 1909.

James Granger Bridgman, born Amherst, Mass. Dec. 1820; grad. Amherst Coll. 1842; went to China, and ar. at Hongkong Feb. 19, 1844; appointed a missionary of the Board, Nov" 25, 1845; ord. Canton, May 31, 1846. In consequence of severe study and impaired health, a feeling of despondency came over him; and during temporary aberration of mind, he inflicted on himself a wound, Dec. 1, 1850, which resulted in his death, Dec. 6, 1850. He was not married; his age was 30. He was much esteemed and beloved. Mr. B. edited Chinese Repository from May 1847 to Sept. 1848.

Samuel William Bonney, son of Rev. William Bonney, born New Canaan, Ct., March 8, 1815; prof. rel. Allen St. Church, New York City, Jan. 1838; studied a few months in New York University 1840; Lane Sem. O, 1841-1844; went as a teacher to China, and ar. Hongkong, March 10, 1845; was at Canton, 1846; appointed an assistant missionary of the Board Oct. 6, 1846; assistant missionary and licensed preacher till 1856; mingled much with the people; in 1847, had visted every house in 24 streets, numbering about 700 houses and shops. Visited his native land 1854; ord. 1856; re-emb. with wife, New York, Aug. 4, 1856; ar. Hongkong, Dec. 1, 1856; resided nearly two years at Macao, on account of the war; returned to Canton near the close of 1858; died of bilious fever, at Canton, July 27, 1864. (See Obituary Herald, Vol.60 p. 374.)

Mrs. Bonney (Catharine Visscher Van Rensselaer) Albany, N.Y.; mar. Cherry Hill, N.Y., July 1856; emb. N.Y. Aug. 4, 1856; returned to U.S. April 25,1867.

In April 1863, went to Peking under Woman's Union Miss. Soc. Removed to Shanghai, Aug. '70. Returned to U. S. Sept. 1871. Published, 1875, a "Legacy of Historical Gleanings", 2 vol. 1879, in Albany, N. Y. Ditto 1888.

William Allen Macy was a missionary at Canton from his appointment, 1849, till his removal to Shanghai, in 1858. For further notice see North China Mission. Died, Shanghai, April 9, 1859.

Daniel Vrooman, Hudson, Ohio; born Ossian, Alleghany Co., N. Y. Aug. 15, 1818; grad. Western Reserve Coll., Hudson, 1849; Theol. Sem. Hudson, 1851; ord. Hudson, Oct. 24, 1851; emb. New York, Dec. 4, 1851; ar. Canton, March 15, 1852; vis. U. S. July 17, 1857; re-emb. New York, July 30, 1859; ar. Canton, Jan. 13, 1860. He labored there till 1865, when the ill health of Mrs. Vrooman induced him to try the effect of a voyage to California, where he was doing what he could for the Chinese emigrants. Spring of 1867, he returned to China and became connected with the U.S.Consulate. 1877-1878 at Canton. 1888 San Francisco, Cal. Died in East Oakland, Cal. March 4, 1895.

Mrs. Vrooman (Elizabeth C. Pitkin, dau. of Rev. Caleb Pitkin) Hudson, Ohio; born Akron, Summit Co., O., June 14, 1826; prof. rel. 1848; mar. Oct. 24, 1851, see above; emb. New York Dec. 4, 1851; died June 17, 1854.

Mrs. Vrooman (Maria Wilberforce Alvord, dau. of Rev. Alanson Alvord) Grass Lake, Mich.; born in Chester, Mass., Feb. 9, 1836; prof. rel. Cong. Ch. Downers Grove, (Now, 1999, Lisle) Ill. 1849; mar. Aug. 12, 1858; emb. New York, July 30, 1859; ar. Canton, Jan. 13, 1860; went to California 1865. Her dau. Mrs. Katharine Vrooman King, Inkston, No. Dak. 1899 - wrote her May 22. Died in Brooklyn, California, Aug. 20, 1866.

Frederick Humphrey Brewster, Wright, Hillsdale Co. Mich.; born Waterloo, Seneca Co. N.Y. Feb. 20, 1822; prof. rel. Buffalo, N.Y., 1837; grad. Williams Coll. 1840; East Windsor Sem. 1850; ord. Enfield, Ct. Feb.25,1852; emb. Boston, July 31, 1852; ar. Canton, January 1, 1853; died there of small pox, Jan. 29, 1853; having been less than a month on missionary ground.

Mrs. Brewster (Mary Gray Byrne) b. Windham, Ct. May 10, 1828; prof. rel. Nov. 1851; mar. April 13, 1852; emb. Boston, July 31, 1852. After the death of Mr. Brewster, she mar. Rev. Charles Finney, Preston, of the Presbyterian Board, Dec. 19, 1854. 1877, still at Canton. Mr. Preston died July, 1877; Mrs. P. ret. to U.S., Oct. '77. May 1878, she is in San Francisco, has charge of the Woman's Home, for Chinese women and girls.

MISSIONARY PHYSICIAN

William Beck Diver, M.D. born Philadelphia, Pa., Aug. 13, 1819; prof. rel. April 1836; studied four years at Jefferson Medical Coll., Philadelphia; emb. New York, May 8, 1839; ar. Macao, Sept. 27, 1839; returned to U.S. July 6, 1841; released, Aug. 24, 1841. Resided in Cincinnati, Ohio.

ASSISTANT MISSIONARIES

Samuel Wells Williams L.L.D. born Utica, N.Y., Sept. 21, 1812; learned the printer's trade; emb. New York, June 15, 1833; arrived Canton, Oct. 26, 1833; was the missionary printer at Canton, but was otherwise active and useful in the mission; was one of the party on board of ship Morrison, in her remarkable voyage to Japan, July and Aug. 1837; visited the U.S. 1845. While in this country he wrote and published, in two large volumes, 12 mo. a work on China, entitled "The Middle Kingdom" &c, containing a large amount of information touching that empire. He re-emb. with wife, New York, June 1, 1848; ar.

Canton, Sept. 15, 1848. He continued in the same relation to the mission, till 1857, when he resigned his position, in consequence of having accepted the post of Secretary in the legation of the United States. The Honorary Degree of Doctor of Laws was conferred on him by Union College in 1854. Returned to U. S. 1860. Ret. to Peking, 1862. Ret. to U.S. Dec. '76. April, 1878, residing in New Haven, Conn. (Graduated Rensselaer Inst. Troy, N.Y.) Died February 16, 1884.

Mrs. Williams (Sarah Symonds Walworth) Plattsburgh, N.Y., born there Nov. 6, 1815; mar. Nov. 25, 1904(?); emb. New York, June 1, 1848; ar. Canton, Sept. 15, 1848; released 1857. April 1878, residing in New Haven, Conn. Mrs. W. d. Jan. 26, 1881

Canton Mission relinquished in October, 1866.

AMOY MISSION

This was an outgrowth from the Canton Mission, and was begun by Mr. David Abeel of that mission in Feb. 1842. It was conducted wholly by members of the Reformed Dutch Church, and on the separation of that church from the American Board of Foreign Missions, this mission was transferred to the Missionary Board of that Church. The separation was agreed in September 1857, and the final transfer effected March 23, 1858.

MISSIONARIES

David Abeel, born New Brunswick, N.J., June 12, 1804; grad. Seminary of the Reformed Dutch Church, New Brunswick, 1826; embarked with Mr. Elijah C. Bridgman, New York, Oct. 14, 1829; went out with a commission from the American Seaman's Friend Society, as a missionary to seamen at Canton and vicinity; continued in that employ till Dec. 27, 1830; (ar. at Canton Feb. 19, 1830;) appointed a missionary of the A.B.C.F.M. Oct. 1830;) sailed from Canton, Dec. 28, 1830 for Java, to ascertain the condition of the Dutch Churches on that Island; ar. at Angier in Java, Jan. 17, 1831; ar. Batavia, Jan. 21; ar. Singapore, June 15, 1831; ar. Bangkok, in Siam, July 1, 1831; returned to Singapore, Nov. 1832; left Siam Autumn of 1833 in impaired health, and ar. New York Sept. 6, 1834; after a visit to England, France and Holland; re-emb. New York in ship Morrison for Canton, Oct. 17, 1838; ar. Canton, April 26, 1839; continued there Feb. 1842; when he commenced a new station at Kolongsu, an island half a mile from Amoy; where, and at Amoy, he "found abundant opportunities for preaching"; left China from enfeebled health, Jan. 18, 1845; ar. New York April 3, 1845; died Albany, Sept. 3, 1846. He published, 1834, a "Journals of a Residence in China and the Neighboring

Elihu Doty, born at Bernville, N.Y., Sept. 20, 1809; prof. rel. Nov.1827; grad. Rutgers Coll. New Brunswick, N.J., 1833; seminary of Ref. Dutch Church New Brunswick, 1835; ord. Bernville, May 16, 1836; emb. with Messrs. Ennis, Nevins, and Youngblood, New York, June 8, 1836; ar. Batavia, Sept. 15, 1836; visited and explored Borneo, Oct. and Nov. 1838; ar. Sambas on the island of Borneo, June 17, 1839, and commenced a mission there; removed to Pontianak, on the same island, Aug. 1841; joined Mr. Abeel at Amoy, June 22, 1844; vis. U.S. March 7, 1846; re-emb. Boston, April 15, 1847; ar. Amoy, Aug. 18,1847; Amoy taken by the insurgents, May 29, 1853; retaken by the imperialists, Nov.11, 1853; Mr. Doty's connection with the A.B.C.F.M. dissolved at his request, March 23, 1858. Died at sea, near New York, 1865.

Mrs. Doty (Clarissa Dolly Ackley) New York, b. Washington, Ct., Dec.7,1806; prof. rel. 1819; mar. New York, May 13, 1836; emb. June 8, 1836; died at Amoy, Oct. 5, 1845.

Mrs. Doty (Eleanor Augusta Smith) b. Parsippany, Morris Co. N.Jersey, July 27, 1823; prof. rel. 1837; mar. Feb. 17, 1847; emb. Boston, April 15, 1847; Died Feb. 28, 1859, at Amoy.

William John Pohlman, born Albany, N.Y., Feb. 17, 1812; graduated Rutgers Coll. New Brunswick, 1834; sem. at N.Brunswick 1837; ord.   Emb. with Mr. Thomson, New York, May 25, 1838; ar. Singapore, Sept. 17,1838; with Mr. Doty visited and explored Borneo, Oct. and Nov. 1838; returned with him to Singapore, Dec. 3, 1838; resided a year in Batavia, in compliance with an ordinance of the Dutch government; joined Mr. Doty at Sambas, in Borneo, 1839; removed to Pontianak, Aug. 5, 1841; left that place with Mr. Doty, April 8,1844; and with him ar. at Amoy, June 22, 1844; drowned on the passage from Hong-kong to Amoy, Jan. 5, 1849. "The first instance in which a missionary of the Board has perished by the dangers of the sea." Annual Report for 1849.

Mrs. Pohlman (Theodosia R. Scudder) New York City; b. Freehold, N.J., Jan. 26, 1811; mar.   ; died Amoy, Sept. 30, 1845.

John Van Nest Talmage, D.D. born Somerville, Somerset Co., N.J., Aug.18, 1819; prof. rel. June 1837; grad. Rutgers Coll. New Brunswick, 1842; Seminary of Ref. Dutch Church, New Brunswick, 1845; ordained Williston, N.J., Aug. 1846; emb. Boston, April 15, 1847; then unmarried; ar. Amoy, Aug.18,1847; vis. U.S. 1849; re-emb. New York, March 19, 1850; ar. Amoy, July 16,1850; released with the other Amoy missionaries, March 23, 1858. 1878, at Amoy. Died in Bound Brook, N.J., Aug. 19, 1892.

Mrs. Talmage (Abby F.   ) Elizabethtown, New Jersey; b.
                                         Arrived Amoy July 16, 1850;
mr.   1850; emb. New York, March 19, 1850. / Died there, Feb.10, 1862.

John Sansome Joralmon   Newark, N.J.; born New York City, Oct. 30, 1828; grad. Rutgers Coll. Theol. Sem. New Brunswick, N.J.; ord. Oct. 2, 1855, at Newark, N.J.; emb. New York, Oct. 25, 1855; ar. Shanghai, Feb. 25,1856;
                                     Ret. U. S. June 1858;
at Amoy   ; released March 23, 1858. / 1871 at Fairview, Ill. 1878 still there.

Mrs. Joralmon (Martha Bogart Condit) Newark, N.J.; b. Chatham,N.J., July 6, 1833; mar. Oct. 23, 1855; emb. Oct. 25, 1855. 1878, at Fairview, Ill., and 1883.

FUH-CHAU MISSION

The "Opium War" of 1840-1, being over, and a treaty of peace having been concluded between China and Great Britain, on the 20th of August, 1842, by which five of the principal ports of the empire, Canton, Amoy, Fuh-Chau, Ningpo, and Shanghai, were opened to commerce and Christian effort, the Missionary Societies of England and America were not slow in availing themselves of their opportunity.

Messrs. Johnson and Peet, who had been laboring among the Chinese in Siam, left that kingdom August 12, 1846, with the view of entering one of the inviting fields, thus opened in China. They arrived in Canton, Nov. 2, in that year. Mr. Johnson left Canton, Nov. 23; and after some delays, He immediately made preparations for a mission there. ..ched Fuh-Chau, Jan. 2, 1847./ Mr. Peet joined him, Sept. 6, 1847.

MISSIONARIES

Stephen Johnson, born Griswold, Ct. Apr. 15, 1803; grad. Amherst Coll. 1827; Auburn Sem. 1832; ord. Griswold, Feb. 21, 1833; emb. with Messrs. Winson, Lyman and Robinson at Boston for Batavia, June 10, 1833; ar Bangkok, in Siam, July 25, 1834; labored there among the Chinese emigrants; vis. U.States, Dec. 7, 1838; re-emb. Boston, Nov. 17, 1840; ar. Bangkok, May,1841; left that place, Aug. 12, 1846; removed to Fuh-Chau, Jan. 2, 1847; and commenced the mission there; returned to U.S. 1853; released July 18, 1854. Jan. 1878; still living in Gouverneur, N.Y. Died at Gouverneur, N.Y., Jan. 14, 1886. (See Herald, Mar. 1886, p. 113.)

Hannah
M. Johnson(/ Maria Preston) Rupert, Vt., daughter of Rev. John B., born Dec. 4, 1808; mar. May 26, 1833; emb. June 10, 1833; returned to U.States Dec. 7, 1838; died at Philadelphia, Jan. 8, 1839.

Mrs. Johnson (Mary Fowler) Oxboro, N. Y.(?) dau. of Edward, Town of Antwerp; born Jan. 8, 1813; mar. Nov. 1, 1840; emb. Boston Nov. 17, 1840; ar. Bangkok, May 1841; died there July 1, 1841, seven weeks after her arrival.

Mrs. Johnson (Caroline M. Selmar) born in Stockholm, Sweden, Dec. 8, 1808; mar. Ningpo, China, Sept. 17, 1849.
(Only the third wife of Mr. Johnson was a member of the Fuh-Chow Mission.)

Lyman Bert Peet, born Cornwall, Vt., March 1, 1809; grad. Middlebury Coll. 1834; AndoverSem. 1837; ord. South Dennis, Mass. Dec. 13, 1837; emb. Boston July 6, 1839; ar. Singapore Oct. 23, 1839; detained there till May 1840; ar. Bangkok May 28, 1840; labored among the Chinese emigrants; left Bangkok Aug. 12, 1846; ar. Canton, Nov. 2, 1846; ar. Amoy, March 19, 1847; joined Mr. Johnson at Fuh-Chau, Sept. 6, 1847; visited U. States March 28, 1857; re-emb. New York Oct. 4, 1858; ar. Fuh-Cheu March 16, 1859. He is still (1869) laboring in that mission; vis. U. S. 1871. Released 1875. Died West Haven, Jan. 11, 1878.

Mrs. Peet (Rebecca Clemens Sherrill) born Orwell, Vt. Dec. 3, 1810; mar. April 14, 1839; emb. July 6, 1839; died Fuh-Chau July 17, 1856.

Mrs. Peet (Hannah Louisa Plympton) of Sturbridge, Mass., born 1823; grad. Mt. Holyoke Sem. 1848; mar. June 6, 1858; emb. New York Oct. 4, 1858; ret. U. S. 1871. Released 1875. Jan. 1878, still in West Haven. Re-appt. and returned to Fuh-Chau with her dau. Mrs. Geo. H. Hubbard; emb. Oct. 18, 1884; arr. Fuh-Chau, Nov. 27, 1884; mar. at Fuh-Chau Nov. 5, 1885 to Rev. Chas. Hartwell. (See page 4#)

Seneca Cummings, born Antrim, N. H. May 16, 1817; prof. rel. Oct. 1838; grad. Dartmouth Coll. 1844; studied Theology at Lane and Union Theol. Seminaries, graduating at the latter 1847; ord. Antrim, Sept. 30, 1847; emb. Philadelphia Nov. 11, 1847; ar. Hongkong March 25, 1848; ar. Fuh-Chau, May 7, 1848; returned to U. States in impaired health Oct. 16, 1855; died suddenly New Ipswich, N.H. Aug. 12, 1856.

Mrs. Cummings (Abigail Mary Stearns) born New Ipswich, N. H. July 24, 1822; prof. rel. 1834; grad. Mt. Holyoke Col.; mar. Oct. 28, 1847; emb. Nov. 11, 1847; ret'd U. S. 1855 (Sister of Mrs. Hartwell, p. 41). Jen. 1878, still residing with her son in New Ipswich, N. H. Ditto 1888. Died New Ipswich, N. H. Nov. 16, 1895.

Caleb Cook Baldwin, born Bloomfield, N. J. April 1, 1820; prof. rel. Sept. 1842; grad. New Jersey Coll., Princeton 1841; Princeton Sem. 1847; ord. Bloomfield, May 25, 1847; emb. Philadelphia Nov. 11, 1847; ar. Fuh-Chau May 7, 1848; visited U. S. March 30, 1858; re-emb. New York, Sept. 27, 1859; ar. Hongkong Jan. 22, 1860; at Fuh-Chau Feb. 7, 1860. Still a member of the mission there 1869. Vis. U. S. 1872. Returned to Fuh-Chau Nov. 1873. Jan. 1878, still at Fuh-Chau. Vis. U. S. arr. San Francisco Apr. 18, 1886; re-emb. San Francisco Sept. 21, 1887; arr. Fuh-Chau Oct. 23, 1887; returned to U. S. arr. San Francisco May 13, 1895. Released Jan. 3, 1899. Died July 20, 1911, E. Orange, N.J. (See Miss'y Herald Sept. 1911, p. 381)

Mrs. Baldwin (Harriet Fairchild) born Bloomfield, N. J. Nov. 5, 1826; prof. rel. Dec. 3, 1843; mar. Sept. 28, 1847; emb. Nov. 11, 1847. Jan. 1878, still at Fuh-Chau. Vis. U. S. arr. San Francisco April 18, 1886; re-emb. San Francisco Sept. 21, 1887; arr. Fuh-Chau Oct. 23, 1887; returned to U. S. arr. San Francisco May 13, 1895. Died at Summit, N. J. July 29, 1896. (See Sept. 1896 Herald, p. 356)

William Lyman Richards, son of Rev. William Richards, missionary at the Sandwich Islands, page   : Brooklyn, N. Y.; born Lahaina, on Maui, one of the Sandwich Islands, Dec. 3, 1823; left the Islands, Dec. 9, 1836; prof. rel. Canonsburg, Pa. 1841; grad. Jefferson Coll. Canonsburg, 1841; Union Theol. Sem., N. York 1846; ord. Brooklyn, Oct. 14, 1847; emb. with Messrs. Cummings and Baldwin, Philadelphia, Nov. 11, 1847; ar. Fuh-Chau, May 7, 1848; died at sea, near St. Helena, on the passage from Hongkong to the U. States, June 5, 1851. He was unmarried. (See obituary in Herald, vol. 47, pp.303, 304)

Justus Doolittle, Middlebury, Elkhart Co., Indiana,: born Rutland, Jefferson Co. N. Y. June 23, 1823; prof. rel. Medina, N. Y. 1834; grad. Hamilton Coll. 1846; Auburn Sem. 1849; ord. Auburn June 20, 1849; emb. Boston, Nov. 23, 1849; ar. Fuh-Chau May 31, 1850: vis. U. States July 18, 1864; re-emb. New York April 7, 1866; arr. Tientsin, Aug. 20, 1866; resigned from ill health, Feb. 9, 1869; 1878 at Clinton, N. Y. (Having been transferred to the North China Mission Nov. 3, 1863, Mr. Doolittle should have been arranged under that head.) Sept. 1872, joined Presbyterian Mission at Shanghai. Ret. to U. S. June 1873. Died at Clinton, N. Y. 1880, June 15. (See obituary notice in Herald Aug. 1880, p. 294)

Mrs. Doolittle (Sophia Acland Hamilton) Auburn, N. Y.; born Fleming, N. Y. March 20, 1820: prof. rel. 1834: mar. June 20, 1849; emb. Nov. 23, 1849; died at Fuh-Chau June 21, 1856.

Mrs. Doolittle (Lucy Emeline Mills) Buffalo, N. Y.; born Guilford, Chenango Co., N. Y. March 13, 1827; prof. rel. 1841: accompanied her brother, Rev. Charles R. Mills, missionary of the Presbyterian Board, to Shanghai, China, where they arrived in Feb. 1857; mar. at Shanghai, Jan. 1859; returned to U. States July 18, 1864; died at Rutland, Jefferson Co., N. Y. Aug. 12, 1865.

Mrs. Doolittle, (Louisa M   Judson) Galesburg, Ill; born Pontiac, Mich. April 20, 1841; mar. Feb. 1, 1866; emb. April 7, 1866: arr. Tientsin, Aug. 20: rem. to Fuh-Chau, Nov. 1868: ret. to U. S. June 1873. 1878 at Clinton, N. Y.

Charles Hartwell, born Lincoln, Mass. Dec. 19, 1825: prof. rel. Amherst Coll. June 1846; grad. Amherst Coll. 1849: East Windsor Sem. 1852: ord. Lincoln, Mass. Oct. 13, 1852; emb. New York Nov. 3, 1852: ar. Fuh-Chau, June 9, 1853; vis. U. S. Oct. 26, 1865: re-emb. N. York Aug. 10, 1867; went by way of San Francisco; ar. Fuh-Chau Oct. 10, 1867. Vis. U. S. July 1877; re-emb. San Francisco Oct. 16, 1878. Dec. 1885 at Fuh-Chau. Vis. U. S. arr. San Francisco June 15, 1890; re-emb. Vancouver Sept. 9, 1891: arr. Fuh-Chau Oct. 8, 1891;

Died Fuh-Chau Jan. 30, 1905. (See April 1905 Herald, p. 166)

Mrs. Hartwell (Lucy E. Stearns), sister of Mrs. Seneca Cummings, page 39 ; born New Ipswich, N. H. April 13, 1827; prof. rel. March 1842; grad. Mt. Holyoke Sem. 1849; mar. Billerica Sept. 6, 1852; emb. Nov. 3, 1852; vis. U.S. Oct. 26, 1865; re-emb. Aug. 10, 1867; vis. U. S. July 1877. Died Foochow July 10, 1883. (See obit. in Herald Oct. 1883, p. 378)

Mrs. Hartwell (Hannah Louisa Plympton Peet). Mar. at Foochow, Nov. 5, 1885; Jan. 1886 at Foochow. Vis. U. S. arr. San Francisco June 15, 1890; re-emb. Vancouver Sept. 9, 1891; arr. Foochow Oct. 1891. Died Dec. 7, 1908. (See obit. Feb. 1909 Herald, p. 63)

Simeon Foster Woodin, Green River, Columbia Co., N. Y.; born Hillsdale, Columbia Co., N. Y. May 11, 1833; prof. rel. in Coll. 1852; grad. Williams Coll. 1855; Union Theol. Sem., N. York 1859; ord. New York, June 19, 1859; emb. New York, Sept. 27, 1859; arr. Fuh-Chau, Feb. 7, 1860. Still there, 1869. Returned to U. S. April 1870. Again at FooChow, June 1872. Jan. 1878, still at FooChow (Nantai). Vis. U. S. arr. May 1883; re-emb. Oct. 18, 1884; arr. Foochow, Nov. 27; Dec. 1885 at Foochow. Vis. U. S. arr. San Francisco, May 27, 1895. Died at Amenia, N. Y. June 28, 1896. (See Aug. 1896 Herald, p. 316)

Mrs. Woodin (Sarah Lee Utley, dau. of Rev. Samuel Utley) Hudson City, N. J.; born Epping, N. H. Dec. 19, 1835; prof. rel. Austerlitz, N. Y. 1853; studied Mt. Holyoke Sem., South Hadley; mar. Concord, N. H. Aug. 10, 1859; emb. Sept. 27, 1859. Vis. U. S. 1870. Ret. to China, June 1872. Sailed from San Francisco, May 1, 1872. Jan. 1878 still at F. Vis. U. S.arr. June 11, 1882; re-emb. San Francisco Nov. 1, 1890; arr. Foochow Dec. 6, 1890. Vis. U. S. arr; San Francisco May 27, 1895. Died July 29, 1932 at Saybrook, Conn.

Joseph Elkanah Walker, son of Rev. Elkanah Walker, miss. to Oregon Indians; born Walker's Prairie (N.E.part Washington Ter.) Feb. 10, 1844; prof. rel. Jan. 1,

1840; grad. Pacific University, Forest Grove, Oregon, 1867. Graduated Bangor Sem. 1871; ord. June 19, 1872, Forest Grove. Sailed from San Francisco, Sept. 1, 1872. Reached Foo Chow Oct. 15. At F. until Nov. 1876, when he removed to Shao-Wu. Jan. 1878 at Shao-Wu. Vis. U. S. arr. May 8, 1881; re-emb. Nov. 6, 1882; arr. Foochow Jan. 19, 1883; Dec. 1885 at Shao-Wu. Vis. U. S. arr. Oberlin, O. Aug. 25, 1891; re-emb. Tacoma, Nov. 15, 1892; arr. Foochow Jan. 4, 1893. Vis. U. S. arr. Vancouver July 1896; re-emb. Vancouver Sept. 11, 1899. Vis. U. S. arr. Forest Grove, Ore. July 23, 1907; sailed Dec. 1, 1908; arr. home Nov. 30, 1914. Sailed Aug. 10, 1916. Died in Foochow June 28, 1922. (Miss. Herald 1922, page 252) DD. 1902.

Mrs. Walker (E. Ada Claghorn) dau. of Dea. James M. Claghorn; born Evans, Erie Co., N. Y. Sept. 17, 1843. Graduated Oberlin Coll. 1870; prof. rel. 1859; taught for two years among Cattaraugus Indians. Sailed from San Francisco, Oct. 1 and arr. Foo Chow, Nov. 11, 1872. Mar. May 21, 1873. Nov. 1876, removed with her husband to Shao-wu. Jan. 1878 at Shao-wu. Vis. U. S. arr. May 8, 1881; re-emb. Nov. 6, 1882; arr. Foochow Jan. 19, 1883; Dec. 1885 at Shau-wu. Vis. U. S. arr. San Francisco June 15, 1890; re-emb. Tacoma Nov. 15, 1892; arr. Foochow, Jan. 4, 1893. Died at Foochow Feb. 22, 1896. (See May 1896 Herald, page 184.

MISSIONARY PHYSICIAN

Dauphin William Osgood, M.D. born Nelson, N. H. Nov. 5, 1845; prof. rel. there, ; studied at no college; studied medicine in Medical Dept. of the University of New York, grad. M.D. there 1869; left New York for San Francisco on the way to Fuh-Chau Nov. 18, 1869. Sailed from San Francisco Dec. 1, and arr. Fuh-Chau in Jan. 1870. Jan. 1878 still at Foochow (Nantai). Died at Foochow, Aug. 17, 1880. (See obit in Herald Dec 1880, p. 488)

Mrs. Osgood (Helen Woolley Cristy) born Charlestown, Mass. April 9, 1846; converted in a revival in New York City, 1858; prof. rel. Broome Street Church.

New York 1859; studied at Normal School, New Britain, Ct.; a teacher in this country; mar. at Greenwich, Conn. Oct. 28, 1869; sailed as above. Greenwich, Ct., has been residence of her parents since 1860, as New York was during ten years previous. Jan. 1878, still at FooChow (Nantai). Returned to U. S. arr. May 8, 1881; released 1881; 1888 Bridgeport, Ct. Died April 1911, New Haven, Conn. (See Herald 1911, p. 285)

ASSISTANT MISSIONARIES

Jennie S. _____ Peet, daughter of Rev. Lyman B. Peet; born emb. with Mr. and Mrs. Hartwell, New York, Aug. 10, 1867; reached Fuh-Chau Oct. 10, 1867. Having March 23, 1868 become the wife of an English missionary her connection with the A.B.C.F.M. ceased. Mar. Rev. John Macgowan of the London Missionary Society, a resident of Amoy. Jan. 1878 in England.

Adelia M. Payson, Kent, Ct.; born Hadley, Mass. Nov. 19, 1833; prof. rel. 1849; some years a teacher in this country; emb. N. York, Oct. 31, 1868; went by way of California; sailed from San Francisco Dec. 3, 1868; ar. Yokohama, Japan, Dec. 31, 1868; ar. Fuh-Chau, Jan. 18, 1869. Jan. 1878, still at Foo Chow (Nantai). Returned 1878 (?). Released Nov. 16,   ; 1887 at Honolulu, H. I. Teaching Chinese. Same June 1893, in con. with the Anglican Ch.

Henry Thomas Whitney, M.D., born Lunenburg, Mass., April 11, 1849. Prof. rel. Keene, N. H. Sept. 1867. Educated at Middlebury Coll. Little more than two years at M. Grad. at University Med. Coll., New York City. Prac. Med. in Brattleboro, Vt. and Milford, N. H. Sailed from San Francisco Feb. 1, 1877. Arr. Foo Chow, March 26. Went, soon after, to Shao-wu, in the interior. Jan. 1878, at Shao-wu. (Ar. Shao-wu, May 18, 1877) Vis. U. S. arr. Apr. 29, 1884; re-emb. San Francisco Oct. 3, 1885; ar. Foochow, Nov. 7. Vis. U. S. arr. San Francisco July 8, 1892; re-emb. San Francisco Oct. 10, 1893; arr. Foochow Nov. 17, 1893. Vis. U. S. Arr. San Francisco May 18, 1898; re-emb. San Francisco Jan. 8, 1901; arr. Foochow Feb. 14. Vis. U. S. arr. San Francisco

July 2, 1910. Sailed Oct. 4, 1911; ar'd home Sept. 3, 1919. Died in Glendale, California Sept. 14, 1924. (Miss'y Herald 1924, page 515)

Mrs. Whitney (Lurie Ann Snover) born Sterling, Mass. Nov. 19, 1848. Prof. Rel. Milford, N. H. Oct. 1, 1876. Educated at High School, Bolton, Mass.; mar. Fitchburg, Mass. July 15, 1876. Sailed as above.Jan. 1878 at Shao-wu. Vis. U.S. arr. Apr. 29, 1884; re-emb. San Francisco, Oct. 3, 1885; arr. Foochow, Nov. 7; vis. U. S. arr. San Francisco, July 8, 1892; re-emb. San Francisco Oct. 10, 1893; arr. Foochow Nov. 17, 1894. Vis. U. S. arr. San Francisco May 18, 1898; re-emb. San Francisco Jan. 8, 1901; arr. Foochow Feb. 14, 1901; vis. U. S. arr. San Francisco July 2, 1910. Sailed Oct. 4, 1911; arr. Home Sept. 3, 1919. Died in Glendale, Calif. on Sept. 25, 1922. (Miss. Herald 1922, p.473)

Ella J. Newton, born Auburn, Worcester Co., Mass. July 17, 1849; prof. rel. Sept. 1864; studied Milford High School; emb. San Francisco Oct. 16, 1878. Arr. Dec. 1878 at Foochow. Vis. U. S. arr. San Francisco May 10, 1889; re-emb. Vancouver Sept. 9, 1891; arr. Foochow Oct. 8, 1891; vis. U. S. arr. San Francisco April 1900; re-emb. Boston May 22, 1901. Died at Foochow Dec. 28, 1907. (See April 1908 Herald, page 179)

(Foochow Mission)

Josiah Blackman Blakely, born Otego, Otsego Co., N. Y. April 23, 1846; prof. rel. Ripon, Wis., January 1864; grad. at Ripon Coll. 1870; grad. at Oberlin Sem. 1873, having taken a part of the course at the Chicago Sem. Ord. Menasha, Wis. Apr. 14, 1874. Sailed San Francisco Oct. 31, 1874; ar. Foochow Dec. 14, 1874. Nov. 1876 removed to Shao-wu, in the interior. Released June 30, 1882. 1888 Minn. Died Jan. 20, 1925.

Mrs. Blakely (Isabella Campbell) born Waupun, Fond du lac Co., Wis., May 17, 1850. Dau. of Rev. Daniel A. Campbell. Prof. rel. autumn of 1868. Educated Ripon Coll., Wis. Teacher. Mar. Sept. 1, 1874, Pine River Waushara Co., Wis. Sailed as above. Nov. 1876 moved to Shao-wu. Released June 30, 1882. 1888 Minn.

George Henry Hubbard, born Woodmont, town of Orange, Ct. Jan. 11, 1855; prof. rel. Jan. 1872; grad. Yale Coll. 1881; Yale Divinity School 1884 emb. Oct. 1884; arr. Foochow, Nov. 27. Dec. 1885 at Foochow. Ord. Sept. 24, 1884, N. Haven, Conn. Vis. U. S. arr. San Francisco May 20, 1893; re-emb. San Francisco Oct. 27, 1894. Vis. U. S. arr. N. Y. May 13, 1901; re-emb. San Francisco Mar. 11, 1903; vis. U. S. arr. May 5, 1911; sailed Oct. 12, 1912; ar'd home July 21, 1920. Sailed Dec. 17, 1921; ar'd home June 27, 1925. Died at N. Haven, Conn. Apr. 15, 1928. (See Herald June 1928, page 256) (Retired to Honor Roll in 1926)

Mrs. Hubbard (Ellen Louisa Peet) dau. of Rev. Lyman B. Peet, formerly of this mission; born Foochow, July 21, 1859; prof. rel. 1870; grad. Mt. Holyoke Sem.; mar. July 24, 1884; emb. Oct. 18, 1884; arr. Foochow Nov. 27. Dec. 1885 at Foochow. Vis. U. S. arr. San Francisco May 20, 1893; re-emb. San Francisco Oct. 27, 1894. Vis. U. S. arr. N. Y. May 13, 1901; re-emb. San Francisco Mar. 1903; vis. U. S. arr. Boston May 26, 1910. Died Feb. 14, 1925 at Foochow, China. (See Miss'y Herald 1925, page 241) (Sailed Oct. 12, 1912; arr. home July 21, 1920; sailed Dec. 17, 1921.)

FOOCHOW MISSION

ASSISTANT MISSIONARIES

Alice Berton Harris, born Windham, Vt., July 23, 1852; prof. rel. Phillipston, Mass. Jan. 1875: studied Mt. Holyoke, Sem.; emb. Sept. 19, 1882; arr. Foochow, Oct. 28; mar. at Foochow, Dec. 4, 1883; Rev. George B. Smyth of the Methodist Mission, and her connection with the Board ceased.

Emily S. Hartwell, dau. of Rev. Charles Hartwell of this mission; born Foochow, April 15, 1859; prof. rel. 1867; studied Wheaton Fem. Sem. Norton, Mass.; emb. Dec.1, 1883; arr. Foochow, Jan. 17. Dec. 1885 at Foochow. Was for several years in the U. S.; re-emb. Aug. 24, 1896; arr. Foochow, Sept. 22. Vis. U. S. arr. Seattle July 1, 1903; re-emb. San Francisco Nov. 15, 1904. Third term Jan. 1, 1905. Left field Mar. 3, 1912; arrived home Mar. 1912. Sailed Aug. 1913. Fourth term Oct. 1913. Left field Dec. 1920; arrived home Feb. 1921: sailed Sept. 1922. On. Feb. 26, 1929, P.C. approved retirement to take effect July 1, 1929. Died in Oberlin, Ohio on Oct. 2/1951 See cards.

Kate Cecilia Woodhull, M. D. born Wading River, N. Y. July 24, 1842; prof. rel. about 1858; studied Ingham Univ., LeRoy, N. Y., Med. Coll. of the N. Y. Infirmary, one year at Univ. of Zurich, Switz. and one in Dresden, Ger.; emb. Oct. 18, 1884; arr. Foochow, Nov. 27. Dec. 1885 at Foochow. Vis. U. S. arr. San Francisco April 12, 1892; re-emb. San Francisco Oct. 10, 1893; arr. Foochow Nov. 17, 1894; vis. the U. S. arr. Vancouver July 1, 1896; re-emb. San Francisco Nov. 18, 1897; arr. Foochow Dec. 24, 1897.
Arrived home May 27, 1912. Died Mar. 25, 1925, Riverhead, N. Y. (See Herald May 1925, page 187)

Hannah Conklin Woodhull, born Wading River, N. Y. July 4, 1844; prof. rel. 1860; studied Packer Inst.; emb. Oct. 18, 1884; arr. Foochow, Nov. 27. Dec. 1885 at Foochow; vis. the U. S. arr. Vancouver July 1, 1896; re-emb. San Francisco Nov. 18, 1897; arr. Foochow Dec. 24, 1897. Arrived home May 27, 1912. Died in Riverhead, N. Y. on Oct. 30, 1922. (Miss'y Herald 1922, page 821)

Elsie Margaret Garretson; born Bound Brook, N. J. March 4, 1847; prof. rel. 1870; studied Knox Sem., Galesburg, Ill.; emb. for the No.China Mission Sept. 1880; arr. Kalgan, Oct. 22; transferred to Foochow June 24, 1884; Dec. 1885 at Foochow. Was for some time in the U. S.; re-emb. arr. Foochow Dec. 24, 1897; vis.U. S. arr. San Francisco Jan. 26, 1906; re-emb. Seattle Nov. 29, 1907; died in Foochow March 4, 1922. (Miss. Herald 1922, page 160) (Arrived home July 20, 1915, sailed Sept. 7, 1916.)

NORTH CHINA MISSION

until 1862 known as the
Shanghai Mission

Shanghai, the most northerly of the Five Ports opened to European and American commerce by the treaty of 1842, and situated near the mouth of the great river Yangtse-kiang, is a large and populous city, and in the midst of a great population. Mr. Bridgman went there in June 1847, to be employed with missionaries from other societies, English and American, in a revision of the Chinese version of the scriptures. He was thus employed at Shanghai nearly all the time until his death in 1861, except the interval occupied by his visit to this country in 1852. Tientsin, eighty miles south-east from Peking, was first occupied by Mr. Blodget in Sept. 1860.

MISSIONARIES

Elijah Coleman Bridgman, D.D., born in Belchertown, Mass. April 22, 1801. prof. rel. April 1814; grad. Amherst College 1826; Andover Sem. 1829; ord. Belchertown, Oct. 6, 1829; sailed from New York for Canton, with Rev. David Abeel, Oct. 14, 1829. He had been expecting to go as a missionary to Greece, a country then occupying largely the public attention. But the Board, wishing to send a missionary to Canton, in fulfilment of the urgent requests of Rev. Robert Morrison, who had many years been a missionary of the London Society there, and "in compliance with the earnest desires of three christian merchants in that place, urged during several preceding years (from 1827) and a free passage being offered in the ship Roman, Cap. Lavender, belonging to these merchants: Mr. Evarts, then corresponding secretary of the A.B.C.F.M. who was at Andover, Sept.23, 1829: attending the Anniversary of the Theological Seminary, proposed to Mr. Bridgman, of the graduating class of that day, to go as a missionary to Canton, and gave him three days to consider the question. Within twenty-four hours Mr. Bridgman decided to go: and, it is believed, never regretted the decision. The decision was the result of earnest, fervent prayer to God. Three weeks after, he embarked for China.

He arrived in Canton, February 19, 1830; and was heartily welcomed by Dr. Morrison. (Dr. Morrison died Aug. 1, 1834 in the 27th year of his missionary life.) He immediately commenced the study of that most difficult language, with a veteran native teacher; preaching on the sabbath, after Mr. Abeel's departure, to seamen and others speaking the English language. He operated, as far as circumstances allowed, through the press and the distribution of books. But obstacles presented themselves on all sides. In march 1839, the difficulties which led to the "opium war" commenced. The hospital was closed, and missionary operations in Canton ceased. A powerful British armament took possession of the port and river in June 1840, and soon after demolished all the defences and took possession of the city without the loss of a man. During two years preceding April 2, 1841, Mr. Bridgman was at Macao, near Canton. A Chinese Christomathy, 730 pages, prepared by him was printed at Canton by Mr. Williams in 1842. He baptized and admitted to the church a chinese convert for the first time, May 3, 1847. He arrived at Shanghai, June 23, 1847. At that place he remained most of his subsequent life, engaged with other missionaries, English and American, in a revision of the Chinese scriptures. In 1852, he with his wife visited the U. States; re-emb. New York Oct. 11, 1852; ar. Canton, April 2, 1853. He was formally transferred from the Canton to the Shanghai Mission Sept. 2, 1854; and died at Shanghai after 32 years faithful service, Nov. 2, 1861.

Mrs. Bridgman (Eliza Jane Gillett) New York City; a member of the Am. Episcopal Mission in China; mar. in China June 28, 1845. She visited U. S. April 22, 1863; re-emb. Feb. 10, 1864, and still remains, 1869, in the North China Mission. Left Peking for Shanghai Oct. 1868. Died at Shanghai Nov. 10, 1871. (Obit Herald April 1872)

Henry Blodget, D.D., born Bucksport, Maine July 13, 1825; prof. rel. ; grd. Yale Coll. 1848; tutor there 1850-1853; studied Theol. at New Haven and Andover ; ord. Jan. 25, 1854; emb. New York April 11, 1854; ar. Shanghai Sept. 1, 1854; began to preach in the Chinese language Sept. 2, 1855; removed

to a new station at Tientsin, Nov. 8, 1860; visited Peking, May 1862; established himself permanently there, Feb. 1864. He visited U. S. May 1869; and sailed from San Francisco for China Feb. 1, 1870. Jan. 1878 still in Peking. Vis. U. S. arr. June 13, 1881; re-emb. Sept. 27, 1883; arr. Peking Nov. 19; Dec. 1885 at Peking. Returned to U. S. arr. San Francisco Nov. 27, 1894. Died May 23, 1903, Bridgeport Ct. (See July 1903 Herald, page 293)

Mrs. Blodget (Sarah Franklin Ripley) Greenfield, Mass.; born March 12, 1825 (?) prof. rel.   mar. Jan. 17, 1854; emb. New York Oct. 25, 1855; ar. Shanghai, Feb. 25, 1856; returned to U. S. Jan. 14, 1860. Has remained in this country to the present time, 1869. She sailed from San Francisco for China with her husband on her return, Feb. 1, 1870. Jan. 1878, still in Peking. Vis. U. S. arr. June 13, 1881; re-emb. Sept. 27, 1883; arr. Peking Nov. 19. Dec. 1885 at Peking. Returning to U. S. arr. Nov. 27, 1894. Died Bridgeport, Ct., Nov. 27, 1914. (See Jan. 1915 Herald, page 45)

William Aitchison, born in Glasgow, Scotland, June 4, 1826; prof. rel. Norwich Ct. March 1841; grad. Yale Coll. 1848; tutor there 1850-1851; New Haven Theol. Sem. 1851; ord. Norwich, Ct. Jan. 4, 1854; embarked with Mr. Blodget (supra) N. Y. April 11, 1854; arrived Shanghai, Sept. 1, 1854. Began to preach in the Chinese language, Sept. 2, 1855; ar. Ping-hu Oct. 1856; returned to Shanghai 1857; died of dysentery on the way from Peking to the seaboard, Aug. 15, 1859, and was buried in the sea. Unmarried.

William Allen Macy, born New York City, Jan. 29, 1825; grad. Yale Coll. 1844; went to China in 1845; conditionally appointed 1849; licensed preacher at Canton; returned to U. S. 1849; re-appointed Nov. 22, 1853; ord. New Haven, Jan. 1854; emb. New York, Nov. 8, 1854; ar. Canton, April 9, 1855; transferred to Shanghai mission, Jan. 1858; died of smallpox at Shanghai April 9, 1859. Unmarried.

Charles Alfred Stanley, Waynesville, Warren Co., Ohio; born Fearing, Washington Co., O. June 24, 1835; prof. rel. Fearing Dec. 31, 1854; grad. Marietta

Coll. 1858; Lane Sem. 1861; ord. Waynesville, June 17, 1861; emb. Boston, July 1, 1862; ar. Shanghai Dec. 23, 1862; ar. Tientsin, March 13, 1863; vis. ., 1872; returned to Tientsin, Nov. 13, 1873. At Tientsin, 1873-1878. Tis. U. S. arr. San Francisco Feb. 11, 1886; re-emb. San Francisco Feb. 1, 1888; arr. Tientsin Apr. 2. Vis. U. S. arr. San Francisco Dec. 11, 1899; re-emb. San Francisco Oct. 23, 1901; vis. U. S. arr. San Francisco Apr. 30, 1910. Died Winthrop Center, Mass. Nov. 10, 1910. (Dec.Herald, page 545 and Jan. 1911 Herald, page 14)

Mrs. Stanley (Ursula Johnson) Waynesville, Warren Co., O.; born Cincinnati, Nov. 19, 1839; prof. rel. Walnut Hill, O. Nov. 1859; some time a teacher; mar. Walnut Hill, Feb. 19, 1862; emb. Boston, July 1, 1862; vis. U. S. 1872. Ret. to Tientsin Nov. 13, 1873. Still at T. Jan. 1878. Vis. U. S. arr. Jan. 24, 1884; re-emb. San Francisco Feb. 1, 1888; arr. Tientsin Apr. 2. Vis. U. S. arr. San Francisco, Dec. 11, 1899; re-emb. San Francisco Oct. 23, 1901. Died . Pei-ta-ho Sept. 8, 1908. (See Dec. 1908 Herald, page 558)

Lyman Dwight Chapin, son of Rev. A. L. Chapin, of Amsterdam, N. Y.; born Jewett, Greene Co., N. Y. Sept. 18, 1836; prof. rel. Amsterdam, Sept. 1853; grad. Amherst Coll. 1858; Union Theol. Sem., N. York 1861; ord. New York July 6, 1862; emb. New York Nov. 1, 1862; ar. Tientsin April 22, 1863; resided at Tientsin 1863-1867 and at Tung Cho from Nov. 1867 to May 1870; visited U. S. 1870; sailed with wife from San Francisco by steamer, May 1, 1871; arr. Tung-cho June 17. Jan. 1878, still at Tung-cho. Returned to U.S. arr. July 9, 1883. Released Sept. 22, 1885. 1886 at Los Angeles, Calif. Died there June 29, 1894. (See Sept. 1894 Herald, p. 363)

Mrs. Chapin (Clara Labaree Evans) Brooklyn, N. Y.; born Orford, N. H. Aug. 16, 1835; prof. rel. Petersham, Mass. May 1854; a teacher eight years; mar. lyn, July 8, 1862; emb. New York Nov. 1, 1862. Ret. to U. S. 1870. Sailed again as above. Jan. 1878 still at Tung-cho. Returned to U. S. arr. July 9, 1883; released Sept. 22, 1885. 1886 at Los Angeles, Cal. Died in Los Angeles, Oct. 22, 1904.

John Thomas Gulick, son of Rev. Peter J. Gulick, missionary of the Board to Sandwich Islands; born March 13, 1832 at Waimea, Kauai; prof. rel. Jan. 1847. He spent some time, 1861-1864, in Japan, and China;(Grad. Williams College 1859.) Studied Theology at Union Seminary, 1859-1861. Appt. April 1864; ord. Canton. Aug. 1864; emb. Hongkong for Tientsin, Sept. 13, 1864; was wrecked on the passage Sept. 22; again emb. Hongkong Oct. 8, 1864; ar. Tientsin Oct. 26; reached Peking Nov. 5, 1864; stationed at Kalgan 1865-1871; vis. U. S. 1871; emb. April 1, 1873 at San Francisco. Residing at Kobe, Japan, since Sept. 1875. Jan. 1878 still at Kobe. In Japan to 1899; 1900-1905 Oberlin. Died Honolulu April 14, 1923

Mrs. Gulick (Emily DeLaCour) born Barnstable, Devonshire, England April 3, 1833. Prof. rel. 1848, Rochester, Eng. Sent out originally by the Woman's Missionary Soc. of London to Hongkong, China to labor there with Miss Baxter. Mar. China 1864. Vis. U. S. 1871. Died Kobe, Japan Dec. 17, 1875. (Obit of Mrs. Gulick in Miss. Herald vol. 72, p. 145). (Second wife Frances Stevens of Osaka)

Chauncey Goodrich, born Hinsdale, Mass. June 4, 1836; prof. rel. July 3, 1854; grad. Williams Coll. 1861; Union (1 year) and Andover (2 years) Seminary 1864; ord. Hinsdale, Mass. Sept. 21, 1864; emb. New York Jan. 21, 1865; arrived Peking August 15, 1865; began a new station at Yucho, Nov. 1870; vis. U. S. 1871; emb. San Francisco July 1, 1872; ar. Shanghai Aug. 11, 1872; 1872-1878 at Tungcho. Jan. 1878 still at Tungcho. Vis. U. S. arr. May 28, 1885; re-emb. San Francisco, Aug. 23, 1887; arr. Tung-cho Oct. 8, 1887; vis. U. S. arr. San Francisco June 3, 1895; re-emb. Vancouver Aug. 24, 1896; vis. U. S. arr. 1901? Wis. June 24, 1902; re-emb. N. Y. July 22, 1903; vis. U. S. arr. San Francisco Mar. 13, 1911. Sailed Aug. 6, 1912. Arr. field Sept. 21, 1912. Died on Sept. 29, 1925 at Peking, China. (See Herald 1925, page 562)

Mrs. Goodrich (Abbie Ambler) Spencertown, Columbia Co., N. Y.; born Austerlitz, Columbia Co., N. Y. July 21, 1836; prof. rel. March 1853; mar. Spencertown, Sept. 8, 1864; emb. New York Jan. 21, 1865; vis. U. S. 1869. Died at Tung-cho near Peking, Sept. 1, 1874. (In U. S. June 1869 to July 1, 1872.)

Mrs. Goodrich (Justina E. Wheeler) (See Mission to Japan) Mar. May 30, 1878; and died Sept. 4, 1878.

Mrs. Goodrich (Sarah B. Clapp) (See Assistant Missionaries North China) Vis. U. S. 1885; re-emb. Aug. 23, 1887· vis.U. S. arr. N. Y. June 3, 1895; Re-emb. Vancouver Aug. 24, 1896. Vis. U. S. arr. San Francisco Oct. 1900. Re-emb. N. Y. July 22, 1903· vis.U. S. arr. San Francisco Mar. 13, 1911. Died Nov. 14, 1923 at Peking.

Mark Williams, born New London, Butler Co., Ohio, Oct. 28, 1834; prof. rel. June 1850; grad. Miami Univ., Oxford, Ohio, 1858; Lane Sem. 1861; ord. Indianapolis, March 1, 1865; emb. New York April 7, 1866; ar. Tientsin, Aug. 20, 1866; stationed at Kalgan 1867. Jan. 1878, still at Kalgan. Returned to U.S. ? ; re-emb. Mar. 15, 1881; ar. Kalgan May 28. Dec. 1885 at Kalgan. Vis. U. S. arr. N. Y. April 25, 1892; re-emb. Vancouver Aug. 28, 1893; ar. Tientsin Sept. 29, 1893. Vis. U. S. arr. N. Y. Oct. 9, 1900; one of the party which escaped from China by way of Mongolia and Russia at time of Boxer uprising. Re-emb. San Francisco May 1, 1902. Arrived home July 3, 1911; sailed July 7, 1912; In Shansi Miss. 1913. /arrived home Aug. 25, 1918; sailed July 29, 1920. Died at sea near Yokohama Aug. 9, 1920. (Miss. Herald 1920, page 457)

Mrs. Williams (Isabella Burgess Riggs, dau. of Rev. Stephen R. Riggs, missionary to the Dakota Indians); born at Lacqui Parle, Minn. Feb. 21, 1840; prof. rel. 1858; studied at Western Female Seminary, Oxford, O.; teacher in the Dakota Mission 1862; mar. Beloit, Wis. Feb. 21, 1866; emb. New York April 7, 1866; at Kalgan 1867-1878. Returned to U. S. ? ; re-emb. Mar. 15, 1881; ar. Kalgan May 28. Dec. 1885 at Kalgan. Died Jan. 26, 1897.

Thomas William Thompson, Worcester, Mass.; born Plymouth, N. H. Aug. 31, 1837; prof. rel. Worcester Jan. 1855; grad. Dartmouth College 1859; studied at Andover Sem. 1859 to Feb. 1862; but went abroad before completing the course; ord. Worcester June 24, 1868; emb. New York for China by way of San Francisco July 9, 1868; ar. Peking Sept. 19, 1868. Previous to ordination he

he had spent more than a year at Kanagawa, Japan, and twenty months at Canton, China, teaching and studying the Japanese and Chinese languages; at Kalgan 1860. Returned to U. S. Sept. 1875. At home Jan. 1878. 1888 at 19 Kendall Street, Worcester, Mass. Died April 24, 1916 in Worcester.

Chester Holcombe, son of Rev. Chester Holcombe, Atlanta Georgia; born Winfield, Herkimer Co., N. Y. Oct. 16, 1842; consecrated to the missionary work by his mother before his birth; prof. rel. Webster, Monroe Co., N. Y. Feb. 1855; grad. Union Coll. 1861; was engaged in teaching and missionary work for the American Sunday School Union in Georgia; studied Theology under private teachers; ord. Lyons, N. Y. Dec. 31. 1868; emb. New York Feb. 9, 1869 for China, by way of Panama and San Francisco; ar. Shanghai April 10; ar. Peking April 27, 1869. Appointed Sec'y and Interpreter to U. S. Legation to succeed Dr. S. Wells Williams. Released May 1, 1877. Jan. 1878, still in Peking. A corporate member of Bd. from 1868 to death. Died at Lyons, N. Y. April 1912.

Mrs. Holcombe,(Olive Kate Sage) Hartford, Ct.; born East Hartford, Ct. Dec. 19, 1847; prof. rel. Jan. 1869; mar. Springfield, Mass. Jan. 31, 1866; emb. Feb. 9, 1869; ar. Peking April 27, 1869. Returned to U. S. May 1874. Released May 1, 1877. Returned to Peking, Nov. 1877.

Joseph L. Whiting, of Jasper, Steuben Co., N. Y.; born Lyndeboro, N. H. Jan. 30, 1835; converted in a revival at Jasper Oct. 1860; prof. rel. there 1861; grad. Geneseo Coll. 1866. Auburn Theol. Sem. 1869; licensed to preach by Ontario Presbytry at Lima, N. Y. in Dec. 1867; ordained Auburn, N. Y. May 2, 1869, N. G. Clark of Am. Board preaching the sermon; sailed with other missionaries from San Francisco Oct. 4, 1869, by steamer for China; arr. Shanghai as early as Nov. 11; at Tientsin Nov. 30; released 1871, to become connected with the Presbyterian Board. 1877, still in Peking. Died August 25, 1906 in Peking.

Mrs. Whiting (Lucy Eliza Jackson) born Norwalk, Huron Co., Ohio, Jan. 2, 1843; converted, summer of 1865; prof. rel. Norwalk, O. Sept. 3, 1865; studied Norwalk

High School and Oberlin Conservatory; final decision to go to the heathen made July 3, 1867; married, Norwalk July 28, 1869; sailed as above. Released as above 1871. 1877, still in Peking.

Devello Z. Sheffield, D.D., born in Gainesville, Wyoming Co., N. Y. Aug. 13, 1841; converted in a revival in Castile, Wyoming Co., N. Y. in the spring of 1866; prof. rel. Castile spring of 1866; studied at the academies in Warsaw, Middlebury and Alexander, three years in Auburn Theol. Sem. ending May 1869; was assisted in seminary course by Hon. William E. Dodge of New York to the extent of $250 a year; previously he had been two years in the army, which cost him a long sickness; licensed to preach by Cayuga Presbytery at Auburn, April 1868; ordained at Auburn May 2, 1869, by said Presbytery, together with Joseph L. Whiting (supra); sailed with said Whiting and McCoy from San Francisco Oct. 4, 1869, by steamer for China; arr. Tungcho Nov. 28, 1869. Jan. 1878, still at Tungcho. Vis. U. S. in 1879; re-emb. San Francisco Sept. 1, 1880; arr. Tientsin Oct. 6. Dec. 1885 at Tung-cho. Vis. U. S. arr. San Francisco June 15, 1890; re-emb. Vancouver July 29, 1891; arr. Tientsin Aug. 29, 1891. Vis. U. S. Arr. San Francisco June 27, 1899; re-emb. San Francisco June 22, 1900; vis. U. S. arr. San Francisco July 2, 1909; re-emb. Boston May 31, 1910. Died July 1, 1913 at Tung-cho, China. (Miss. Herald #109, page 358 and 378) DD in 1891.

Mrs. Sheffield (Eleanor W. Sherrill) born at Pike, Wyoming Co., N. Y. March 2, 1847; converted in a revival there Feb. 1860; prof. rel. there 1860; studied at Pike Seminary; has been a teacher; married, Pike July 27, 1869. Sailed as above. Jan. 1878, still at Tung-cho. Vis. U. S. in 1879; re-emb. San Francisco Sept. 1, 1880; arr. Tientsin Oct. 6. Dec. 1885 at Tung-cho. Vis. U. S. arr. San Francisco June 15, 1890; re-emb. Vancouver Aug. 28, 1893; arr. Tientsin Sept. 29, 1893. Vis. U. S. arr. San Francisco June 27, 1899; re-emb. San Francisco Oct. 19, 1900; vis. U. S. arr. San Francisco July 2, 1909; re-emb. Boston May 31, 1910; arrived home July 1, 1916; sailed July 1917; arrived home 1924; sailed Aug. 22, 1925. Retired to Honor Roll List in 1925. Died June 7, 1933 at Honolulu.

Daniel Charles McCoy, born in Clayton, Adams Co., Ill. May 30, 1836; converted in a revival at Clayton, winter of 1852; prof. rel. Clayton 1853; studied at Clayton Academy and at Yellow Springs Academy, Kossuth, Iowa; one year in Knox College, Galesburg, Ill.; three years in Auburn Theol. Sem. ending May 6, 1869; like the preceding, received $250 annually during the seminary course from William E. Dodge of New York; assisted himself by teaching; was an agent of the Am. Bible Society two years; licensed by Schuyler Presbytery Sept. 1, 1869, and ordained same day, at Clayton; sailed with other missionaries (see above) from San Francisco Oct. 4, 1869; ar. at Peking, China, Nov. 29, 1869; released 1871, to be connected with Presbyterian Board.

Mrs. McCoy (America H. Pollock) dau. of Samuel Pollock, now of Burlington, Iowa; born at Hart Mills, Ripley Co., Ind., Dec. 2, 1842; prof. rel. Feb. 1861; studied Yellow Springs Academy, Kossuth, Iowa; a teacher; married Burlington, Iowa July 14, 1869; sailed as above. 1877, Mr. and Mrs. M. still in Peking. Released as above.

Isaac Pierson, born August 11, 1843 at Orange, Essex Co., N. J.; grad. Yale Coll. 1866; Andover Theol. Sem. 1869; preached as "stated supply" at Harwich Port, Mass. 1869-1870; ord. Hartford, Ct., March 30, 1870; sailed from San Francisco, Sept. 1, 1870 for China; ar. Shanghai Oct. 4; was at Peking Oct. 27; began a station, with Dr. Treat, at Yu Cho Nov. 10, 1870; violently assaulted there in the street, Dec. 3, 1871. 1872-1876 at Pao-ting-foo; ret. to U. S. June 1876. Sailed from San Francisco Sept. 12, 1877. Arr. Pao-ting-fu Nov. 16, 1877. Vis. U. S. arr. San Francisco Dec. 6, 1889; released Feb. 10, 1891. Died in Berkeley, Calif. on July 15, 1919. (Miss. Herald 1919, page 356)

Mrs. Pierson (Sarah Elisabeth Dyer) dau. of Rev. E. Porter Dyer; born Stow, Mass. Aug. 1, 1845; prof. rel. 1865; grad. at Mt. Holyoke, 1866; taught school at Springfield, Ohio; Worcester and Cambridge, Mass. 1866 - Feb. 1877; mar. July 10, 1877. Sailed Sept. 12, 1877. Arr. Pao-ting-fu Nov. 16, 1877. Died

Jan. 12, 1882 (See Miss. Herald May 1882)

(infra)
Pierson (Flora J. Hale)/Dec. 1885 at Pao-ting-fu. Vis. U. S. arr. San Francisco Dec. 6, 1889; released Feb. 10, 1891.

Arthur Henderson Smith, born Vernon, Conn., July 18, 1845. Son of Rev. Albert Smith DD, pastor of Cong. Ch. in that town. Prof. rel. in 1865 at Beloit; grad. at Beloit College in 1867 with valedic. Two years at Andover and grad. at Union Sem. in 1870. Studied Medicine in New York in winter 1870-71. Supplied for brief terms, ch. in Ann Arbor, Mich., Appleton, Wis., So. Chicago and Clifton, Ill. Sailed from San Francisco, July 1, 1872; reached Tientsin Aug. 17. Jan. 1878, still in the field;(ord. May 29, 1872.) Vis. U. S. arr. June 2, 1885; returned to China 1886; returned to U. S. arr. July 13, 1893; DD in Beloit 1894; re-emb. New York, April 27, 1895; arr. Shanghai Aug. 28, 1895; called home by the Prud. Com. to assist in the million dollar campaign, San Francisco Jan. 12, 1906; LLD in Whitman 1906; re-emb. Seattle, July 6, 1906; arrived home Sept. 14, 1910;/sailed Apr. 3, 1912; arrived home after 4th term July 14, 1926. Retired from active service March 10, 1925. Died Aug. 31, 1932 at Claremont, Cal.

Mrs. Smith (Emma Dickinson) born near Janesville, Wis. Oct. 23, 1849; prof. rel. 1864; educated at Beloit High School and Fox Lake Sem., grad. there 1869 (and Oberlin College one winter) mar. Sept. 7, 1871; ar. Tientsin Aug. 17, 1872. Still there Jan. 1878. Vis. U. S. arr. June 2, 1885; returned to China 1886. Returned to U. S. arr. July 13, 1893; vis. U. S. arr. San Francisco Mar. 9, 1909. Sailed Apr. 3, 1912; arrived home etc. as above. Died Jan. 28, 1926 at Tungchow, China. (See Herald, March 1926, pages 118, 119, 120)

MISSIONARY PHYSICIAN

Lurel Otis Treat, M.D., son of Rev. Selah Burr Treat, Home Secretary of the A.B.C.F.M.; born Newark, N. J., Feb. 28, 1840; prof. rel. Essex St. Ch., Boston, January 2, 1859; grad. Williams Coll. 1863; received his medical education in

Boston and New York; emb. New York, Sept. 21, 1867; reached Peking Dec. 6,

He first indulged the Christian hope during a revival in Boston 1858. He studied six years in the Boston Latin School, four years in Williams Coll. two years in the Harvard Medical college in Boston, and two years in the Bellevue Medical Coll. New York, graduating there Feb. 1866. Near the close of the late war, he was an acting assistant surgeon four months in the army. His father, Rev. S. B. Treat, grad. Yale Coll. 1824; mar. Dec. 25, 1827; practiced law several years; resided in what is now South Windsor, Ct. from 1826 to 1830; in Penn Yan, Yates Co., N. Y. from 1831 to 1833, and there first united with the curch of Christ; was a member of the Andover Sem. 1833-35; ordained pastor, Newark, N. J. March 23, 1836; removed to New York, and was editor of Biblical Repository 1840-42; came to Boston March 1843, and was editor of the Missionary Herald; in Sept. 1843 was elected Recording Secretary of the A.B.C.F.M. and since Sept. 1847 has been one of its secretaries for correspondence, still residing in Boston. Died March 28, 1877.

Dr. Treat, at first stationed at Peking, was at Tientsin 1869; with Mr. Goodrich and Mr. Pierson commenced a new station at Yu Cho in the interior Nov. 10, 1870. Remained at Yu cho nearly two years. At Pao-ting-fu with Mr. Pierson from summer of 1872 to the end of 1873. Impaired health occasioned his return to U. S. the following spring. He reached Boston May 30, 1874. Released by Prudential Committee Oct. 16, 1877. April 1878, residing in Boston. Died June 20, 1880 at Luzerne, N. Y.

ASSISTANT MISSIONARIES

Mary Elizabeth Andrews, born Cleveland, Ohio Dec. 13, 1840; prof. rel. April 1857; emb. New York for China via San Francisco March 21, 1868; ar. Tung Chou June 12, 1868; was there 1872. Ret. to U. S. May 1874. Ret. to China Oct. 1876. Ja. 1878 still at Tung-cho; vis. U. S. arr. Cleveland, O. Aug. 3, 1886; re-emb. Vancouver Aug. 7, 1892; arr. Tientsin Sept. 1892; Vis. U. S. arr. San Francisco Oct. 1900; re-emb. Oct. 23, 1901. Vis. U. S. arr. Seattle May 13, 1908; re-emb.

...n Francisco Oct. 20, 1909. Began 5th term Nov. 22, 1909. In 1925 she was ...tired by the W.B.M. and put on the veteran list. Died in Chuhu, Monterey (?) April 19, 1936

Mrs. Harriet Porter, Prairie du Chien, Wisconsin, daughter of Rev. Jeremiah Porter, a veteran Home Missionary of the West; born Green Bay, Wis. Nov. 22, 1846; prof. rel. March 1856; emb. New York March 21, 1868; reached Peking, June 13, 1868; was there 1872. Ret. to U. S. Nov. 1876; re-emb. San Francisco May 1, 1879. Returned to U. S. arr. San Francisco April 28, 1886; released June 18, 1886. 1888 with her brother in Chicago, Ill. (20 Bryan Block) Re-app. Mar. 26, 1894; arr. Tientsin Oct. 26, 1894. Vis. U. S. arr. Victoria, B.C. June 1904; re-emb. San Francisco Feb. 6, 1906. Released Aug. 8, 1911. Died Jan. 10, 1929 La Mesa, Cal. (See Herald, March 1929, page 126)

Phineas Rice Hunt, Bath, N. Y.; born Arlington, Vt. Jan. 30, 1816; prof. rel. Bath June 1831; learned the printer's trade. emb. Boston July 30, 1839; ar. ...as March 19, 1840. He took charge of the large printing establishment of the A.B.C.F.M. at that place, and conducted it with great ability and success twenty-seven years. For the amount of work done in that establishment, see Madras Mission. On the relinquishment of the Madras Mission, 1866, Mr. and Mrs. Hunt being the only missionaries of the Board then and there remaining, they came to the U. States June 26, 1867. Being transferred to the North China Mission, they embarked at New York March 21, 1868, for said mission, by way of Aspinwall and San Francisco; ar. Shanghai May 19 and reached Peking June 13, 1868; was there 1872. Jan. 1878, still at Peking. Died Peking May 30, 1878, typhus fever.

Mr. Hunt also visited the U. S. in 1854; re-emb. June 2, 1855, and reached Madras, July 27, 1855.

Hunt (Abigail Nims) Conway, Mass.; born Sangerfield, N. Y. Dec. 9, 1808; prof. rel. Conway, March 1822; mar. Boston July 26, 1839. Died Peking, March 29, 1877. (Obit in Miss. Herald. vol. 73, p. 210)

Gilbert Tompkins Holcombe, brother of Chester Holcombe, missionary of the
Board; born Winfield, Herkimer Co., N. Y. May 12, 1845; prof. rel. Newark, N.J.
April 1, 1864; studied Union Coll. a year and a half; and half a year at Chicago
Theol. Sem.; emb. New York with his brother Feb. 9, 1869; purposing to itinerate
in China, and sell Bibles and Tracts; ar. Peking April 27. Returned to U. S.
1870. 1878, acting pastor Elkhart, Ind. 1883 Glenwood, Iowa.

Mary Anica Thompson, born Kaltsville, Saratoga Co., N. Y. Jan. 12, 1845; studied
at Grove Hill Seminary, New Haven, Ct., where in the autumn of 1860 she was
hopefully converted; prof. rel. at Rosendale, Wisconsin, the residence of her
parents, Nov. 3, 1861; sailed with Messrs Whiting, Sheffield and McCoy and their
wives for China from San Francisco Oct. 4, 1869. Returned to U. S. in ill
health, 1872.

Jane Eliza Chapin, of Springfield, Illinois; born Greensboro, Vt. May 18,
prof. rel. 1851; educated in Monticello Sem. (Ill.) and Ipswich Fem. Sem.;
sailed with Rev. Lyman D. Chapin and wife in steamer from San Francisco for
China, May 1, 1871; ar. Tung-cho June 17; at Peking 1872. Still at Peking Jan.
1878. Vis. U. S. arr. about June 1, 1883 ; re-emb. Sept. 19, 1885; arr.
Peking Nov. 9, 1885; vis. U. S. arr. San Francisco April 17, 1900; re-emb. San
Francisco Oct. 23, 1901. Vis. U. S. arr. San Francisco Sept. 9, 1905. Released
May 29, 1906. Living at Springfield, Ill. 1913. Died June 23, 1914. (See
Herald Aug. 1914, p. 342)

Naomi Diament, born Cedarville, N. J. Sept. 7, 1834; prof. rel. June 1849;
educated at Mt. Holyoke and Western Fem. Sem., Oxford, O. Engaged for some time
in teaching. Sailed from San Francisco Feb. 1, 1870. 1870-1876 stationed at
Kalgan. Autumn 1876, trans. to Peking. Jan. 1878, still in Peking. Vis. U.S.
in 1882; re-emb. May 29, 1883; arr. Tientsin May 4. Dec. 1885 at Kalgan. Died
May 3, 1893, at Kalgan. (See Herald July 1893, p. 271)

Jane Gertrude Evans, born Orford, N. H. Nov. 7, 1838. Educated in Fitchburg,
Mass. and Brooklyn, N. Y. Taught in Brooklyn twelve years. Prof. rel. 1857.

sailed from San Francisco Oct. 1, 1872. Reached Tung-cho Nov. 22. Has labored there, to present time, (Jan. 1878). Vis. U. S. arr; July 3, 1883; re-emb. San Francisco Sept. 2, 1884. Dec. 1885 at Tung-cho. Vis. the U. S. in 1893; re-emb. San Francisco Aug. 7, 1894. Vis. U. S. arr. San Francisco June 9, 1902. Died Charlestown, N. H. Sept. 9, 1904. (See Oct. 1904 Herald)

Henry Dwight Porter, M.D., son of Rev. Jeremiah Porter, born Green Bay, Wis., Aug. 19, 1845. Prof. rel. March 1857; grad. Beloit Coll. 1867; grad. Andover 1870; grad. Chicago Medical Coll. 1872; ord. May 29, 1872. Sailed San Francisco July 1, 1872. Arr. Tientsin Aug. 17. Jan. 1878, still at Tientsin. Returned U. S. Nov. 23, 1878; re-emb. San Francisco Sept. 13, 1879; arr. Shanghai Oct. 16. Dec. 1885 at Shantung. Vis. U. S. arr. San Francisco May 23, 1888; re-emb. San Francisco April 5, 1890; Vis. U. S. arr. N. Y. June 13, 1901. Died Oct. 23, 1916. (See Miss'y Herald 1916, p. 542)

Porter (Elizabeth Colton Chapin) born Milwaukee, Wis., Nov. 27, 1848; prof. rel. June 28, 1868; studied Beloit High School, Rockford Fem. Sem., Miss Porter's Sch., Farmington, Ct.; mar. April 2, 1879; emb. San Francisco Sept. 13, 1879; arr. Shanghai Oct. 16. Dec. 1885 at Shantung. Vis. U. S. arr. San Francisco May 23, 1888; re-emb. San Francisco April 5, 1890. Vis. U. S. arr. San Francisco July 1899. LaMesa, Calif. 1913. Died at Beloit, Wisc. November 24, 1930.

Myron Winslow Hunt (son of P. R. Hunt); born Madras, India Dec. 5, 1846. Prof. rel. 1864. Grad. Amherst Coll. 1870. Grad. Union Sem. 1873. Ord. Brooklyn, N. Y. June 25, 1873. Sailed from San Francisco Aug. 1873 and arr. Peking Sept. 19. Ret. to U. S. 1876. Mar. 1878 in Kansas. Centralia under A.H.M.S. Died at Falls City, Neb. 1881, Aug. 10, leaving 3 children, Myron, Jesse and a dau. Mary, who are now, Mar. 1901, Mary and Jesse with the mother in Cleveland, O. Myron is in Melia, Montana.

Mrs. Hunt (Laura A. White) born Sinclairville, N. Y. Mar. 10, 1849; prof. rel. March 1866. Educated, Norwalk (O.) High School. Teacher! Mar. May 28, 1873,

sailed from San Francisco Oct. 1, 1872. Reached Tung-cho Nov. 22. Has
..ared there, to present time, (Jan. 1878). Vis. U. S. arr; July 3, 1883; re-
emb. San Francisco Sept. 2, 1884. Dec. 1885 at Tung-cho. Vis. the U. S. in
1893; re-emb. San Francisco Aug. 7, 1894. Vis. U. S. arr. San Francisco June 9,
1903. Died Charlestown, N. H. Sept. 9, 1904. (See Oct. 1904 Herald)

Henry Dwight Porter, M.D., son of Rev. Jeremiah Porter, born Green Bay, Wis.,
Aug. 19, 1845. Prof. rel. March 1857; grad. Beloit Coll. 1857; grad. Andover
1870; grad. Chicago Medical Coll. 1872; ord. May 29, 1872. Sailed San Francisco
July 1, 1872. Arr. Tientsin A ug. 17. Jan. 1878, still at Tientsin. Returned
U. S. Nov. 23, 1878; re-emb. San Francisco Sept. 13, 1879; arr. Shanghai Oct. 16.
Dec. 1885 at Shantung. Vis. U. S. arr. San Francisco May 23, 1888; re-emb. San
Francisco April 5, 1890; Vis. U. S. arr. N. Y. June 13, 1901. Died Oct. 23,
1916. (See Miss'y Herald 1916, p. 542)

Porter (Elizabeth Colton Chapin) born Milwaukee, Wis., Nov. 27, 1848; prof.
rel. June 28, 1868; studied Beloit High School, Rockford Fem. Sem., Miss
Porter's Sch., Farmington, Ct.; mar. April 2, 1879; emb. San Francisco Sept. 13,
1879; arr. Shanghai Oct. 16. Dec. 1885 at Shantung. Vis. U. S. arr. San Francisco May 23, 1888; re-emb. San Francisco April 5, 1890. Vis. U. S. arr. San
Francisco July 1899. LaMesa, Calif. 1913. Died at Beloit, November 24, 1930, Wis.

Myron Winslow Hunt (son of P. R. Hunt); born Madras, India Dec. 5, 1846. Prof.
rel. 1864. Grad. Amherst Coll. 1870. Grad. Union Sem. 1873. Ord. Brooklyn,
N. Y. June 26, 1873. Sailed from San Francisco Aug. 1873 and arr. Peking Sept.
19. Ret. to U. S. 1876. / 1878 in Kansas. Centralia under A.H.M.S. Died at
Falls City, Neb. 1881, Aug. 10, leaving 3 children, Myron, Jesse and a dau.
Mary, who are now, Mar. 1901, Mary and Jesse with the mother in Cleveland, O.
M is in Melia, Montana.

Mrs. Hunt (Laura A. White) born Sinclairville, N. Y. Mar. 10, 1849; prof. rel.
March 1866. Educated, Norwalk (O.) High School. Teacher: Mar. May 28, 1873,

Srs lk, O. Sailed as above. Ret. to U. S. 1876. March 1888 Kan. In course of time married a Mr. Rensseller R. Herrick. He has since died and she is now,/1901, living 726 East Prospect St., Cleveland, O.

William Parmelee Sprague, born E. Bloomfield, New York June 20, 1843. Grad. Amherst 1870; grad. at Andover 1873, having been at New Haven Sem. part of the course. Ord. May 8, 1873. Sailed from New York Jan. 28, 1874, and reached Tientsin April 15. At Kalgan 1874 to Jan. 1878. Vis. U. S. in 1880; re-emb. Sept. 3, 1881; arr. Tientsin Oct. 14; Dec. 1885 at Kalgan. Vis. U. S. arr. San Francisco May 28, 1889; re-emb. N. Y. Mar. 11, 1891; arr. Tientsin May 8, 1891; vis. U. S. arr. N. Y. Oct. 9, 1900; one of the party which escaped from China through Mongolia and Russia. Re-emb. Seattle Aug. 26, 1902; returned to U. S. arr. N. Y. July 5, 1910; released Aug. 30, 1910. Died Feb. 9, 1919. (Miss'y Herald 1919, p. 142)

Mrs. Sprague (Viette I. Brown) born Newark, Wayne Co., N. Y. 1846; profl rel. Shortsville, N. Y. 1873; grad. Mt. Holyoke Sem. 1871; arr. Tientsin Sept. 23, 1885; mar. Tientsin Sept. 30, 1893; vis. U. S. arr. N. Y. Oct. 9, 1900; re-emb. Seattle Aug. 26, 1902; returned to U. S. arr. N. Y. July 5, 1910; released Aug. 30, 1910. Died

Mrs. Sprague (Margaret S. Henderson) born Dec. 4, 1844, Edinburgh; prof. rel. 1857; mar. July 16, 1873 at New Haven, Ct. Sailed as above. Jan. 1878 at Kalgan. Vis. U. S. in 1880; re-emb. Mar. 29, 1883; arr. Tientsin May 4. Dec. 1885 at Kalgan. Vis. U. S. arr. San Francisco May 28, 1889. Died at Rochester, N. Y. Jan. 5, 1891. (See Mar. Herald 1891)

Lyman Hudson Roberts, born Hartford, Ct. 1851; prof. rel. Aug. 3, 1863; grad. Yale 1873 and Yale Sem. 1876. Ord. Sept. 12, 1877. Emb. S.F. Oct. 11, 1877. Arr. Peking Dec. 6, 1877. Dec. 1885 at Kalgan. Vis. U. S. arr. San Francisco Sept. 11, 1887; re-emb. San Francisco Mar. 20, 1889; arr. Tientsin April 29, 1889; vis. the U. S. arr. Vancouver July 1, 1896; re-emb. Vancouver Mar. 28, 1898; arr. Kalgan May 30, 1898; vis. U. S. arr. N. Y. Oct. 9, 1900; one of

the party which escaped from China through Mongolia and Russia at time of Boxer uprising; re-emb. Vancouver May 7, 1901; returned to U. S. arr. San Francisco June 21, 1906; released Aug. 14, 1906. S̶t̶i̶l̶l̶ ̶l̶i̶v̶i̶n̶g̶ ̶1̶9̶3̶6̶ Died May 15, 1945 at Wethersfield, Conn.

Mrs. Roberts (Grace L. Howe) dau. of Hon C. M. Howe, who lives Worcester, 18 Maple St.; born Marlboro, Mass. Sept. 5, 1854. Grad. Marlboro High School 1874; prof. rel. 1875. Taught in M. two years. Mar. Sept. 19, 1877. Emb. Oct. 11, 1877. Arr. Peking Dec. 6, 1877. Vis. U. S. arr. San Francisco Sept. 11, 1887; re-emb. San Francisco Mar. 20, 1889; arr. Tientsin April 29, 1889; vis. U. S. arr. San Francisco June 6, 1894; re-emb. San Francisco Oct. 23, 1901; returned to U. S. arr. San Francisco June 21, 1906; released Aug. 14, 1906.

William Scott Ament, born Sept. 14, 1851, Owasso, Mich.; prof. rel. 1865; grad. Oberlin Coll. 1873. At Union Sem. two years, graduating at Andover, 1877. Ord. Owasso Sept. 5, 1877. Sailed from San Francisco Oct. 11, 1877. Ar. -ting-fu Dec. 10, 1877. Returned to U. S. arr. May 16, 1885. Released July 14, 1885. Re-appt'd Feb. 28, 1888; emb. San Francisco Aug. 30, 1888; arr. Tientsin Oct. 7, 1888; vis. U. S. arr. San Francisco May 21, 1897; re-emb. Vancouver Sept. 12, 1898; arr. Peking Oct. 8. Vis. U. S. arr. San Francisco April 27, 1901; re-emb. San Francisco May 9, 1902; returned to U. S. arr. San Francisco Dec. 25, 1908, where he died Jan. 6, 1909. (See Feb. 1909 Herald, p. 85)

Mrs. Ament, (Mary Alice Penfield) born Oberlin, Ohio July 4, 1856; prof. rel. Oberlin Jan. 1, 1870; educated at Oberlin Coll. and Berea Coll., Ky. Taught for a time. Mar. at Cleveland, Aug. 23, 1877. Sailed as above. Ar. Pao-ting-fu Dec. 10, 1877. Vis. U. S. in 1880; re-emb. Sept. 3, 1881; arr. Tientsin Oct. 14. Returned to U. S. arr. May 16, 1885. Released July 14, 1885. Re-appt'd Feb. 28, 1888; emb. San Francisco Aug. 30, 1888; ar. Tientsin Oct. 7, 1888; vis. U. S. arr. San Francisco May 21, 1897; re-emb. San Francisco May 9, 1902. Vis. U. S. arr. Sept. 1906; re-emb. Seattle Aug. 4, 1908; returned to U. S. arr.

San Francisco Dec. 25, 1908; re-emb. Seattle Sept. 19, 1910; arr. home June 11, 1914; sailed Aug. 7, 1915; arr. home July 9, 1918. Resigned May 27, 1919.

Franklin Munroe Chapin, born Portland, Me. April 19, 1853; prof. rel. July 1875; grad. Dartmouth Coll. 1877; Hartford Theol. Sem. 1880; ord. Keene, N. H. May 20, 1880; emb. San Francisco Sept. 1, 1880; arr. Kalgan Oct. 22. Dec. 1885 at Pang-chuang. Vis. U. S. arr. June 11, 1890; re-emb. Vancouver Sept. 9, 1891; arr. Tientsin Oct. 3, 1891. Vis. U. S. arr. San Francisco Oct. 1900; re-emb. San Francisco Oct. 18, 1901; returned to U. S. arr. San Francisco Nov. 8, 1906; released Dec. 4, 1906. Living 1908. *Died Aug. 1, 1940, at Manhattan, Kansas*

Mrs. Chapin (Flora Maria Barrett) born Winchester, Cheshire Co., N. H. June 29, 1851; prof. rel. Nov. 1, 1868; studied Greenfield and Keene High Schools; mar. June 30, 1880; emb. as above. Dec. 1885 at Pang-chuang. Vis. U. S. arr. June 11, 1890; re-emb. Vancouver Sept. 9, 1891; arr. Tientsin Oct. 3, 1891; vis. U. S. arr. San Francisco Oct. 1900; re-emb. San Francisco Oct. 18, 1901; returned to U. S. arr. Nov. 8, 1906; released Dec. 4, 1906.

William Herbert Shaw, born South Weymouth, Mass. June 1, 1856; prof. rel. Braintree 1871; grad. Amherst Coll. 1877, Union Theol. Sem. 1880; ord. Braintree July 13, 1880; emb. Sept. 1, 1880; arr. Pao-ting-fu Oct.; returned to U. S. after the death of his wife, arr. May 31, 1884. Dec. 1895 in U. S. 1888 at 76 Chauncy St., Boston. Died at Braintree, Mass. Feb. 8, 1915.

Mrs. Shaw (Sarah Lizzie Burnham) born Haverhill, Mass. March 13, 1857; prof. rel. 1871; studied Braintree High School; mar. Aug. 4, 1880; emb. Sept. 1, 1880; arr. Pao-ting-fu Oct.; died Kobe, Japan Nov. 22, 1882. (See Herald Feb. 1883, p.47)

Henry Poor Perkins, born Ware, Hampshire Co., Mass. Dec. 24, 1856; prof. rel. Ware about 1870; grad. Williams Coll. 1879; studied two years at Hartford Theol. Sem.; ord. Ware Sept. 6, 1882; emb. San Francisco Oct. 7, 1882. Dec. 1885 at Tientsin. Vis. U. S. arr. San Francisco May 9, 1892; re-emb. San Francisco Sept. 12, 1893; arr. Tientsin Oct. 18, 1893. Vis. U. S. arr. San Francisco

Oct. 1900; re-emb. Boston Aug. 28, 1901; vis. U. S. arr. Worcester July 18, 1910. Died at Claremont, Cal. Jan. 3, 1933.

Mrs. Perkins (Estella Lille Akers, M.D.) born Buxton, York Co., Me. ? 21, 1856; prof. rel. Bath 1876; studied Bath High School and Woman's Medical Coll. Chicago; went to China under Meth. Board about 1881; mar. Oct. 29, 1885; 1886 at Tientsin. Vis. U. S. arr. San Francisco May 9, 1892; re-emb. Sept. 12, 1893; arr. Tientsin Oct. 13, 1893; vis. U. S. arr. San Francisco Oct. 1900; re-emb. San Francisco Oct. 15, 1902; vis. U. S. arr. Worcester July 18, 1910. Died Aug. 13, 1929, Claremont, Calif. (See Missionary Herald, Oct. 1929, page 390)

Harlan Page Beach born So. Orange, N. J. April 4, 1854; prof. rel. 1864; grad. Yale Coll. 1878, Andover Theol. Sem. 1883; ord. July 19, 1883; emb. San Francisco Sept. 27, 1883; arr. Peking Nov. 19. Dec. 1885 at Tung-cho. Vis. U. S. arr. San Francisco Feb. 21, 1890; released Sept. 15, 1891. Died March 4, 1933. (See M-H. May, 1933)

M. Beach (Lucy Lucretia Ward) born Chicago, Ill. Oct. 16, 1855; prof. rel. April ? ; studied Ferry Hall Sem., Lake Forest, Ill. and Lake Forest Univ.; mar. June 29; 1883 as above. Died September 1, 1945 Winter Park, Florida.

ASSISTANT MISSIONARIES

Willis Clark Noble, born New Haven, Ct. June 27, 1854; prof. rel. March 1871; emb. San Francisco Aug. 1, 1878; arr. Peking Oct. 8. Dec. 1885 at Peking. Vis. U. S. arr. San Francisco May 23, 1888. Reappt'd May 5, 1891; emb. Vancouver, Sept. 18, 1892; arr. Pao-ting-fu Nov. 7, 1892; vis. U. S. arr. San Francisco April 17, 1900; released April 29, 1902.

Mrs. Noble (Willa J. Gibson) born Hamden, New Haven Co., Ct. Nov.13, 1852; prof. rel. April 1870; mar. Dec. 25, 1877; emb. San Francisco Aug. 1, 1878; arr. Peking Oct. 8. Dec. 1885 at Peking. Vis. U. S. arr. San Francisco May 23, 1888; re-appt'd May 5, 1891; emb. Vancouver Sept. 18, 1892; arr. Pao-ting-fu Nov. 7,

vis. U. S. arr. New Haven, Ct. Dec. 26, 1897; released April 29, 1902.

Sarah Boardman Clapp, born Waunatosa, Milwaukee Co., Wis. Nov. 28, 1855; prof. rel. 1870; studied Rockford Fem. Sem., Rockford, Ill. emb. San Francisco Sept. 13, 1879; arr. Shanghai Oct. 16; mar. Rev. Chauncey Goodrich, 1880. Vis. U. S. arr. May 28, 1885. Returned to China, and after the siege returned to the U.S. in 1901.

Ada Haven, born Brookline, Mass. March 21, 1850; prof. rel. about 1860; studied grammar and high schools of Chicago; emb. San Francisco Sept. 13, 1879; arr. Shanghai Oct. 16. Dec. 1885 at Peking. Vis. U. S. arr. Chicago Jan. 23, 1891; re-emb.   .; mar. Rev. Dr. C. W. Mateer of the Presbyterian mission 1900; released Nov. 13, 1900. Died 1937. (See Missionary Herald, December, 1937, p 978)

Virginia Cox Murdock, M. D. born Zanesville, O., April 1, 1850; prof. rel. Bloomington, Ill. Feb. 1879; studied Normal Univ., Normal, Ill., Woman's Medical Coll. Philadelphia, grad. med. dept. Univ. of Mich., Ann Arbor; emb. Feb. 26, 1881; arr. Tientsin April 10. Dec. 1885 at Kalgan. Vis. U. S. arr. San Francisco June 27, 1890; re-emb. San Francisco Oct. 8, 1891; arr. Tientsin Nov. 18, 1891; vis.U.S. arr. San Francisco Jan. 1, 1898. Released Oct. 25, 1898. Re-appt'd Mar. 21, 1899; re-emb. Vancouver Aug. 21, 1899. Vis. U. S. arr. N. Y. Oct. 9, 1900; one of the party which escaped from China by way of Mongolia and Russia at the time of the Boxer uprising; released March 4, 1902. Died Sept. 14, 1929, in Oakland, Calif. age 70 years. (See Herald Jan. 1929, pages 47 and 48)

Mary Anna Holbrook, M.D. born E. Abington,(now Rockland) Plymouth Co., Mass., July 10, 1854; prof. rel. July 1869; studied Mt. Holyoke Sem. and Mich. Univ. Sch. of Medicine; emb. Sept. 3, 1881; arr. Tientsin Oct. 14. Dec. 1885 at Tung-cho. Vis. U. S. arr. July 1887; transferred to Japan Aug. 6, 1889. Died at E. Haven, Conn. Dec. 2, 1910. (See Miss'y Herald Jan. 1911, p. 4)

Flora Josepha Hale, born Fredonia, Licking Co., O., March 28, 1851; prof. rel. 1868; grad. at Adrian Coll. 1871; emb. San Francisco Mar. 29, 1883; arr.

Tientsin May 4. Mar. Rev. Isaac Pierson at Peking Aug. 1, 1884. Dec. 1885 Pao-ting-fu. Ret. 1889. Released Feb. 10, 1891. 1900, 8 Wareham St., Medford, Mass.

Edwin Edgerton Aiken, born Newington, Hartford Co., Ct. March 1, 1859; prof. rel. about 1871, Rutland, Vt.; grad. Yale Coll. 1881, Yale Theol. Sem. 1884; ord. New Haven, Ct. May 20, 1885; emb. Oct. 3, 1885; ar. Peking Nov. 17, 1885; vis. U. S. arr. San Francisco July 31, 1890; re-emb. Vancouver Oct. 15, 1892; arr. Tientsin Nov. 9; Vis. U. S. arr. San Francisco Dec. 11, 1899; re-emb. San Francisco Oct. 15, 1902. Released March 1912. (Arrived home Apr. 30, 1911. Member of intermission com. engaged in revision of the mandarin. bible.) Returned to Peiping early in 1913; sailed Dec. 16, 1912. In China 1938. See card. Passed away January 5, 1951 in New Haven, Conn.

Mrs. Aiken (Maud Lockwood) born
mar. New York Oct. 6, 1892; emb. Vancouver Oct. 15, 1892; arr. Tientsin
ed at Tientsin Oct. 28, 1899. (See Jan. 1900 Herald, p. 5)

Mrs. Aiken (Rose E. Merrill) born Hartford, Ct. Oct. 26, 1882; united with Howard Av. Cong. Ch. 1896; studied in publ schools. Mar. Fairhaven, Conn. Oct. 5, 1902; emb. San Francisco Oct. 15, 1902. Arrived home Apr. 30, 1911 etc. Released Mar. 1912. In China 1938. See card.

Irenaes J. Atwood, Transferred fr. Shanse Miss. Vis. U. S. arr. San Francisco April 22, 1888; re-emb. San Francisco Aug. 13, 1889; vis. U. S. arr. San Francisco May 20, 1899; re-emb. San Francisco March 7, 1901. In 1890 re-transferred to Shanse.

Mrs. Atwood (Annette Williams) Transferred fr. Shanse Miss. Vis. U. S. arr. July 1887; re-emb. San Francisco Aug. 13, 1889; vis. U. S. arr. San Francisco y 20, 1899; re-emb. Vancouver July 28, 1902; In 1890 re-transferred to Shanse.

MISSIONARY PHYSICIANS

Robert Palmer Peck, M.D., born Racine, Wis. April 30, 1848; prof. rel. Racine 1862; studied Rush Medical Coll. Chicago; practiced med. in Chicago, Racine and Beloit; emb. Sept. 1, 1880; arr. Pao-ting-fu Oct. Dec. 1885 at Pao-ting-fu. Vis. U. S. arr. N. Y. April 10, 1890; re-emb. San Francisco Sept. 6, 1892. Vis. U. S. arr. San Francisco July 1, 1899. re-emb.   ; arr. Shanghai Jan. 17, 1901. Released Nov. 3, 1903.

Mrs. Peck (Celia Stella Flagg) born Racine, Wis. Oct. 13, 1850; prof. rel. Jan. 1, 1864; studied Chicago High Schl; mar. July 15, 1874; emb. Sept. 1, 1880; arr. Pao-ting-fu Oct.   Dec. 1885 at Pao-ting-fu. Vis. U. S. arr. San Francisco June 1889; re-emb. San Francisco Sept. 6, 1892; vis. the U. S. arr. San Francisco June 1897; released Nov. 3, 1903.

Charles Phelps Williams Merritt, M.D., born Piscataway, Middlesex Co., N. J. July 1, 1852; prof. rel. Metuchen, N. J. 1870; grad. Rutgers Coll. 1871; studied Coll. of Physicians & Surgeons, N. Y. City; emb. Sept. 2, 1885; arr. Pao-ting-fu Oct. 20, 1885; vis. U. S. arr. Vancouver May 3, 1893; released June 3, 1895. Died Feb. 16, 1925 in Canadea, N. Y. (See Miss. Herald 1925, p.222)

Mrs. Merritt (Anna C. Lord) born Fulton, Oswego Co., N. Y. Jan. 13, 1854; prof. rel. 1869; studied H. C. Inst., Adams; Fairfield Sem. "Maplewood", Pittsfield and private school in New Brunswick; emb. Sept. 2, 1885; arr. Pao-ting-fu Oct. 20, 1885; vis. U. S. arr. Vancouver May 3, 1893; released June 3, 1895. Died Clifton Springs January 21, 1937. Her husband had practised there for thirty years.

SHANSI MISSION

This mission was commenced in 1881.

MISSIONARIES

Martin Luther Stimson, born Waterbury, Washington Co., Vt. July 6, 1856; prof. rel. Oberlin, O., Jan. 1879; grad. Dartmouth Coll. 1878, Oberlin Theol. Sem. 1881; ord. Oberlin July 26, 1881; emb. Sept. 3, 1881; arr. Tientsin Oct. 14. Dec. 1885 at Tai-ku. Vis. U. S. arr. Vancouver, May 2, 1889; released March 25, 1890. Re-appt'd July 5, 1898 and designated to the Micronesia Mission. Released 1908. Died November 4, 1936, at Coral Gables, Fla.

Mrs. Stimson (Emily Brooks Hall) dau. of Rev. H. B. Hall, formerly missionary to Jamaica under the A.M.A.; born Brainerd, Jamaica, W. I. Sept. 13, 1857; prof. rel. Dover, O. 1871; studied Oberlin Coll.; mar. July 6, 1881; emb. Sept. 3, 1881; arr. Tientsin Oct. 14. Dec. 1885 at Tai-ku. Vis. U. S. arr. Vancouver 2, 1889; released Mar. 25, 1890. Reappointed July 5, 1898, and designated to the Micronesia Mission. Still living 1936, Coral Gables, Florida. Died June 22, 1943 at Rochester, N. Y.

Linnaeus J. Atwood, M.D., born Lake Mills, Jeff.Co., Wis., Dec. 4, 1850; prof. rel. Lake Mills 1864; grad. Ripon Coll. 1878, Oberlin Theol. Sem. 1881; ord. Oberlin June 25, 1881; emb. Aug. 30, 1882; arr. Tai-yuen-fu Nov. 1. Dec. 1885 at Tai-ku. Transferred to the North China Mission June 14, 1887; transferred back to this mission in 1890; vis. U. S. arr. San Francisco May 20, 1899; re-emb. San Francisco Mar. 7, 1901; vis. U. S. arr. San Francisco Mar. 29, 1909. Died Oct. 1, 1913 in Tacoma, Wash. (Miss'y Herald #109, page 508)

Mrs. Atwood (Annette Williams) born Delavan, Walworth Co., Wis., Aug. 23, 1851; prof. rel. Delavan 1865; studied Delavan Episcopal Sem.; mar. Dec. 25, 1878; emb. Aug. 30, 1882; arr. Tai-yuen-fu Nov. 1. Dec. 1885 at Tai-ku. Transferred the No. China Mission June 14, 1887. Transferred back to this mission in 1890; vis. U. S. arr. San Francisco May 20, 1899; re-emb. Vancouver July 29, 1902; vis. U. S. arr. San Francisco Nov. 6, 1908; vis. U. S. arr. San Francisco Mar. 29, 1909. Died Mar. 9, 1912. (See Miss. Herald May 1912, p. 223)

70

Chauncy Marvin Cady, born Summer Hill, Pike Co., Ill., March 6, 1854; prof. rel. Oberlin, O. 1871; grad. Oberlin Coll. 1877; Oberlin Theol. Sem. 1881; ord. Oberlin June 25, 1882; emb. Aug. 30, 1882; arr. Tai-yuen-fu, Nov. 1; transferred to Japan mission Nov. 4, 1884.

Charles Daniel Tenney, born Boston, June 29, 1857; prof. rel. Troy, O. Mar. 9, 1873; grad. Dartmouth Coll. 1878, Oberlin Theol. Sem. 1882; ord. Oberlin June 25, 1882; emb. Aug. 30, 1882; arr. Tai-yuen-fu Nov. 1. Dec. 1885 at Tai-ku. Released April 6, 1886. 1888 Tutor to the Emperor's children, Tientsin, No. China. Died March 14, 1930 /Palo Alto, California.

Mrs. Tenney (Annie Runcie Jerrell) born Fairton, N. J. Feb. 18, 1859; prof. rel. Bridgeton, N. J. 1865; studied Jay Hall & Wellesley Coll.; mar. March 1882; emb. Aug. 30, 1882; arr. Tai-yuen-fu Nov. 1. Dec. 1885 at Tai-ku. Released April 6, 1886. 1888 Tientsin, No. China.

Francis Marion Price, born Milroy, Rush Co., Ind. 1851; prof. rel. 1868; after taking the junior and part of the middle year in Oberlin Sem. completed Coll. course graduating from Oberlin Coll. 1882, and Theol. Sem. 1883; ord. Oberlin July 1, 1883; emb. Sept. 6, 1883; arr. Tai-yuen-fu Nov. "; returned to U. S . arr. Nov. 25, 1884; released Mar. 24, 1885. Re-appt'd Dec. 14, 1887; arr. Taiku, Shanse, May 4, 1887; returned to U. S. arr. S an Francisco July 9, 1890; Transferred to Micronesia Jan. 15, 1894. Died September 4, 1937 at Berkeley, Calif.

Mrs. Price (Sarah Jane Freeborn) born Winterset, Iowa, Dec. 1, 1855; prof. rel. 1866; studied at Oberlin, O.; mar. Milroy, Ind. Jan. 3, 1872; emb. S ept. 6, 1883; arr. Tai-yuen-fu Nov.; returned to U. S. arr. Nov. 25, 1884; released Mar. 24, 1885. Re-appt'd Dec. 14, 1887; emb. with Dr. and Mrs. Osborne from San Francisco Aug. 23, 1887; returned to U. S. arr. San Francisco July 9, 1890. transferred to Micronesia Jan. 15, 1894. Died Aug. 2, 1916. He married 1917 Mrs. Jennie Reeves, living in Berkeley 1937.

Dwight Howard Clapp, born Middlefield, Geauga Co., O. Nov. 1, 1849; prof. rel. Kirtland, O., July 1867; grad. Oberlin 1879; Oberlin Theol. Sem. 1884; ord. Oberlin, June 22, 1884; emb. San Francisco Sept. 2, 1884. Dec. 1885 at Taiku. Vis. U. S. arr. Vancouver May 22, 1894; re-emb. Vancouver Sept. 16, 1895; arr. Tientsin Oct. 12, 1895. Killed in Boxer uprising 1900. (See Missionary Herald Nov. 1900 and 1900 Annual Report.

Mrs. Clapp (Mary Jane Rowland) born Clarksfield, Huron Co., O. Feb. 18, 1845; prof. rel. 1862; studied Lake Erie Sem., Painesville, O.; mar. June 3, 1884; emb. San Francisco Sept. 2, 1884. Dec. 1885 at Tai-ku. Vis. U. S. arr. Vancouver May 22, 1894; re-emb. Vancouver Sept. 16, 1895; arr. Tientsin Oct. 12, 1895; killed in Boxer uprising 1900.

James Brettle Thompson, born Harbor Grace, N. F. May 24, 1858; prof. rel. St. Johns, N. F., April 1876; eight years a home missionary in New Brunswick; Oberlin Theol. Sem. 1885; ord. Oberlin, June 3, 1885; emb. Sept. 2, 1885; arr. Tai-ku Oct. 21, 1885; vis. U. S. in 1896; re-emb. San Francisco Sept. 2, 1897; arr. Tientsin Oct. 2; vis. U. S. arr. San Francisco Dec. 2, 1899; released Jan. 23, 1900. Died April 10, 1932 in Minneapolis.

Mrs. Thompson (Tinnie DeEtta Hewett) See Vol. 11, p. 147. Mar. Tientsin, Oct. 25, 1892. Vis. U. S. in 1896; re-emb. Vancouver Sept. 12, 1898. Died at Jen T'sun, Shansi, Aug. 23, 1899. (See Nov. 1899 Herald, p. 519)

MISSIONARY PHYSICIANS

Daniel Edward Osborne, born Chardon, O., Aug. 3, 1857; prof. rel. Ann Arbor, Mich., 1879; grad. Ann Arbor 1879 and 1884, also studied medicine at Univ. of Mich.; emb. San Francisco Sept. 2, 1884. Dec. 1885 at Tai-ku. Returned to U. arr. San Francisco June 1, 1886; released June 18, 1886. Re-appt'd May 17, 1887; emb. San Francisco Aug. 23, 1887; arr. Tai-ku Oct. 22, 1887. Returned to U. S. arr. San Francisco Nov. 1888. Released Nov. 20, 1888.

Mrs. Osborne (Mary Margaret Alabaster) born Niagara Falls, N. Y., March 8, 1862; prof. rel. 1874; studied Auburn, N. Y. Academic High Sch. and Ann Arbor High Sch.; mar. May 17, 1882; emb. San Francisco Sept. 2, 1884. Dec. 1885 at Tai-ku. Returned to U. S. arr. San Francisco June 1, 1886; released June 18, 1886. Re-appt'd May 17, 1887; emb. San Francisco Aug. 23, 1887; arr. Tai-ku Oct. 22, 1887. Arr. San Francisco Nov. 1888. Released Nov. 20, 1888.

HONG-KONG MISSION

This mission was commenced in 1883 with special reference to the religious needs of that class of the Chinese who have resided for a time in the U. S. and have returned to China.

MISSIONARIES

Charles Robert Hager, M.D., born Nanikon, Canton Zurich, Switzerland, Oct. 27, 1851; prof. rel. Little Shasta, Cal.; grad. Theol. Sem., Oakland, Cal. May 1882; ord. San Francisco Feb. 15, 1883; emb. Feb. 24, 1883; arr. Hong Kong Mar. 31. Dec. 1885 at Hong Kong. Vis. U. S. arr. San Francisco May 23, 1888; re-emb. San Francisco Nov. 28, 1888; arr. Hong Kong Dec. 27, 1888; vis. U. S. on account of ill health, after a stay of several months in Switzerland, arr. N. Y. Sept. 19, 1891; grad. Med. Coll. Nashville, Tenn. June 1894; re-emb. Francisco Aug. 28, 1894; arr. Hong Kong Sept. 24, 1894. Vis. U. S. arr. San Francisco May 27, 1904; re-emb. N. Y. July 4, 1905; returning via. Switzerland, via. U. S. arr. San Francisco Mar. 14, 1910. Released Mar. 1912. Died July 13, 1917 in Claremont, California. (See Herald Sept. 1917, p.397)

Mrs. Hager (Lizzie W. Blackman) born
mar. Chicago, June 20, 1894; emb. San Francisco Aug. 28, 1894; arr. Hong Kong Sept. 24, 1894; died at Canton, March 7, 1895.

Mrs. Hager (Marie vonRausch) born Mottlingen, Wurtemberg, Germany; Mar. 6, 1865; united with German Evangelical Church 1877; for three years had charge of the Basel Mission Kindergarten school at Hong Kong; mar. at Hong Kong Dec. 31, 1896; vis. U. S. arr. San Francisco May 27, 1904; re-emb. N. Y. July 4, 1905, returning via Switzerland. Released Mar. 1912. Living with her three ldren in Claremont, California in 1917. Died in Claremont, Calif. on Nov. 22, 1918.

MISSION TO SIAM

This mission may be said to have grown out from the Mission to Canton. Mr. Abeel (page 211) having spent a year in the service of the Seamen's Friend Society there, was appointed a missionary of the American Board, and in that capacity arrived at Bangkok, the capital of Siam, July 1, 1831, and commenced the American mission there. He was compelled by ill health to leave that place in 1833, but was succeeded by Messrs Robinson and Johnson, July 1834.

The Mission was discontinued in October, 1848.

Missionaries.

David Abeel--with some interruption from ill health, which compelled him to retire for a season to Singapore--distributed Chinese books and tracts, and performed other missionary service at Bangkok, till obliged by prostrate health finally to leave that place in the autumn of 1833. See p. 211. Unmarried. Died, Albany, N.Y., Sept. 4, 1846.

Charles Robinson, Lee, Mass: born Lenox, Mass. Dec. 30. 1801: prof. rel. Dec. 1815: grad. Williams Coll. 1829: Auburn Seminary 1832: ord. Lenox, Jan. 16, 1833: emb. with his fellow-student Mr. Johnson (p. 215) and with Munson and Lyman (pp. 243-245) at Boston for Batavia, June 10, 1833: ar. Singapore, Oct. 1833: arr. Bangkok, July 25, 1834: labored there, amid great discouragements, more than eleven years: in the Siamese department of the mission. Compelled by declining health, he left the mission, Nov. 1845: and died on his passage from St. Helena to the U.S. March 3, 1847. See Obituary notice, Herald, vol. 43, p. 228.

Mrs. Robinson (Maria Church) Riga, Monroe Co. N.Y.: born West Poultney, Feb. 1, 1807: prof rel. May 1827: mar. Riga, N.Y. April 1, 1833: returned to U.S. 16, 1847. Died Brooklyn, N.Y., Jan. 9, 1886.

(missing page, copied and sent from Boston)

Stephen Johnson was a fellow-student of Mr. Robinson at Auburn, and accompanies him to Siam; labored in the Chinese department of the mission; removed to Fuh-Chau June 1847. (See Fuh-Chau Mission) The two former wives were members of this mission. 1878, Gouverneur, N. Y. Died Gouverneur Jan. 14, 1886. (See Herald, Mar. 1886, p. 113)

Dan. B. Bradley, M.D., Penn-yan- N. Y.; born Marcellus, N. Y. July 18, 1804; emb. Boston, July 2, 1834; ar. Amherst, in British Burmah, Dec. 6, 1834; arr. Singapore, Jan. 12, 1835; ar. Bangkok July 18, 1835; went out as a physician; opened a dispensary Aug. 5, 1835; commenced tract distribution Sept. 15, 1838; ord. at Bangkok Nov. 5, 1838; successfully vaccinated more than a thousand natives, and was otherwise useful as a physician; at length, he embraced some new religious views; returned to U. S. 1847; released Dec. 14, 1847. He is still, 1869, a missionary in Siam, under the Am. Miss. Associa. Died at Bangkok June 23, 1873. See article in August, 1929 Missionary Herald.

Mrs. Bradley (Emilie Royce) born Clinton, N. Y. July 12, 1811; mar.   ; died at Bangkok Aug. 2, 1845.

Samuel R. Robbins, born Marietta, O. Aug. 25, 1811; grad. Univ. of Ohio 1830; appt'd July 7, 1835; Andover Sem. 1835; emb. Boston July 1, 1836; expected to commence a mission in Sumatra; ar. Borneo April 24, 1837; ar. Bangkok April 24, 1838; returned to U. S. (Boston) March 20, 1840; released April 14, 1840. Deceased July 1846.

Mrs. Robbins (Martha R. Pierce) born Enfield, Ct. May 18, 1813; mar. May 1836. Returned to U. S. March 1840; released April 14, 1840. Died Aug. 1841. (Converted at age of 14.)

Nathan S. Benham, Byron, N. Y.; born Shandaken, N. Y. Aug. 23, 1810; grad. Western Reserve Coll., Hudson, O. 1835; appt'd Dec. 12, 1837; at the Theol. Sem. Hudson, 1838; emb. Boston, July 6, 1839; ar. Singapore Oct. 23, 1839; reached Bangkok March 1, 1840; drowned in the Meinam River April 6, 1840, one

month after his arrival. (See Miss'y Herald Nov. 1840, p. 464)

Mrs. Benham (Maria H. Nutting) born Groton, Mass. Jan. 17, 1814; mar. returned to U. S. May 1842; released Oct. 21, 1845. 1858, said to have been (?, possibly ,84) Anne married to Dr. Knapp. Mrs. Knapp died at Clear Lake, Minn. Jan. 18, 1884.

Jesse Caswell, born Middletown, Vt. April 17, 1809; grad. Middlebury Coll. 1832; appt. Feb. 28, 1837; Lane Sem. 1837; City Missionary, Cincinnati 1837-1839; emb. Boston July 6, 1839; arr. Singapore, Oct. 23, 1839; reached Bangkok Jan. 1, 1840; labored with great zeal and earnestness and not without some encouraging tokens of success; at length was recalled for some aberration in Christian doctrine, at the same time with Dr. Bradley, and released Dec. 14, 1847. Died Sept. 25, 1848. (Ord. Shoreham, Vt. Jan. 22, 1839.)

Mrs. Caswell (Anna T. Hemenway) born Shoreham, Vt. Aug. 4, 1812. 1862, resided in Rockford, Ill. Died at Rockford, Ill. Feb. 25, 1890.

Henry Sewell Gerrish French, born Boscawen, N. H. April 27, 1807; grad. Yale Coll. 1834; Andover Sem. 1837; ordained Sept. 19, 1837; emb. Boston July 6, 1839; ar. Singapore Oct. 23, 1839; a printer by trade, and spent some months at Singapore with Mr, North, learning to manufacture type; ar. Bangkok, May 28, 1840; died at Bankok of consumption Feb. 14, 1842. (See Miss. Herald Nov. 1842, p. 461)

Mrs. French (Sarah C. Allison) Concord, N. H.; born Castine, Me. Nov. 22, 1810; mar.   ; emb. July 6, 1839; returned April 1844. Died in Greeley, Col. Apr. 9, 1862.

Asa Hemenway, born Shoreham, Vt. July 6, 1810; grad. Middlebury Coll. 1835; Andover Sem. 1838; ord. Jan. 22, 1839; emb. with the three preceding missionaries Boston, July 6, 1839; ar. Singapore, Oct. 23, 1839; reached Bangkok Jan. 1, 1840; after ten years of faithful service was left the last missionary of the Board in Siam; returned to U. S. July 2, 1850. Afterwords preached Ripton, Vt. 1851-1860. Jan. 1878 at Manchester, Vt. Ditto 1887. Died Feb. 26, 1892 in same town.

Mrs. Hemenway (Lucia Hunt) born Shoreham, Vt. Nov. 21, 1810.

Lyman Bart Peet and wife embarked at Boston, July 6, 1839, in the same vessel (ship Arno) with Messrs. Benham, Caswell, French and Hemenway, at Boston, July 6, 1839; ar. Singapore Oct. 23, 1839; ar. Bangkok May 28, 1840; and labored in Siam till Aug. 12, 1846; when with Mr. Johnson, they left for Fuh-chau. (See Fuh-Chau mission.)

MISSIONARY PHYSICIAN

Stephen Tracy, M.D., brother of Rev. Joseph Tracy, of Ebinezer C. Tracy, editor of Boston Recorder, of Rev. Miron Tracy, Strongsville, Ohio, and of Rev. Ira Tracy, missionary of the Board (See mission to Singapore and to Canton); born Hartford, Vt. Feb. 25, 1810; prof. rel. Sept. 1826; studied at Dart. Coll. but did not graduate; emb. Boston July 1, 1836; ar. Singapore Dec. 17, 1836; reached Bangkok April 24, 1838; from ill health returned to U. S. March 28, 1840; released April 28, 1840. Lived at Andover, Mass. many years. Died there Jan. 13, 1873.

Mrs. Tracy (Alice Hewitt Dana) born Pomfret, Vt. Feb. 27, 1815; mar. Pomfret, Vt. May 10, 1836; emb. Boston July 1, 1836; returned 1840. Died Lansing, Mich., March 18, 1898.

ASSISTANT MISSIONARY

Mary E. Pierce, born Butternuts, N. Y. Oct. 22, 1815; emb. with Mr. Benham and other missionaries Boston, July 6, 1839; ar. Bangkok Jan. 1, 1840; a teacher; died at Bangkok Sept. 22, 1844.

The Mission to Siam was discontinued by vote of the Prudential Committee Oct. 10, 1848, agreeably to the recommendation of the Board at the previous Annual Meeting.

MISSION TO SINGAPORE

Singapore is an island near the extremity of the Malayan Peninsula, about two degrees north of the equator. It was occupied as a missionary station by the London Missionary Society, as early as 1826, and probably some years before. Being the centre of an extensive commerce, and subject to the British government, it afforded favorable opportunities for the operations of a Christian press, and the wide dissemination of religious truth. An extensive printing establishment at this place had been under the direction of the society just mentioned, though not owned by them. That society declining to purchase it, the establishment was sold to the American Board in January 1834; Messrs Johnson and Robinson, then in Singapore on their way to Siam, acting as agents in the purchase. (See missions to Fuh-chau and Siam.) Mr. Tracy soon after removed from Canton, and took charge of the establishment at Singapore.

This mission was discontinued in 1843.

MISSIONARIES

Ira Tracy, born in Hartford, Vermont, Jan. 15, 1806; prof. rel. 1820; grad. Dart. Coll. 1829; Andover Sem. 1832; was ordained at White River Village, Hartford, Sept. 26, 1832; his brother, Rev. Joseph Tracy, preaching the sermon; sailed from New York for China, June 15, 1833; arr. in Canton Oct. 26, 1833; arr. Singapore, July 24, 1834; went to Southern Hindoostan for the health of himself and wife, Nov. 1839; returned to U. S. and arr. Philadelphia Aug. 7, 1841; released Aug. 25, 1846. Died Bloomington, Wis. Nov. 10, 1875.

Mrs. Tracy (Adeline White, sister of Sarah G. White, wife of Asa B. Smith (see Sandwich Islands); born Brookfield, Mass. Sept. 25, 1809; emb. Boston, July 2, 1834, with Dr. Bradley (see Mission to Siam); married at Singapore Jan. 15, 1835; returned U. S. Aug. 1841; released Aug. 25, 1846. Died Streetsboro, Ohio April 1851.

James Taylor Dickinson, born at Lowville, Lewis Co., N. Y. Oct. 27, 1806; prof.

rel. Montreal, C.E. Aug. 1827; grad. Yale Coll. 1828; studied one year, or more, at Andover Sem. and a further time at New Haven; ordained pastor, Norwich, Ct. April 4, 1832; emb. Boston, July 20, 1835; arr. Singapore Feb. 6, 1836; sailed thence in the brig Himmaleh, owned by Olyphant & Co., christian merchants of Canton, and at their expense, on a tour of missionary exploration, Jan. 30, 1837; visited the islands of Celebes, Ternate, Mindanao, and Borneo; and returned to Singapore June 22, in the same year. For the benefit of his health, he visited Canton in 1838, and returned to Singapore in March 1839. Unmarried. Released Oct. 20, 1840. He was afterwards a teacher in the Singapore Institution for three years. 1857, in Durham, Conn. 1877 in Middlefield, Conn, where he died July 22, 1884.

Matthew Boyd Hope, M.D., Philadelphia, Pa.; born Armagh, Pa.   1812; grad. Jefferson Coll. 1830; grad. Princeton 1834; appt'd April 12, 1834; ord. 1835 by Pby. Huntington; emb. Boston July 1, 1836, with Mr. Travelli; arr. Singapore Dec. 17, 1836; health failing he returned April 2, 1838; released May 5, 1840. Unmarried. 1846-54 prof. Rhetoric Princeton Coll. 1854-59 prof. Rhet. and Polit. Economy. Died Dec. 17, 1859. His M. D. was from the University of Pennsylvania.

Joseph Secondo Travelli, born Philadelphia, Pa. April 21, 1809; prof. rel. 1827; graduated Jefferson Coll., Canonsburg, Pa. 1833; Western Theol. Sem., Alleghanytown, Pa. 1836; emb. Boston July 1, 1836 with Mr. Hope; arr. Singapore Dec. 17, 1836; sailed from that port on his return home, March 4, 1841; arr. Salem, Mass. July 6, 1841; released July 4, 1843. 1877, a teacher in Sewickley, Penn. Ditto 1887.

Mrs. Travelli (Susan Irwin) born Alleghanytown, Pa. Aug. 22, 1815; prof. rel. 1832; mar. March 31, 1836; embarked with husband as above; in greatly impaired health sailed from Singapore October 1840; arr. New York Feb. 1841. Died before 1862.

(The printing establishment purchased at Singapore for the Board in 1834, comprised two presses, a fount of Roman type, two founts of Malay, one of Arabic, two of Javanese, one of Siamese, and one of Bugis; also apparatus for casting types in all these languages and for book-binding.)

Dyer Ball, M.D. was a member of this mission from May 1838 when he embarked at New York in ship Albion, bound for Batavia, till June 1841, when he went to Macao in China for the benefit of Mrs. Ball's health. (See Canton mission). Died Canton, March 27, 1866.

Mrs. Ball - See Canton Mission.
1878, residing with her son at Hongkong.

George Warren Wood, and his first wife, were missionaries at Singapore, from May 25, 1838, when they embarked at New York for Batavia, till her death at Singapore March 9, 1839. He left that island in June 1840. See a further notice of him in the Western Turkey Mission.

Mrs. Wood - See Western Turkey Mission.
Died March 9, 1839.

ASSISTANT MISSIONARIES

Alfred North, was the missionary printer at Singapore, from the time of his arrival there, Feb. 6, 1836, till the relinquishment of the mission there in 1843. See a further account of him in Madura Mission. Died March 3, 1869.

Mrs. North - See Madura Mission. Died Jan. 13, 1844.

MISSION TO JAPAN

In the year 1829, Mr. William Ropes, a christian merchant of Boston, was residing in Brookline, Mass. Feeling a deep interest in the missionary enterprise, he proposed to a few christians in sympathy with him that they should assemble at his house and observe the Monthly Concert for Prayer. At their first meeting of this sort, the question arose- To what special object shall we devote our contributions? On the table before them lay a Japanese basket of rare workmanship, brought probably by one of his ships from the Eastern seas. Taking it in his hands, he suggested that the moneys collected at these monthly gatherings should be devoted to the evangelization of Japan. The proposal was accepted and month after month, for many years, prayer was offered and money contributed in that room for this purpose. In these meetings, and in the ladies' sewing-circle connected therewith, more than six hundred dollars were, in the end, raised and paid into the treasury of the Board.

At that time, and during two hundred years previous, Japan was inaccessible to the gospel. Christianity was held in supreme detestation; the cross and its allied emblems were annually trampled under foot; and death to a native was the certain consequence of embracing the christian religion. Moreover, all commercial intercourse with the western world was resolutely denied, except to the Dutch at the single port of Nagasaki. But God has had purpose of mercy towards these poor idolators. In a very remarkable manner, by solemn treaties, Japan has within a few years been opened to the commerce and to the religion of the Christian world. Clergymen, as well as merchants, may now reside in that remarkable empire; and no danger is now apprehended from prudent efforts to make known there the salvation of the gospel.

At the meeting of the Board, held at Pittsburgh, Oct. 5-8, 1869, it was unimously resolved to establish a mission to Japan.

MISSIONARY

Daniel Crosby Greene, D.D., son of Rev. David Greene, secretary of the A.B.C.F.M. from Oct. 3, 1828 to Sept. 12, 1848; his mother being Mary Evarts, dau. of Jeremiah Evarts, secretary or treasurer from Sept. 1811 till his death May 10, 1831, whose wife was Mehitable, dau. of Roger Sherman, the eminent statesman of Revolutionary fame; born in Roxbury, now Boston Highlands, Mass. Feb. 11, 1843; prof. rel. Westborough, Mass. Sept. 1863; prepared for college at the High School, Windsor, Vt. during his father's residence there; studied one year at Middlebury Coll. and three years at Dartmouth Coll. grad. there 1864; one year at the seminary in Chicago, two at Andover, ending 1869; ord. Westboro, Mass. July 28, 1869; sailed from San Francisco for Yokohama, Nov. 4, 1869; arr. Yokohama Nov. 30. April 1870 removed to Kobe. June 1874 removed to Yokohama to assist in translating Bible into Japanese. Jan. 1878, still at Yokohama. Vis. U. S. in 1880; D.D. 1880; arr. in returning at Yokohama Nov. 30, 1881. Dec. 1885 at Kioto. Vis. U S. arr. Boston Sept. 23, 1888; re-emb. San Francisco Mar. 22, 1890; arr. Tokyo Apr. 10, 1890; vis. U. S. arr. Vancouver May 18, 1897; re-emb. San Francisco Oct. 29, 1898; arr. Tokyo Nov. 18; vis. U. S. arr. San Francisco Apr. 3, 1908; re-emb. San Francisco Sept. 14, 1909; LL.D. 1909, Dartmouth. Died Hoyama Japan Sept. 15, 1913. (See Miss. Herald, Nov. 1913)

Mrs. Greene (Mary Jane Forbes) born Charlestown, Mass. Oct. 3, 1845; studied at Mt. Holyoke Sem. South Hadley, Mass. and in 1862, experienced the grace of God; prof. rel. Westboro, Mass. Sept. 1864; grad. Mt. Holyoke Sem.; married at Westboro July 29, 1869; sailed as above. Jan. 1878, still at Yokohama. Vis. U. S. in 1880-81. Dec. 1885 at Kioto. Vis. U. S. arr. Boston Sept. 23, 1888; re-emb. San Francisco Mar. 22, 1890; vis. U. S. arr. Vancouver May 18, 1897; re-emb. San Francisco Oct. 29, 1898; arr. Tokyo Dec. 18. Vis. U. S. arr. San Francisco April 3, 1908; re-emb. San Francisco Sept. 14, 1909. Died at Tokyo April 17, 1910. (See June Herald, page 561)

Orramel Hinckley Gulick, son of Rev. Peter J. Gulick, missionary to the Sandwich Islands; born at Honolulu, Oahu, Haw. Is. Oct. 7, 1830. (For a further account see Mission to Sandwich Islands) Appointed to the Japan Mission   ; and sailed from San Francisco for that country, with wife, Feb. 1, 1871. Arr. Kobe, Mar. 3, 1871; Jan. 1878, still at Kobe; vis. U. S. arr. July 26, 1881; re-emb. Jan. 26, 1882; arr. Kobe Feb. 24, transferred to No. Japan Miss. Oct. 1883. Dec. 1885 at Nugata. At Honolulu 1912.

Mrs. Gulick (Anna Eliza Clark) dau. of Rev. E. W. Clark; born at Honolulu Oct. 8, 1833; prof. rel. 1847; educated at Mt. Holyoke Sem. Taught one year. Mar. in Honolulu May 19, 1855. Sailed as above. Jan. 1878, still at Kobe; vis. U. S. arr. July 26, 1881; re-emb. Jan. 26, 1882; arr. Kobe Feb. 24; transferred to No. Japan Miss. Oct. 1883. Dec. 1885 at Nugata. *Died Oct. 9, 1938, at Honolulu, T.H. - Aged 105.*

Jerome Dean Davis, D.D., born Groton, Tompkins Co., N. Y. Jan. 17, 1838; prof. rel. Groton, N.Y. March 1852; grad. at Beloit Coll. 1866 and at Chicago Sem. 1869. Spent four years in the army. Pastor at Cheyenne, Wyoming Ter. 2 1/2 years. Ord. June 1, 1869 at Dundee, Ill. Appt. July 11, 1871; sailed from San Francisco Nov. 1, 1871; arr. Kobe Dec. 1. Jan. 1878 at Kioto to which city he was trans. in autumn of 1875. Vis. U. S. arr. Nov. 8, 1881; re-emb. Nov. 1883. Dec. 1885 at Kioto. Vis. U. S. arr. San Francisco Apr. 28, 1886; re-emb. San Francisco Feb. 12, 1887; arr, Kyoto Mar. 10, 1887; vis. U. S. arr. San Fran. May 21, 1894; re-emb. San Fran. Sept. 12, 1895; vis. U. S. arr. San Francisco June 8, 1904; re-emb. San Fran. Nov. 25, 1905; vis. U. S. arr. Montreal July 3, 1910. Died at Oberlin, O. Nov. 4, 1910; (See Dec. 1910 Herald page 545. See Jan. 1911 Herald page 11)

Mrs. Davis (Sophia D. Strong; born Naperville, Dupage Co., Ill. Aug. 29, 1843; dau. of Rev. Ephraim Strong; prof. rel. 1857; educated at Rockford Fem. Sem.; mar. July 15, 1869 in Dundee, Ill. Sailed as above. Jan. 1878 at Kioto; vis. U.S. arr. Nov. 8, 1881; re-emb. Nov. 1883; Dec. 1885 at Kioto. Died at sea between Kobe and Yokohama April. 6, 1886. (See Herald June 1886, p. 214)

Mrs. Davis (Frances Hooper) (infra) Mar. Kyoto July 1888; vis. U. S. arr.
San Francisco May 21, 1894; re-emb. San Francisco Sept. 12, 1895; vis. U.S.
re-emb. San Francisco Oct.23, 1901; vis. U. S. arr. San Francisco June 8, 1904;
re-emb. San Francisco Nov. 20, 1906; vis. U. S. arr. Montreal July 3, 1910.
Sailed Dec. 19, 1911; arr. home July 9, 1918; sailed Sept. 2, 1919; arr. home
Feb. 1920. Died July 12, 1922 at Denver. Colo.

Marquis Lafayette Gordon, M.D., born Waynesburg, Greene Co., Penna. July 18, 1843; prof. rel. Jan. 1866, Cumberland Pres. Ch., Waynesburg, Penna.; grad. Waynesburg Coll. 1868; grad. Andover Sem. 1871; grad. in med. from Long Island Coll. Hospital, Brooklyn, N. Y. June 1872. Took one course of lectures at Coll. of Phys. & Sur., New York City; spent three years in the army; taught two or three years; ord. Waynesburg Aug. 6, 1872. Sailed from San Francisco Sept. 1, 1872; arr. Yokohama Sept. 24.; stationed at Osaka 1872-77; returned to U. S. June 1877; re-emb. San Francisco Oct. 1, 1878; vis.U. S. arr. San Francisco Dec. 19, 1885; re-emb. Aug. 23, 1887; arr. Kobe Sept. 15, 1887; returned to U. S. arr. San Francisco June 1891; re-emb. San Francisco Sept. 27, 1892; arr. Yokohama Oct. 15, 1892; vis. U. S. arr. San Francisco May 20, 1899. Died at Auburndale, Mass. Nov. 4, 1900.

Mrs. Gordon (Agnes Helen Donald) born Andover, Mass. Sept. 3, 1852; prof. rel. Nov. 13, 1870; educated at Punchard School, Andover. Taught school more than three years; mar. July 30, 1872; stationed at Osaka 1872-77; sailed as above. Ret. to U. S. June 1877; re-emb. Oct. 1, 1878; vis. U. S. arr. San Fran. Dec. 19, 1885; re-emb. San Francisco Aug. 23, 1887; arr. Kobe Sept. 15, 1887; returned to U. S. arr. San Francisco June 1891; re-emb. San Francisco Sept. 12, 1893; arr. Kyoto Oct. 13, 1893; vis. U. S. arr. San Francisco May 20, 1899; re-emb. San Francisco March 7, 1901; arr. vis. U. S. Boston, March 3, 1904; returned to field 1906; arr. home Jan. 23, 1916; sailed Sept. 7, 1916; arr. home May 1921; sailed Sept. 7, 1922; arr. home Apr. 18, 1924; returned after a few months; retired June 1925. Died Dec. 29, 1940, at Pasadena, Calif.

John Laidlaw Atkinson, born Danby Wiske Village, Yorkshire, England, Aug. 12, 1842; prof. rel. Cedar Falls, Iowa, educated at Retford, England; grad. Chicago Sem. 1869; ord. Iowa Falls, Iowa, Sept. 1, 1869; sailed from San Francisco Sept. 1, 1873; arr. Kobe Sept. 28, 1873; Jan. 1878, still at Kobe; vis. U. S. arr. Sept. 10, 1882; re-emb. June 22, 1883; arr. Kobe Jan. 3. Dec. 1885 at Kobe; vis. U. S. arr. San Francisco May 30, 1891; re-emb. San Francisco Oct. 25, 1892; arr. Yokohama Nov. 17; vis. U. S. arr. Vancouver June 6, 1900;

re-emb. Oct. 1901. Died Kobe Feb. 17, 1908. (See April 1908 Herald, page 172)

Mrs. Atkinson (Carrie Electa Guernsey) born Charlestown, Mass. Sept. 4, 1848; dau. of Rev. Jesse Guernsey; prof. rel. Dubuque, Iowa 1868; educated at Iowa Coll., Grinnell, Iowa. Mar. July 29, 1869; sailed as above. Arr. Kobe Sept. 28, 1873; Jan. 1878, still at Kobe; vis. U. S. arr. Sept. 10, 1882; re-emb. June 22, 1883; arr. Kobe Jan. 3. Dec. 1885 at Kobe; vis. U. S. arr. San Fran. May 30, 1891; re-emb. San Francisco Oct. 25, 1892; arr. Yokohama Nov. 17. Via. U. S. arr. Vancouver June 6, 1900. Died at Kobe, Japan, April 18, 1906. (See July 1906 Herald, page 316)

Granville M. Dexter, born Dedham, Maine May 1, 1839; living on Pacific coast since 1859; common school education; grad. Pacific Theolog. Sem., Oakland, 1873; ord. June 29, 1873 at Oakland; sailed from San Francisco Oct. 1873; ar. Kobe, Oct. 31, 1873; returned to U. S. 1875; released 1875; Jan. 1878 preaching in Pacheco, Cal.; at Cottonwood, Cal. 1895-6.

Mrs. Dexter (Florence Allene Ashley) born Albion, Noble Co., Ind. June 2, 1848; prof. rel. Baptist Ch., Brooklyn, Cal. May 1865; studied in pub. schools of Ohio and Cal.; mar. Pacheco, Cal. July 2, 1873; released ......; 1896 at Cottonwood, Cal.

Horace Hall Leavitt, born Lowell, Mass. July 8, 1845; prof. rel. 1858; uniting with High St. Ch., Lowell; educated at Lowell High School, Williams College, grad. 1869 and Andover Sem. grad. 1873; ord. June 19, 1873, at Cambridge, Mass., Dr. Mark Hopkins preaching the sermon. Sailed from San Francisco Oct. 1873; arr. Kobe Nov. 15; stationed at Osaka 1873-75. Ret. to U. S. 1875; sailed again from San Francisco March 1, 1876. Jan. 1878, at Osaka; returned to U. S. arr. May 8, 1881; released Jan. 3, 1882; 1887 No. Andover, Me. 1904 Somerville, Mass. Ditto 1912. Died April 30, 1920.

Mrs. Leavitt (Mary Augusta Kelley) born Roxbury, Mass. Mar. 24, 1853; prof. rel.

May 1872; uniting with Pilgrim Cong. Cj., Cambridgeport. Educated at Tilden Sem., Lebanon, N. H. and Mt. Holyoke; mar. Jan. 19, 1876; sailed from San Francisco March 1, 1876. Jan. 1878, at Osaka. Returned to U. S. arr. May 8, 1881; released Jan. 3, 1882; 1887 No. Andover, Me. Died Oct. 15, 1914 in Somerville.

Wallace Taylor, M.D., born Cadiz., Harrison Co., Ohio June 18, 1835; prof. rel. Oberlin O., June 1865; educated at Normal Sch., Lebanon, O., Oberlin Coll., grad. 1867 (M.A. 1871) and Oberlin Sem. grad. 1873; grad. M.D. 1870 at Michigan Univ., Med. Dept., Ann Arbor Mich.; ord. Oberlin, O. Sept. 30, 1873; sailed from San Francisco Dec. 1, 1873; ar. Kobe Jan. 1, 1874; Jan. 1878 at Kioto; vis. U. S. arr. San Francisco Apr. 28, 1886; re-emb. San Francisco Nov. 9. arr. Kobe Dec. 1887; vis. the U. S. in 1896; re-emb. San Francisco Oct. 30, 1897; arr. Kobe Nov. 20, 1897; vis. U. S. arr. San Francisco Apr. 22, 1906; re-emb. San Francisco Oct. 24, 1907; arrived home June 23, 1912. Died in Oberlin, Feb. 3, 1923. (Miss'y Herald 1923, page 169)

Mrs. Taylor, (Mary Felicia Wisner) born Nunda, N. Y. April 12, 1842; prof. rel. Oberlin 1861; educated at Oberlin. Spent some time in teaching. Mar. at Oberlin, O. Aug. 4, 1869; sailed as above; arr. Kobe Jan. 1, 1874. Jan. 1878 at Kioto; vis. U. S. arr. San Francisco Apr. 28, 1886; re-emb. San Francisco Nov. 9, 1887; arr. Kobe Dec. 1887; vis. U. S. arr. San Francisco June 23, 1892; re-emb. San Francisco Oct. 24, 1907; arr. U. S. June 23, 1912. Died at Oberlin, Ohio July 17, 1925. (See Miss'y Herald 1925, page 496)

John Kinne Hyde DaForest, born Westbrook, Conn. June 25, 1844, son of Rev. Wm. A. Hyde; prof. rel. Jan. 1, 1863; educated at Phillips Acad. (Andover), Yale Coll. grad. 1868, Yale Sem. grad. 1871; ord. at Mt. Carmel Conn., May 27, 1871. Pastor at Mr. Carmel; was in the army; sailed from San Francisco Oct. 31, 1874. Jan. 1878, at Osaka. Vis. U. S. arr. April 7, 1882; re-emb. Nov. 22, 1883; arr. Osaka Dec. 1884; Dec. 1885 at Osaka; vis. U. S. arr. N. Y. May 11, 1890; re-emb. San Francisco Oct. 1, 1890; arr. Yokohama Oct. 19, 1890; vis. U. S. arr. San Francisco May 21, 1894; re-emb. San Francisco Dec. 21, 1895; vis. U. S. arr. Seattle

June 16, 1903; re-emb. San Francisco Nov. 18, 1903; vis. U. S. arr. Boston May 20, 1907; re-emb. San Francisco Sept. 25, 1908. Died at Tokyo, O. May 8, 1911. (See June 1911 Herald)

Mrs. DeForest (Sarah Elizabeth Starr) born Guilford, Conn., July 9, 1845; prof. rel. Sept. 1862; educated at Guilford Institute; engaged for a time in teaching; mar. Guilford, Conn., Sept. 23, 1874. Sailed as above. Arr.   ; Jan. 1879 at Osaka. Vis. U. S. arr. April 7, 1882; re-emb. Nov. 22, 1883; arr. Osaka Dec. 1884. Dec. 1885 at Osaka; vis. U. S. arr. San Francisco May 21, 1894; re-emb. San Francisco Dec. 21, 1895; vis. U. S. arr. Boston, May 20, 1907; re-emb. San Francisco Sept. 25, 1908. Died at Kyoto (Sendai), Dec. 23, 1915. (See Miss. Herald Feb. 1916, p. 54)

Edward Toppin Doane, born Tompkinsville, Staten Island, N. Y. May 30, 1820; embarked for Micronesia, June 4, 1854. (See Micronesia Mission) In 1875, transferred to Japan Mission and sailed from San Francisco Nov. 1, 1875; arr. Yokohama Nov. 23. Dec. 1875-April 1877 at Kioto. Returned to U. S. June 1877. Formally released Nov. 1, 1877. Returned to Micronesia. Died Honolulu May 15, 1890.

Mrs. Doane (Clara Hale Strong) born Oct. 4, 1841. Embarked for Micronesia May 20, 1865. Visited U. S. 1863; returning, reached Ponape Sept. 19, 1871; left San Francisco for Japan Sept. 1, 1873; arr. Kobe Sept. 28, 1873; Oct. 1875 went to Kioto, with Mr. and Mrs. Davis. Returned to U. S. June 1877. Released Nov. 1, 1877. (See Micronesia Mission)

Dwight Whitney Learned, born Canterbury, Windham Co., Conn., Oct. 12, 1848. Son of Rev. Robert Coit Learned. Prof. rel. July 1865, uniting with Plymouth (Ct.) Cong. Ch.; educated at Williston Sem. (Easthampton, Mass.) Yale Coll. grad. 1870. Had no theolog. course; ord. Kidder, Mo. July 7, 1875. Sailed from San Francisco Nov. 1, 1875. Arr. Yokohama Nov. 23. March 1876, stationed at Kioto. Jan. 1878 still at Kioto. Vis. U. S. arr. San Francisco June 23, 1892; returned to Japan arriving at Kyoto Nov. 21, 1893; vis. U. S. in 1910 and re-

emb. San Francisco Feb. 28, 1911; arr. home Oct. 7, 1928. Retired Jan. 13, 1925.

Mrs. Learned (Florence Helena Rohard) born White-Eyes Plains, Coshocton Co., Ohio, March 20. 1857; prof. rel. 1869; educated at Thayer Coll., Kidder, Mo.; engaged in teaching; mar. July 7, 1875, at Kidder, Mo. Sailed as above. Jan. 1878, still at Kioto; vis. U. S. arr. May 31, 1883; re-emb. Oct. 7, 1885; Dec. 1885 at Kioto; vis. U. S. arr. San Francisco June 23, 1892; re-emb. San Fran. Feb. 27, 1894; arr. Kyoto Mar. 22, 1894; vis. U..S. arr. San Francisco Apr. 15, 1910; re-emb. San Francisco Feb. 28, 1911. Arr. home Sept. 12, 1916. Sailed Apr. 12, 1917; arr. home May 1, 1924; sailed Oct. 14, 1924; arr. home Oct. 7, 1928. Retired Jan. 13, 1925

William Willis Curtis, born Waukesha, Waukesha Co., Wis. June 29, 1845, son of Rev. Otis Freeman Curtis; prof. rel. Emerald Grove, Wis. 1861; grad. Beloit Coll. 1870 and Chicago Sem. 1873; ord. Calumet, Mich. Aug. 10, 1873. Was pastor at Calumet, Mich. from July 1873 to Oct. 1876; acting pastor at Hancock, Mich. Dec. 1876 to Sept. 1877; Sailed from San Francisco Nov. 3, 1877; arr. Kobe Nov. 28, 1877; Jan. 1878, station Osaka; vis. U. S. arr. July 25, 1883; Dec. 1885 in U. S.; re-emb. San Francisco Oct. 19, 1886; arr. Yokohama Nov. 6, 1886; vis. U. S. arr. San Francisco Dec. 10, 1896; released June 28, 1900; vis. U. S. arr. San Francisco Apr. 15, 1910; at Oberlin, O. 1912. Died April 11, 1913. (See Miss. Herald June 1913, p. 262.)

Mrs. Curtis (Delia Eliza Harris) born Leon, Waushara Co., Wis. Oct. 14, 1856, dau. of Rev. James W. Harris; prof. rel. 1870; educated at Evansville Sem., Madison Univ. and Oberlin Coll.; spent some time in teaching; mar. Aug. 31, 1877, at Evansville, Rock Co., Wis. Sailed as above. Arr. Kobe Nov. 28, 1877. Died at Osaka Oct. 12, 1880.

Mrs. Curtis (Lydia V. Cone) born Madison, Lake Co., O., May 1854; prof. rel. 1869; grad. Oberlin Coll. 1880; taught in Doane Coll. eight years; mar. Painesville, O. Feb. 25, 1885; emb. San Francisco Oct. 19, 1886; arr. Yokohama Nov. 6, 1886; vis. U.S. arr. San Francisco Dec. 10, 1896; released June 28, 1900. Died Aug. 29, 1929 at Elmira, N. Y. See Dro. 1929 Mis. Her. p. 478

1886; vis. U. S. arr. San Francisco Dec. 10, 1896; released June 28, 1900.

s Cary Jr., born Foxborough, Mass., April 20, 1851; prof. rel. 1866, uniting with Cong. Ch. in Foxborough; fitted for coll. in Foxborough; grad. at Amherst 1872, and at Andover Sem. in 1877; ord. Foxborough Nov. 15, 1877; sailed San Francisco Feb. 7, 1878; Dec. 1885 at Okayama; vis. U. S. arr. N. Y. May 6, 1888; re-emb. San Francisco Oct. 3, 1889; arr. Yokohama Oct. 23, 1889; vis. U. S. arr. N. Y. May 1898; returned arr. Yokohama Nov. 1899; vis. U. S. arr. Boston July 22, 1908; re-emb. San Francisco Nov. 2, 1909; died July 23, 4? 1932 at Bradford, Mass.; (arrived home July 9, 1918; resignation accepted May 11, 1920.) Died July 23, 1932, at Bradford, Mass.

Mrs. Cary (Ellen Maria Emerson) born Francestown, N. H. April 25, 1856; prof. rel. July 1873; educated at Francestown and at Abbott Academy, Andover, Mass. Spent some time in teaching; mar. Nashua, N. H. Dec. 18, 1877; sailed San Francisco Feb. 7, 1878; Dec. 1885 at Okayama; vis. U. S. arr. N. Y. May 6, 1888; re-emb. San Francisco Oct. 3, 1889; arr. Yokohama Oct. 23, 1889; vis. U. S. arr. N. Y. May 1898; vis. U. S. arr. Boston July 22, 1908; re-emb. San Francisco Nov. 2, 1909; arrived home July 9, 1918; sailed Oct. 8, 1932; arr. field Oct. 19, 1932. (Retired May 1920) Died Dec. 26, 1946 at Bradford, Mass.

James H. Pettee, born Manchester, N. H. July 16, 1851; prof. rel. 1868; Manchester High School; grad. D. C. 1873 and Andover Theo. Sem. 1877; ord. at Manchester 1878, May 8.; married Aug. 1, 1878; emb. Oct. 1, 1878; vis. U. S. arr. July 19, 1885; re-emb. N. Y. Oct. 12, 1887; arr. Kobe Jan. 13, 1888; vis. U. S. arr. San Francisco Apr. 22, 1898; D.D. 1898, Dartmouth and Grinnell; re-emb. San Francisco Dec. 13, 1899; vis. U. S. arr. Seattle July 23, 1909; re-emb. San Francisco Nov. 22, 1910; arrived home July 23, 1918; died in 18 Oton, Mass. Feb. 17, 1920. (See Miss. Herald 1920, page 444)

Mrs. Pettie (Isabella Wilson) born Westford, Mass. Nov. 8, 1853; dau. of Rev. Thomas Wilson; prof. rel. July 1870; Stoughton High School and Abbott Academy. Sailed from San Francisco for Japan Oct. 1, 1878; vis. U. S. arr. July 13, 1885; re-emb. N. Y. Oct. 12, 1887; arr. Kobe Jan. 13, 1888; vis. the U. S. arr. San Francisco May 10, 1897; vis. U. S. arr. Seattle July 23, 1909; re-emb. San Francisco Nov. 22, 1910; arr. home July 23, 1918; resignation effected April 1, 1922. Died August 14, 1937, at Decatur, Ill.

Robert Henry Davis, born Frederica, Kent Co., Del., Aug. 28, 1844; prof. rel. Amherst 1866; grad. Amherst Coll. 1868; Bangor Theol. Sem. 1871; ord. as evangelist Hiram, Me., Nov. 12, 1874; emb. Oct. 1, 1878; transferred to Northern Japan Mission 1883. (See Northern Japan Mission) Dec. 1885 at Nugata. Died at Milford, Del. Feb. 20, 1899. (See Herald April 1899, p. 162)

Mrs. Davis (Frances Wadsworth Rounds) born Peoria, Roria Co., Ill., June 24, 1852; prof. rel. Hiram, Me., Jan. 1874; studied common schools of Stoneham, Mass.; mar. May 11, 1874; emb. Oct. 1, 1878; transferred to No. Japan Mission 1883. Dec. 1885 at Nugata.

John Thomas Gulick, transferred to this mission from No. China, Sept. 1875. Dec. 1885 at Osaka; vis. U. S. arr. Boston Nov. 13, 1888; re-emb. San Francisco, Oct. 17, 1889; arr. Yokohama Nov. 5, 1889; vis. U. S. arr. San Francisco July 1899; 1903 in Oberlin; 1905 Oakland and went to Honolulu in 1906. Still there in 1911. Died in Honolulu on Apr. 14, 1923. (See Miss. Herald 1923, page 258)

Mrs. Gulick, (Frances Amelia Stevens) (infra) Dec. 1885 at Osaka; vis. U. S. arr. Boston July 29, 1888; re-emb. San Francisco Oct. 17, 1889; arr. Yokohama Nov. 5, 1889; vis. U. S. arr. San Francisco July 1899; 1899-1903 in Oberlin, O. 1905 Oakland, Calif.; 1906 in Honolulu. Died April 23, 1928 in Honolulu.

George Allchin, born Plumstead, Kent, Eng. Jan. 10, 1852; prof. rel. Ontario 1874; studied Williams Coll.; grad. Bangor Theol. Sem. 1880; ord. Middlebury, Vt.

Aug. 14, 1881; emb. Aug. 5, 1882; arr. Osaka Nov. 12. Dec. 1885 at Osaka; vis. U. S. arr. San Francisco April 25, 1891; re-emb. San Francisco Oct. 25, 1892; arr. Yokohama Nov. 17; vis. U. S. arr. San Francisco June 13, 1901; re-emb. Boston Apr. 10, 1902; vis. U. S. arr. Boston July 6, 1910; re-emb. Sept. 18, 1911; arr. field Oct. 4, 1911; arr. home July 16, 1919. Was in Siberia under Red Cross several months in 1919. Died Nov. 21, 1935, New York City.

Mrs. Allchin (Nellie Maria Stratton) born Boston, Mass. June 28, 1860; prof. rel. Melrose July 1872; studied Mt. Holyoke Sem.; mar. June 29, 1882; emb. Aug. 5, 1882; arr. Osaka Nov. 12. Dec. 1885 at Osaka; vis. U. S. arr. San Francisco April 25, 1891; re-emb. San Francisco Oct. 25, 1892; arr. Yokohama Nov. 17; vis. U. S. arr. San Francisco June 13, 1901; re-emb. San Francisco Dec. 3, 1903; vis. U. S. arr. Boston July 6, 1910; re-emb. as above. Died in New York City Dec. 30, 1921. (Miss. Herald 1922, page 45)

Marshall Richard Gaines, born Granby, Hartford Co., Ct., Nov. 15, 1839; prof. rel. Granby 1857; grad. Yale Coll. 1865; studied Yale Theol. Sem. nearly three years; in 1883 was granted his degree; ord. Meriden, N. H. July 30, 1884; taught in Olivet Coll., Hartford, Pub. High Sch., Litchfield, Conn. and Meriden, N. H.; emb. Oct. 7, 1884; arr. Yokohama Oct. 29. Dec. 1885 at Kioto; ret. to U. S. 1889; connection with Board ceased Sept. 3, 1889. See minutes Com'ie? vol. 21, p. 286. Died in Staten Isl,(Brighton)June 16, 1924. (Miss'y Herald 1924, page 387)

Mrs. Gaines (Louise Walker) born Concord, N. H. Oct. 26, 1840; prof. rel. So. Hadley 1860; grad. Mt. Holyoke Sem. 1862; mar. Aug. 20, 1868; emb. Oct. 7, 1884; arr. Yokohama Oct. 29. Dec. 1885 at Kioto. Died in 1924.

Chauncey Marvin Cady, transferred to this mission from the Shanse Mission Nov. 4, 1884. Dec. 1885 at Kioto; returned to U. S. arr. San Francisco Sept. 12, 1892; released April 25, 1893. Died Stratford, Ct., Nov. 5, 1925.

Mrs. Cady (Virginia Alzade Clarkson) (infra)

mar.   ; returned to U. S. arr. San Francisco Sept. 12, 1892; released April 25, 1893. (See page 94) *Died Nov. 26, 1940, at Stratford, Conn.*

MISSIONARY PHYSICIANS

John Cutting Berry, M.D., born Phipsburg, Me., Jan. 16, 1847; prof. rel. at Bath, Me., in autumn of 1864; educated at Monmouth Academy; studied medicine at Portland and Brunswick, Me., and Philadelphia, graduating at Jefferson Med. Coll. Practiced medicine at Ferry Village, Me.; sailed from San Francisco May 1, 1872; ar. Kobe May 27. 1872; stationed at Kobe 1872-1877; returned to U. S. May 1877; re-emb. San Francisco Oct. 1, 1878; vis. U. S. arr. Apr. 17, 1884; re-emb. Oct. 17, 1885; returned to U. S. via Europe arr. N. Y. July 14, 1895; released Mar. 3, 1896.

Mrs. Berry (Maria Elizabeth Gove) born Bath, Me., Dec. 18, 1846; prof. rel. 1862; uniting with Cong. Ch. in Bath. Educated at Bath and at Abbott Academy, Andover, Mass.; mar. Bath, Me., April 10, 1872; sailed as above. At Kobe 1872-1877; ret. to U. S. May 1877; re-emb. Oct. 1, 1878; vis. U. S. arr. April 17, 1884; re-emb. Oct. 17, 1885; vis. U. S. arr. N. Y. July 14, 1895; released Mar. 31, 1896. Died Dec. 16, 1932.

Arthur Herman Adams, M.D., born Florence, Erie Co., Ohio, Nov. 24, 1847; prof. rel. spring of 1866, Sandusky, O.; educated at Sandusky High School, Ohio Wesleyan Univ., Yale Coll., grad. 1867 and Yale Sem., grad. 1872. Grad. M.D. Yale Med. Coll.   ; licensed to preach April 5, 1871; sailed from San Francisco Oct. 31, 1874; returned to U. S. Oct. 11, 1878 on account of his wife's health. He died while on the passage from San Francisco to Yokohama Nov. 23, 1879; (See Herald Feb. 1880) *Nural Oaska.*

Mrs. Adams (Sarah Catherine Thomas) born Meath, Bradford Co., Penna. Aug. 14, 1849, dau. of Rev. Thomas Thomas; prof. rel. March 1866; educated at Towanda, Penn.,

Franklin and Ithaca, N. Y. Spent some time in teaching. Mar. Aug. 31, 1874, at Stevensville, Penn.; sailed as above. Released Aug. 15, 1882. 1889 at Antwerp, Belgium. Died March 27, 1925 at Wyalusing, Penn.

Mary Anna Holbrook, M.D. Transferred from North China Aug. 6, 1889; emb. San Francisco Oct. 3, 1889; arr. Yokohama Oct. 23, 1889; vis. U. S. arr. Boston via Tacoma May 17, 1894; re-emb. Vancouver Aug. 27, 1894; arr. Kobe Sept.; vis. U.S. arr. San Francisco Dec. 10, 1896; released Feb. 4, 1898; re-appt'd Nov. 12, 1901; re-emb. San Francisco April 15, 1902; returned to U. S. arr. San Francisco Oct. 23, 1905; released Jan. 1, 1907. Died Dec. 2, 1910 at E. Haven, Conn. (See Miss. Herald Jan. 1911, p. 4) (See North China Mission)

Secular Agent.

DeWitt Clinton Jencks, born Killingly, Conn., March 26, 1841; prof. rel. 1865, at Killingly; educated at W. Killingly and E. Greenwich, R. I.; installed Ass't. Miss'y at Lynn, Mass. Jan. 25, 1877; sailed from San Francisco March 1, 1877; ar. Kobe April 16, 1877; Dec. 1885 at Kobe; vis. U. S. arr. N. Y. July 9, 1887; rel. Oct. 1, 1889. Died Nov. 25, 1923.

Mrs. Jencks (Sarah Maria Smith) born Pomfret, Conn., Jan. 23, 1856; dau. of Rev. Henry B. Smith, Greenfield Hill, Conn.; prof. rel. 1866; educated Newtown, Ct., and Southport, Ct. Teacher. Mar. Greenfield Hill, Oct. 25, 1876; sailed as above; ar. Kobe Aprill 16, 1877; Dec. 1885 at Kobe; vis. U. S. arr. July 9, 1887; rel. Oct. 1, 1889; Died May 19, 1911 at Colorado Springs, Colo. (See Missionary Herald Sept. 1911, page 415)

Corresponding Member.

Joseph Neesima, born in Yeddo, Japan, 1844.

Educated at Phillips Academy (Andover), Amherst College and Andover Seminary. Ord. Sept. 24, 1874, in Mount Vernon Church, Boston; sailed San Francisco Oct. 31, 1874; ar. Kobe 1874; summer of 1875, moved to Kioto; Jan. 3, 1876, married to

Yamamoto Yaye (sister of the blind counsellor Yamamoto), who was baptized the previous day, and received into church fellowship. March 1878 at Kioto; vis. U. S. in 1884; re-emb. San Francisco Nov. 19, 1885; arr. Kioto Dec. 17, 1885. Died near Tokyo Jan. 23, 1890. (See April Herald 1890, p. 147)

ASSISTANT MISSIONARIES

Eliza Talcott, born Vernon, Conn., May 22, 1836; prof. rel. 1852, at Rockville, Ct., educated at Farmington, Conn., and at State Normal School, New Britain. Teacher, several years. Sailed from San Francisco March 1, 1873; arr. Kobe Mar. 31, 1873; Jan. 1878, still at Kobe; vis. U. S. arr. June 1, 1884; re-emb. Aug. 18, 1885; arr. Okayama Sept. 8. Dec. 1885 at Kobe; vis. the U. S. arr. San Francisco May 12, 1896; re-emb. San Francisco June 6, 1900. Died at Kyoto, Japan, [Kobe?] Nov. 1, 1911. (See Miss'y Herald Jan. 1912, p. 12)

Julia Elizabeth Dudley, born Naperville, Dupage Co., Ill. Dec. 5, 1840; prof. rel. 1858; educated at Naperville Acad. & Rockford Sem. Teacher, several years. Sailed, San Francisco, March 1, 1873; ar. Kobe. Mar. 31. Jan. 1878; still at Kobe; vis. U. S. in 1882; re-emb. Sept. 27, 1883; arr. Kobe Oct. 26. Dec. 1885 at Kobe; vis. U. S. arr. San Francisco May 6, 1893; re-emb. arr. Yokohama Mar. 15, 1895; returned to America in 1901. Died La Jolla Cal,, July 12, 1906. (See Oct. 1906 Herald, page 462)

Mary E. Gouldy, born McLean, N. Y. Feb. 6, 1843; Normal School 1861; two years at Mt. Holyoke Sem.; sailed San Francisco Oct. 1, 1873; ar. Kobe Oct. 31; 1873 to present time (March 1878) at Osaka; vis. U. S. in 1882; re-emb. Feb. 24, 1883; arr. Kobe, April 2. Dec. 1885 at Osaka. Died April 25, 1925 in New York City.

Julia Ann Eliza Gulick, dau. of Peter J. Gulick (see Mission to Sandwich Islands) born Honolulu, June 10, 1845; Punahou School and Spring Garden Inst., Phila.; appt'd June 24, 1873; sailed San Francisco June 1874; ar. Kobe 1874; at Kobe 1874 to present time (March 1878); transferred to No. Japan Miss. Oct. 1883; released May 23, 1911. Died in May 1936 at Honolulu.

Frances Amelia Stevens, born Akron, Ohio, June 28, 1848, dau. of Rev. Wm. R. Stevens; prof. rel. River Falls, Wis., Mar. 7, 1864; educated at Oberlin. Teacher. Sailed from San Francisco Nov. 1, 1875; station Osaka; Jan. 1878 still at Osaka; ar. Kobe Nov. 25, 1875; mar. Rev. John T. Gulick, Kobe, May 31, 1880. Died April 29, 1928. (See Herald June 1928, page 256)

Justina E. Wheeler, Durham, Ct., born   ; prof. rel.   ; uniting with a Baptist Church; education limited. Dressmaker; sailed San Francisco Nov. 1, 1875; ar. Kobe Nov. 25, 1875; 1875 to present time (March 1878) at Osaka; May 30, 1878, mar. Rev. C. Goodrich (See North China Mission) Died Sept. 4, 1878. (See Herald Dec. 1878)

Martha Jane Barrows, born Middlebury, Vt., July 26, 1841; prof. rel. April 1858; educated at Middlebury and Mt. Holyoke; sailed from San Francisco March 1, 1876; station, Kobe. Jan. 1878, still at Kobe; vis. U. S. arr. July 18, 1885; re-emb. San Francisco Nov. 29, 1887; arr. Kobe Dec. 24, 1887; vis. U. S. arr. San Francisco March 2, 1892; re-emb. San Francisco Aug. 16, 1892; arr. Kobe Sept. 7, 1892; vis. U. S. arr. San Francisco Nov. 21, 1898; re-emb. San Francisco June 30, 1900; arr. Yokohama July 19; vis. U. S. arr. San Francisco July 30, 1907; re-emb. San Francisco Sept. 13, 1910; arrived San Francisco Nov. 28, 1924. Died at Claremont, Cal. March 13, 1925. (See Miss. Herald April 1925)

Alice Jennette Starkweather, born Hartford, Conn., Aug. 3, 1849; prof. rel. April 1865, uniting with 1st Cong. Ch., Hartford; educated at Hartford Ladies' Sem. Teacher. Sailed from San Fran., Mar. 1, 1876; station, Kioto. Jan. 1878 at Kioto; returned to U. S. arr. May 31, 1883; released Mar. 31, 1885. 1888 Elgin, Ill.

Julia Wilson, born New York City, Dec. 6, 1845; prof. rel. about 1861, uniting with (Dutch) Reformed Ch., Washington Sq., New York City. Educated in New York, 12th St. Normal Sch. and Prof. Aubert's French Institute. Teacher and city missionary. Sailed San Fran. Sept. 12, 1877; ar. Kobe Oct. 6. (Returned to U.S. 1879 or 1880)

Harriet Frances Parmelee, born Twinsburg, Ohio, May 13, 1852; prof. rel. April 1, 1866; educated at Twinsburg, Hudson, and Painesville, Ohio. Mission work in New York City for four months. Sailed from San Fran. Sept. 12, 1877; arr. Kobe Oct. 6, vis. U. S. arr. July, 29, 1882; Dec. 1885 in U. S.; released Aug. 9, 1887. 1888 Twinsburg, O.; reappointed Feb. 10, 1891; re-emb. San Francisco April 2, 1891; arr. Yokohama April 20, 1891; vis. U. S. arr. San Francisco Dec. 11, 1899; re-emb. San Francisco Oct. 23, 1901; arrived home Dec. 9, 1909; sailed April 10, 1912; arrived home May 11, 1922; retired March 25, 1924; sailed July 31, 1924. Died in Kyoto, Japan Jan. 8, 1933.

Virginia Alzade Clarkson, born Newburyport, Mass. Feb. 11, 1851; converted about 1864; united with 2nd Pres. Ch., Newburyport. Taught nearly nine years. Grad. at Newburyport High Sch. and Salem State Normal Sch. and Mt. Holyoke; sailed from San Fran. Nov. 3, 1877; arr. Kobe Nov. 28; vis. U. S. arr. July 12, 1882; released Apr. 2, 1883; re-appt'd Mar. 31, 1885; re-emb. Aug. 18, 1885; arr. Kyoto Osaka Sept. 8; Rev. Chauncy M. Cady. (See page 90) Died Nov. 26, 1940, at Stratford, Conn.

Fannie Adelia Gardner, born York, Medina Co., O., Jan. 30, 1849; prof. rel. 1865; studied Oberlin; employed school teaching and book-keeping; emb. Oct. 1, 1878; arr. Kobe Oct. 26. Dec. 1885 at Osaka; vis. U. S. arr. San Francisco March 21, 1887; re-emb. San Francisco Feb. 4, 1890; arr. Yokohama Feb. 22, 1890; vis. U. S. arr. San. Francisco May 21, 1894; released Aug. 29, 1899. Died Jan. 10, 1930, at Moorhead, Miss.

Abby Maria Colby, born Manchester, N. H. July 9, 1847; prof. rel. Holyoke, Mass. May 1863; studied Glenwood Ladies Sem., W. Brattleboro, Vt. and N. E. Hospital for women and children, Boston Highlands; emb. May 31, 1879; arr. Kobe May 24. Dec. 1885 at Osaka; vis. U. S. arr. San Francisco June 15, 1890; re-emb. San Fran. June 25, 1892; arr. Kobe July 10, 1892; vis. U. S. in 1895; re-emb. Vancouver Aug. 23, 1897; arr. Osaka Sept. 4, 1897; vis. U. S. and re-emb. N. Y. Aug. 31, Did Jan. 5, 1917 at Osaka. (See Miss. Herald Mar. 1917, page 108.)

Anna Young Davis, born Milford, Sussex Co., Del., Feb. 13, 1851; prof. rel. Feb. 1868; studied Mt. Holyoke Sem.; engaged in teaching; emb. Sept. 13, 1879; arr.

Kobe Oct. 10; Dec. 1885 at Kioto; vis. U. S. arr. N. Y. June 14, 1888; released May 12, 1891. Mrs. Frank Swann - died July — 1944, Los Angeles, California.

Emilie Louise Kellogg, born Oakham, Worcester Co., Mass. June 22, 1856; prof. rel. St. Louis, 1871; studied Mary Inst. and Washington Univ., St. Louis; emb. Sept. 1, 1880; arr. Kobe Oct. 1; mar. Sept. 23, 1882, Rev. Marcus Taft of the Am. Meth. Episcopal Miss. in China; released Oct. 17, 1882.

Emily Maria Brown, born Granger, Fillmore Co., Minn., May 16, 1858; prof. rel. Salt Lake City, Utah, May 1877; studied Carleton Coll., Northfield, Minn.; emb. Nov. 24, 1883; Dec. 1885 at Kobe; vis. U. S. arr. N.Y. May 29, 1893; re-emb. Feb. 13, 1897; arr. Kobe Mar. 7, 1897; vis. U. S. arr. San Francisco Jan. 15, 1900; released Sept. 30, 1902. Died at Claremont, Calif. May 31, 1925. (NO Herald notice.)

Mary Adelaide Daughaday, born Guilford, Chenango Co., N. Y., March 2, 1845; prof. rel. 1858; studied Newburgh Acad. & Maplewood Sem., Pittsfield, Mass.; engaged in teaching and mission work at Yonkers, N. Y. previous to going out; emb. Feb. 24, 1883; arr. Kobe April 2. Dec. 1885 at Osaka; vis. U. S. in summer of 1888; re-emb. San Francisco Nov. 28, 1888; arr. Osaka Dec. 24; vis. U. S. and re-emb. San Francisco April 1, 1897; vis. U. S. arr. Montreal Sept. 16, 1907; re-emb. San Francisco Feb. 26, 1909. Died in Sapporo, Japan on July 1, 1919. (See Miss. Herald 1919, page 320)

Frances Hooper, born Worcester, Mass. Dec. 8, 1854; prof. rel. July 7, 1872; studied public schools of Worcester; taught in public sch. Washington, D. C.; emb. Feb. 24, 1883; arr. Kobe April 2. Dec. 1885 at Kioto; mar. Rev. J. D. Davis, D.D. at Kyoto, July 1888. (supra) Died July 12, 1922 in Denver, Colo.

Susan Annette Searle, born Niles, Berrien Co., Mich., Oct. 11, 1858; prof. rel. June 1870; studied Wellesley Col.; engaged for some time in teaching; emb. Sept. 27, 1883; arr. Kobe Oct. 26. Dec. 1885 at Kobe; vis. U. S. arr. San

Francisco April 15, 1891; re-emb. San Francisco Sept. 27, 1892; arr. Yokohama Oct. 15, 1892; vis. U. S. arr. Boston May 10, 1901; re-emb. Vancouver Aug. 18, 1902; arrived home Feb. 24, 1910; sailed Aug. 22, 1911; arrived home July 1915; sailed Jan. 8, 1915; arrived home Sept. 26, 1921; sailed Aug. 24, 1922. L.H.D. Carleton Col. 1922. Retired Jan. 1, 1929. Died in Claremont, Cal. on Oct. 25, 1951. See card.

Effie Burton Gunnison (Mrs. C. B. Mouser), born Fairfield, Solano Co., Cal., June 13, 1860; prof. rel. May 1881; studied Girls High School and Irving Inst., San Francisco; engaged for some time in teaching; emb. Sept. 19, 1885; arr. Kobe Oct. 19, 1885; released July 20, 1897. Died Aug. 21, 1946 at Stockton, Calif.

NORTHERN JAPAN MISSION

This mission was commenced Oct. 1883.

MISSIONARIES

Orramel Hinckley Gulick, Transferred to this mission from the Japan mission Oct. 1883. (supra) Dec. 1885 at Nugata; vis. the U. S. arr. Feb. 17, 1893; went to Honolulu to reside for one year arr. there Jan. 27, 1894. At Honolulu 1912. Died in Honolulu Sept. 19, 1923. (Missionary Herald 1923, page 549)

Mrs. Gulick (Ann Eliza Clark) Transferred to this mission from the Japan Mission Oct. 1883 (supra) Dec. 1885 at Nugata; vis. the U. S. arr. Feb. 17, 1893; went to Honolulu to reside for one year arr. there Jan. 27, 1894. Died Oct. 9, 1938, at Honolulu, T.H. - aged 105.

Robert Henry Davis, Transferred to this mission from the Japan mission Oct. 1883 (supra) Dec. 1885 at Nugata; vis. U. S. arr. N. Y. Mar. 5, 1887; released Nov. 29, 1887. Died Milford, Delaware, Feb. 20, 1899. (See April Herald 1899, page 162)

Mrs. Davis (Frances Wadsworth Rounds) Transferred as above. Dec. 1885 at Nugata; vis. U. S. arr. N.Y. Mar. 5, 1887; released Nov. 29, 1887.

MISSIONARY PHYSICIAN

Doremus Scudder, M.D. son of Rev. H. M. Scudder, formerly of Madras and Arcot Miss., born New York City, Dec. 15, 1858; prof. rel. Jan. 1872; grad. Yale Coll. 1880; studied two years in Union Theol. Sem.; grad. Chicago Medical School 1884; emb. Feb. 4, 1884. Dec. 1885 at Nigata; vis. U. S. arr. San Francisco Oct. 1889; released Sept. 7, 1891. 1891, Chicago. 1895, settled over Cong'l Ch., Woburn, Mass.
At Honolulu 1912. Died July 28, 1942 in Claremont, California.

Mrs. Scudder (Eliza Canfield Kendall) see Vol. II p. 162; mar. Nugata June 21,

1888; returned to U. S. arr. San Francisco Oct. 1889; released Sept. 7, 1891; 1891, Chicago. 1895, Woburn, Mass. Died at Honolulu, June 26, 1914. (See Herald Aug. 1914, page 368)

ASSISTANT MISSIONARIES

Catherine Sophia Scudder, dau. of Rev. Henry M. Scudder, formerly of the Madras and Arcot Missions; born Madras, India 1851; prof. rel. 1863; studied Mills Sem., Cal.; emb. Feb. 4, 1884; Dec. 1885 at Nugata; vis. U. S. arr. San Francisco Oct. 1889; died Passadena, Cal., Feb. 14, 1890. (See Herald, April 1890)

Julia Ann Eliza Gulick, Transferred to this mission from the Japan mission Oct. 1883 (supra) Dec. 1885 at Nugata. Vis. U. S. arr. San Francisco April 28, 1886; re-emb. San Francisco Nov. 9, 1887; arr. Japan Dec. 1887; vis. U. S. in 1899; re-emb. San Francisco Dec. 9, 1899; arr. Yokohama Dec. 15; vis. U.S. arr. San Francisco July 14, 1908. Resigned May 1911.

WORK IN PAPAL LANDS

MISSION TO AUSTRIA

In the year 1871, at the Annual Meeting in Salem, Mass., it was decided to be expedient for the Board to commence operations in some of the Nominally Christian Lands. Attention was specially directed to Spain, Mexico and Austria, and in the course of the following year, missions were established in these countries.

The Austrian Empire has in its 19 provinces, about 35,000,000 inhabitants, of different races, German, Slavic, Magyar. Most of the people are Catholics; in Hungary, a majority are Protestants.

Henry Albert Schauffler, born Sept. 4, 1837.(See Western Turkey and European Turkey Missions) Returned to U. S. 1870; appointed by Prudential Committee to commence the new mission in Austria, and sailed from New York May 18, 1872. In October 1872, located in Prague, Bohemia. In 1874, removed to Brunn, Moravia. At Brunn, until present time, March 1878. Returned to U. S. arr. N. Y. April 18, 1881; released Nov. 21, 1882; 1888 Cleveland, O. Died Cleveland, O. February 15, 1905. See Volume III on NEAR EA St

Mrs. Schauffler (Clara E. Gray) born Oct. 3, 1842. (See Western Turkey and European Turkey Missions) Sailed N. Y. May 18, 1872; at Brunn 1874-1878. Died at Cleveland, Ohio Sept. 4, 1883. (See obit. in Herald Oct. 1883, p.379)

Albert Warren Clark, born Georgia, Franklin Co., Vt., June 27, 1842; prof. rel. Jan. 1857, at Georgia, Vt.; grad. at University of Vermont 1865; two years in Union Sem. and one in Hartford Sem., grad. there in 1868; ord. Nov. 19, 1868, at Gilead (Hebron) Conn. Pastor of Cong. Ch. in Gilead, 1868 to Aug. 1, 1872; sailed, N. Y., Oct. 5, 1872; station Prague Nov. 1, 1872 to Mar. 3, 1874, when he took up his residence in Innsbruck, the chief city of the Tyrol; August 1875 re-emb. to Gratz, Styria. March 1878, still there. Vis. U. S. arr. Apr. 1884; re-emb. Oct. 4, 1884; arr. Prague Oct. 20. Dec. 1885 at Prague; vis. U. S. Aug. 1892; re-emb. Oct. 25. 1892; arr. Prague Nov. 4; vis. U. S. arr. N. Y. Aug. 12

1904; re-emb. N. Y. July 8, 1905; between Oct. 1913 and May 15, 1914 he and his family were in Scotland in the interests of the Bible distribution work in Bohemia; arrived home Sept. 8, 1917. Died in Boston, Mass. on June 7, 1921. (Miss'y Herald 1921, page 240)

Mrs. Clark (Nellie Mosher Spencer) born Cornish, Sullivan Co., N.H., June 7, 1842; prof. rel. July 1862, Claremont, N. H.; educated at Franklin Academy, Vt. Teacher. Mar. July 1, 1868 at Claremont, N.H; sailed as above; at Innsbruck 1874; 1875-1878 at Gratz. Died at Prague Dec. 10, 1881.

Mrs. Clark (Ruth Elizabeth Pirie) born Bourlen, St. Boswells, Scot. Aug. 16, 1862; prof. rel. LaTour, Italy 1879; studied Waldensian Coll., LaTour, Italy and Tlaiserswerth, Ger.; mar. March 20, 1884; vis. U. S. in 1884 as above. Dec. 1885 at Prague; vis. U. S. arr. N. Y. Aug. 12, 1904; re-emb. N. Y. July 8, 1905; arrived home Sept. 8, 1917. Died at Herrnhut, Germany, Nov. 2,1934.

Edwin Augustus Adams, born Franklin, Norfolk Co., Mass. Oct. 21, 1837; prof. rel. May 1862, West Medway, Mass.; grad. Amherst Coll., 1861; at Union and Andover Sem., grad. Andover 1868; ord. North Manchester, Conn., Sept. 3, 1868; pastor at N. Manchester 1868-1872; sailed N. Y. Oct. 5, 1872; ar. Prague Nov. 1, 1872; at Prague 1872 to present time (March 1878); vis. U. S. in 1879; re-emb. June 17, 1879; returned to U. S. arr. June 11, 1882; released Mar. 1, 1882; 1888 Chicago, Ill. Died Apr. 9, 1927. (See Herald May 1927, page 201)

Mrs. Adams (Caroline Amelia Plimpton) born Walpole, Mass. Feb. 22, 1842; prof. rel. May 1863; educated Worcester and Abbott Fem. Sem., Andover. Teacher. Mar. May 16, 1866, Walpole, Mass.; sailed as above; at Prague 1872-1878; returned to U. S. arr. June 11, 1882; released Mar. 1, 1882; 1888 Chicago,Ill. Died Nov. 12, 1929 at Walpole, Mass. (See Herald Jan. 1929, page 48)

Walter Scott Alexander, born Killingly, Conn., Aug. 29, 1835; prof. rel. Worcester, Mass. May 1, 1852; grad. Yale Coll., 1858; grad. Andover Sem. 1861; ord. Pomfret, Conn., Nov. 22, 1861; pastor at Pomfret, Nov. 1861 to Feb. 1866; pastor at Racine, Wis. Feb. 1866 to Aug. 1, 1872; sailed Oct. 23, 1872; proceeded to Italy and early in 1873 was authorized to commence a mission in Florence. Was not connected with Miss. to Austria. (See Mission to Italy)

Mrs. Alexander (Constance Eldredge) born Boston, Mass. Feb. 14, 1833; prof. rel. at age of 18 in Pomfret, Conn.; educated at E. Greenwich, R. I., Pomfret and Boston; mar. Pomfret, May 15, 1866; sailed as above; 1873-1874 in Florence. Returned to U. S. 1874; rel. 1874. (See Mission to Italy)

Edwin Cone Bissell, born Schoharie, N. Y., March 2, 1832; prof. rel. Rockville, Conn., about 1850; "Prepared" at Monson Acad.; grad. Amherst Coll. 1855; grad. Union Sem. 1859; ord. Sept. 21, 1859 at Westhampton, Mass.; pastor Cong. Ch. at Winchester 1873; sailed N. Y. Sept. 6, 1873; ar. Vienna Oct. 15. In 1874 at Innsbruck; in August 1875, removed to Gratz, Styria; March 1878 at Gratz; released July 30, 1878; Prof. in Theol. Sem., Hartford, Ct. 1888; afterward Prof. in the McCormack Sem. Died at Chicago, Ill. April 10, 1894.

Mrs. Bissell (Emily Pomeroy) born Somers, Tolland Co., Conn., Nov. 16, 1837; prof. rel. Somers, Conn., 1857; educated Mt. Holyoke and Brooklyn (N.Y.) Heights Sem.; mar. Sept. 6, 1859 at Somers, Conn.; sailed as above; 1875 to March 1878 at Gratz. Released July 30, 1878; 1888 Hartford, Ct.

MISSION TO ITALY

Walter Scott Alexander, born Killingly, Conn., Aug. 29, 1835. (See Mission to Austria) Sailed N. Y. Oct. 23, 1872, intending to join Mission to Austria; early in 1873, it was decided by The Prud. Com. that it was expedient to commence a mission to Italy and obedient to the wishes of the Com., Mr. A. went to Florence and remained there until autumn of 1874, when ill health obliged him to return to the United States. Released 1874; 1876 to present time (Mar. 1878). a.p. at New Orleans, La.; 1887 Cambridge, Mass. Died at Cambridge, Mass. May 15, 1900.

Mrs. Alexander (See Mission to Austria) Ret. U. S. 1874; released 1874; 1887 Cambridge, Mass.

Luther Halsey Gulick, M.D., born Honolulu, June 10, 1828. (See Mission to Spain) In 1873 Dr. G. was trans. to Mission to Italy and left Barcelona for Florence July 26, 1873. In Autumn of 1874, the Board decided to discontinue this mission, and Dr. G. having visited the Missions of the Board in Turkey and in Austria returned to U. S., reaching N. Y. May 1875. The following Dec. he went to Japan, under A.B.S. Released 1875. See volume on ISLANDS.

Mrs. Gulick (See Mission to Spain) Released 1875.

Mission discontinued 1874.

MISSION TO NORTHERN MEXICO

Monterey, State of New Leon, was the residence for a number of years of Miss Melinda Rankin, who carried on missionary work with a large degree of success. In 1873, the work and property of Miss Rankin at Monterey were trans. to the American Board. The work was at that time carried on by one missionary only, Mr. Beveridge.

John Beveridge, born Shelby, Ohio; ordained 1869, by Presb'y; *Procured by Melinda Rankin, Monterey, May 1869. Cont. her work. See Twenty Yrs among the Mexicans by Melinda R. chs. pp. 215 M.H. 1873* returned to U. S. 1875; released 1875. Died in Cuthbert, Georgia Feb. 18, 1882.

Edward Pierrepont Herrick of Middle Haddam, Conn.; born Clintonville, N. Y. Feb. 12, 1846; spent two years in Hopkins Gram. Sch., New Haven; grad. Yale Sem. 1871; pastor at Middle Haddam; left New Orleans, Dec. 21, 1873; ar. Monterey, Jan. 15, 1874, having had a long and exhausting stage-ride of about 300 miles from Matamoras; returned to U. S. 1875; released 1875;(ordained 1871;) pastor Sherman, Conn. 1876 to present time (Mar. 1878) Ditto 1887.

Mrs. Herrick, (Pamela Goodrich Wheeler) born New Haven, New Haven Co., Ct. July 10, 1843; prof. rel. in 1855 at New Haven; educated in private schools, New Haven; mar. May 25, 1871 at New Haven; sailed as above; returned U. S. as above; released 1875.

James Kellogg Kilbourn, born Bridgewater, Ct. 1841; prof. rel. 1858; grad. Beloit College 1868; spent one year at Chicago Sem. and grad; Andover Sem. 1872; appointed Dec. 23, 1873; acting pastor at Hartland, Wis., about one year; left for Mexico early in March 1874 and arr. Monterey Mar. 29, 1874; at Monterey 1874-1877; released Sept. 1877; when the mission was trans. to Presbyterian

Board. Vis. U. S. Feb. 1878; returned to Western Mexico Miss..

Mrs. Kilbourn (Emma Henderson) born   ; studied Whitewater, Wis. Nor. Sch.; mar. Jan. 1, 1879; joined Miss. Jan. 22, 1879. (See Western Mexico.

Carrie M. Strong, of Middle Haddam, Ct.; born Haddam, Ct. 1833; educated in Boston and at State Normal School, New Britain, Conn. Teacher, sixteen or eighteen years, part of this time at Glastonbury, Conn. Sailed from New Orleans Dec. 21, 1873; ar. Monterey Jan. 15, 1874; 1874–1877 at Monterey; released Sept. 1877, by transfer of Mission to Presbyterian Board; vis. U. S. Feb. 1878.

In September 1877 this mission was transferred to the Presbyterian Board.

NORTHERN MEXICO MISSION

This mission was re-opened in 1882.

Japes Demarest Eaton, born Lancaster, Wis., Mar. 18, 1848; prof. rel. March 1866; grad. Beloit 1869; at Chicago Theol. Sem. 1869-70; Andover 1870-72; ord. Lancaster, Wis., Dec. 1872; joined the mission Nov. 1882; Dec. 1885 at Chihuahua; vis. U. S. in the summer and autumn of 1891; vis. U. S. arr. Sept. 23, 1910; returned July 14, 1911; left field Dec. 1912; resigned Feb. 27, 1912, but re-appt. and were in field Aug. to Dec. 1912. Retired in 1913. Died Dec. 9, 1928 at Los Angeles. (See Herald Feb. 1929, page 87; also Herald March 1929, pages 126, 127, 128.) DD 1897.

Mrs. Eaton (Gertrude Clifford Pratt) born Meriden, New Haven Co., Ct. April 28, 1853; prof. rel. Montclair, N. J. June 1869; studied Vassar Coll. and Dresden, Ger.; mar. May 13, 1875; joined the mission Nov. 1882; Dec. 1885 at Chihuahua; vis. U. S. in 1891; returned, arr. home Sept. 23, 1910; returned to field July 14, 1911; left field Dec. 1912; resigned Feb. 27, 1912.

George Albinus Dutton, born Norwich, Vt., Sept. 15, 1854; prof. rel. Norwich July 1868; grad. Dartmouth Coll. 1880; Hartford Theol. Sem. May 1883; ord. Norwich Sept. 5, 1883; joined the mission March 28, 1884; died of small-pox at Chihuahua June 8, 1885. (See Herald Aug. 1885, p. 305)

Alden Buel Case, born Gustavers, Trumbull Co., O., July 25, 1851; prof. rel. April 1867; grad. Tabor Coll. 1878; Yale Divinity School 1881; ord. New Haven, Ct. May 22, 1881; joined the mission Oct. 20, 1884. Dec. 1885 at Chihuahua; returned to the U. S. for a period and rejoined the mission Nov. 5, 1894; released June 9, 1896. Died October 27, 1932 at Pomona, California

Mrs. Cane (Myra Gertrude Rice) born Magnolia, Iowa, April 8, 1857; prof. rel. 1873; studied Tabor Coll., Iowa; mar. May 31, 1881; joined the mission Oct. 20, 1884; Dec. 1885 at Chihuahua; after visiting U. S. rejoined mission Nov.. 5, 1894. At Pomona California in 1932.

MISSION TO WESTERN MEXICO

David F. Watkins, born Dec. 26, 1845; Bridgend, Wales. grad. Pacific Theol. Sem., Oakland, Cal., 1872; ord. Sept. 19, 1872 at Nortonville, Cal.; sailed San Francisco Oct. 1872; ar. Guadalajara, Nov. 7, 1872; at Guadalajara 1872-1876; vis. U. S. 1876; March 1878 in U. S.; released Sept. 27, 1881; 1888 · Cal. Join Methodist South Mission 1881.

Mrs. Watkins (Edna M. Parker)

Sailed as above; at Guadalajara 1872-1876; vis. U. S. 1876; March 1878 in U. S.; 1888 Cal.

John Luther Stephens, born Swansea, Wales, Oct. 19, 1847; prof. rel. Petaluma, Cal., about 1866; spent 2 1/2 years in a Baptist Coll. in Petaluma, Cal. Grad. Pacific Theolog. Sem. 1872; had been clerk and teacher. Supplied at 1st Cong. Ch., South Vallejo, Cal., for a short time; ord. Sept. 19, 1872 at S. Vallejo, Cal.; sailed San Francisco Oct. 1872; ar. Guadalajara Nov. 7, 1872; remained in G. until Dec. 2, 1873, when he went to Ahualulco, a town of 5000 inhab., about 40 miles from Guadalajara. After three months of faithful and successful labor in this place, he was assassinated on the morning of March 2, 1874. (Obit. Miss. Herald May 1874)

G. F. G. Morgan,

grad. Pacific Theolog. Sem. 1872; ordd Oct. 15, 1872 at Cloverdale, Cal.; appointed May 5, 1874; sailed S. F., June 7, 1874; ar. Guadalajara June 21, 1874; returned to U. S. 1875; released 1875; 1876-to present time (Mar. 1878) p., Grass Valley, Cal.; 1887 San Francisco, Cal.

John Edwards, born Jan. 26, 1846, Llanwiddarw, Caermarthenshire, So. Wales?
prof. rel. Oct. 1858; grad. at Brecon Memorial Coll. 1871; ord. Bethlehem
Ch., Blaenavon, Monmouthshire; supplied a ch. at Blaenavon for some time;
sailed N. Y. Jan. 26, 1875; ar. Guadalajara April 24, 1875; March 1878 still
at G.; released 1880; 1888 Lansford, Pa.

Mrs. Edwards (Mary Jane Roberts) born Nov. 25, 1852, at Victoria, Monmouthshire, England; prof. rel. 1867 at Blaenavon; educated Ebbw Vale,
Monmouthshire and New Castle, Emlyn, Wales; mar. Blaenavon, June 1873;
sailed from N. Y. Jan. 26, 1875 and ar. Guadalajara April 24, 1875; 1875-1878
at Guadalajara. Released   ; 1888 Lansford, Pa.

James Kellogg Kilbourn, transferred from No. Mexico to this miss. Started
for this miss. Jan. 22, 1879; arr. Guadalajara Feb. 21, 1879; returned to
U. S.   ; released April 13, 1880; 1887 Genesee, Wis.

Mrs. Kilbourn (Emma Henderson) Reached Guadalajara Feb. 21, 1879; released
April 13, 1880; 1887 Genesee, Wis.

Matthew A. Crawford, born Girvan, Scotland, Nov. 28, 1850; prof. rel. 1864
or 1865; grad. Monmouth Coll. 1870; studied first and third years Chicago
Theol. Sem. and second year Yale Theol. Sem.; ord. Greenville, Ill. 1879;
joined the mission 1882. Dec. 1885 at Guadalajara. Died at Hermosillo,
Mexico April 3, 1894. (See Herald June 1894, p. 232)

Mrs. Crawford (Hattie J. Sturges) dau. Rev.A. A. Sturges of the Micronesia
mission; born Ponape, L. I. Jan. 26, 1853; prof. rel. Honolulu 1865; studied
Denmark Acad, Iowa and Oxford Sem., O., mar. Dec. 27, 1881; joined the
mission 1882; Dec. 1885 at Guadalajara.

John Howland, D.D., son of Rev. W. W. Howland of the Ceylon Mission; born Jaffna, Ceylon, March 13, 1854; prof. rel. Conway, Mass. Nov. 1869; grad. Amherst Coll. 1876; from 1877 to 1879 principal Union Graded Sch., Danielsonville, Conn.; grad. Hartford Theol. Sem. 1882; ord. Danielsonville June 1882; started for the mission Oct. 5, 1882; ar. Nov. Dec. 1885 at Guadalajara ar. home June 7, 1913; ret'd to field Oct. 25, 1914; arr. home Nov. 26, 1927. (L.H.D. Amherst 1926.) Retired 1928.

Mrs. Howland (Sara Brewster Chollar) born Danielsonville, Windham Co., Ct. Oct. 24, 1857;[1] prof. rel. Danielsonville, 1874; studied Packer Coll. Inst. Brooklyn, N. Y.; mar. Aug. 9, 1882; started for mission Oct. 5, 1882; arr. Nov. Dec. 1885 at Guadalajara; vis. U. S. arr. Danielson, Conn. Sept. 1905; arr. home June 7, 1913; arr. field Oct. 25, 1914; arr. home Nov. 26, 1927; retired 1928.

Mary Martyn Bissell, born Spencer Acad., Ind. Ter., Jan. 6, 1848; prof. rel. Antona, Ill. 1867; grad. Wheaton Coll. 1873; ord. Hartford, N. Y. Sept. 5, 1882; joined the mission in Nov. 1882; Dec. 1885 at Tlajamulco; transferred to Northern Mexico Nov. 4, 1890. (See vol. IX, p. 495) Pomona, Calif. 1912. Died June 1, 1920 at Port Angeles, Wash. (Miss. Herald 1920, page 476)

Mrs. Bissell (Ella Norwood) born Hartford, N. Y. Sept. 30, 1852; prof. rel. Jan. 1865; studied Dryden Sem., N. Y. and Wheaton Coll., Ill.; mar. Aug. 9, 1877; joined the mission Nov. 29, 1882. Dec. 1885 at Tlajamulco; transferred to No. Mexico Nov. 4, 1890. (See Vol. IX, page 128)

Isabel Maria Hoskins, born Lawrence, Kan., Sept. 14, 1855; prof. rel. Victoria, Ill. 1869; studied Rockford Sem. and Knox Coll.; engaged for some time in teaching; joined the mission Nov. 1882; vis. U. S. 1887-8; re-emb. New Orleans Ap. 18, 1889; arr. Guadalajara April 26, 1889.

MISSION TO SPAIN

Luther Halsey Gulick, M.D., born Honolulu, June 10, 1828. (See Sandwich Islands) Sailed from Boston for Spain, Dec. 19, 1871. After careful exploration, took up his residence in Barcelona, March 6, 1872. In 1873, trans. to Italy, and removed to Florence. In 1875 (May) returned to U. S. December 1875 went to Japan as agent of American Bible Society to take charge of their work in Japan and China. Ar. Yokohama Jan. 2d, 1876. Still in Japan. March 1878. Died at Springfield, Mass. April 8, 1891.

Mrs. Gulick (Louisa Lewis) born New York City, Nov. 10, 1830. (Mission to Sandwich Islands) Resided in Spain and Italy as above. April 1877 went out to join her husband in Japan. March 1878 still in Japan. Died Japan June 14, 1894.

William Hooker Gulick, born Kauai, Sand. Is. Nov. 18, 1835; prof. rel. Honolulu; educated at Punahou School. S. I. and Union Theol. Seminary; civil war veteran; engaged in teaching and in business for several years; sailed Boston Dec. 19, 1871; early in 1872 commenced operations in Santander, a city of 21,000 inhab. on N. W. coast of Spain. Has remained there to present time (March 1878). Ord. Aug. 2, 1874; vis. U. S. in 1880; re-emb. Aug. 13, 1881; Dec. 1885 in Spain; vis. U. S. arr. N. Y. May 4, 1891; during summer visited the Hawaiian I.; returned to Spain early in 1892; returned to U. S. in 1912; sailed Sept. 2, 1913; arr. home Aug. 1919. Died Apr. 14, 1922 in Boston, Mass. (Miss. Herald 1922, page 218)

Mrs. Gulick (Alice Winfield Gordon Kittredge) dau. of James M. Gordon, treas. A.B.C.F.M. 1854-1865; born Boston, Mass., Aug. 8, 1847; prof. rel. Sept. 4, 1864 at Auburndale; educated at Mt. Holyoke Sem; 1868-1870 teacher at Mt. Holyoke.; mar. Mr. Gulick Dec. 12, 1871, at Auburndale; 1872-1878 at Santander. Vis. U. S. in 1880; re-emb. Aug. 13, 1881; Dec. 1885 in Spain; vis. U. S. arr.

June 10, 1887; re-emb. July 21, 1887; vis. U. S. arr. Boston July 27, 1890; re-emb. Boston June 25, 1892; vis. the U. S. in 1897-9; labored among the Spanish prisoners at Portsmouth, N. H. during the war of 1898; re-emb. Boston Feb. 1, 1899; arr. Biarritz, France to which place the International Inst. had been removed during the war. Feb. 17, 1899; returned to U. S. arr. N. Y. Oct. 7, 1899; re-emb. Boston May 22, 1901. Died London Sept. 14, 1903. (See Nov. 1903 Herald).

Thomas Lafon Gulick, born Sand. Is., April 10, 1839; prof. rel. Honolulu about 1854; grad. at Williams Coll. 1865; Union and Andover, grad. at A. 1868; preached for a time in New York City and Chicago; ord. North Manchester, Conn. May 15, 1870; sailed N. Y. May 17, 1873; ar. Santander July 5, 1873; In 1875 removed to Madrid and in Feb. 1876 went to Zaragoza, Province of Aragon, a city of 70,000 inhab. March 1878 at Zaragoza; returned to U. S arr. Jan. 14, 1883; released Oct. 23, 1883; 1887 Makawao, H. I. Died in Africa in Kijabi, British East Africa, June 15, 1904. (See Miss. Herald Nov. 1904, page 457)

Mrs. Gulick (Alice Elmina Walbridge) born Ithaca, N. Y. Feb. 21, 1843; prof. rel. 1859, Ithaca; educated at Ithaca Acad. Teacher. Mar. Nov. 25, 1872, in Chicago; sailed as above; March 1878 at Zaragoza; returned to U. S. arr. Jan. 14, 1883; released Oct. 23, 1883; 1887 Makamao, H. I. Died in Honolulu Jan. 14, 1911, having been there since 1909.

Gustave Alexy, born May 21, 1833, at Rozsnyo, Hungary. United with a Lutheran Ch. in Hungary; grad. in languages at Turin and Milan; grad. at Union Sem., N. Y. in 1871; ord. New York City June 10, 1872; sailed N. Y. July 13, 1872; at Barcelona Aug. 21, 1872. Had formerly spent two years in Barcelona. April 1874, returned to U. S. Released 1874. Died in New York City Jan. 29, 1880.

Miss Hannah Blake, an English lady, was employed at Barcelona in 1872 as a teacher.

Susie Frances Richards, born Rahway, N. J. March 23, 1856; prof. rel. Auburndale 1870; grad. Newton High Sch. 1874; engaged in teaching for several years; emb. Aug. 13, 1880; Dec. 1885 in San Sebastian. Returned to U. S., 1888; married Theodore Woodman Gore of Auburndale 1889.

SOUTHERN ASIA

The first missionaries sent out by the American Board were Adoniram Judson, Gordon Hall, Samuel Newell, Samuel Nott, and Luther Rice. They were sent to India, but their instructions, delivered to them Feb. 7, 1812, left it to their discretion at what particular point to fix their station. They were ordained at Salem, Feb. 6, 1812. Judson and Newell, with their wives, sailed from Salem in the brig Caravan, Feb. 19. Nott, Hall, and Rice, with the wife of Mr. Nott, sailed from Philadelphia in the Harmony, Feb. 18. The party first named arr. at Calcutta, June 17; the other party arr. there Aug. 8, 1812.

None of these missionaries were suffered to remain. The government, then and there existing, ordered them away. Mr. and Mrs. Newell embarked for the Isle of France (Mauritius) and there Mrs. Newell died. Mr. Judson and Mr. Rice became Baptists, and their connection with the A.B.C.F.M. soon after ceased. Messrs Hall and Nott embarked for Bombay, Nov. 20, which place they reached Feb. 11, 1813; which date is regarded as the commencement of the Mahratta Mission.

Adoniram Judson, son of Rev. Adoniram Judson, pastor of the Cong. Ch. in Malden, Mass.; afterwards of Plymouth, Mass.; born Malden, Aug. 9, 1788; (House now standing on Main St., Malden and occupied by Geo. Wilson, heirs, 1894) grad. Brown Univ., Providence 1807; Andover Sem. 1810; signed the application to the Gen. Assoc. of Mass. at Bradford June 27, 1810; ord. Salem Feb. 6, 1812; emb. Salem Feb. 19; ar. Calcutta June 17, 1812; notified the Baptist missionaries at Serampore Aug. 27, that he and Mrs. Judson had changed their sentiments on the subject of baptism; they were immersed Sept. 6. This event led to his withdrawment from the mission. He was released Sept. 15, 1813. (Mr. Judson was taken into the service of the

Baptist Board of Missions; commenced a mission at Rangoon in Burmah, July 1813; during the Burmese war, from May 1824 to Feb. 1826, he suffered great severities from the Burman government, from which he was freed by the advance of the British army on the capital; via. U. S. and died at sea, April 12, 1850.)

Mrs. Judson (Ann Hasseltine) born Bradford, Mass. Dec. 22, 1789; prof. rel. Sept. 14, 1806; mar. Feb. 5, 1812; died at Amherst in British Burmah Oct. 24, 1826. The first American female, it is supposed, who resolved to go on a Foreign Mission. See Memoir of Mrs. Judson by Rev. James D. Knowles.

Luther Rice, born Northboro, Mass. March 25, 1783; grad. Williams Coll. 1810; Andover Sem. 1811; ord. Salem, Feb. 6, 1812; sailed from Philadelphia with Messrs Hall and Nott, Feb. 18, 1812; arr. Calcutta, Aug. 8, 1812; embraced Baptist views Oct.; was immersed Nov. 1, 1812; withdrew from the Mission Oct. 3, 1812; released Sept. 15, 1813. (Took passage with Mr. Judson and Mrs. Judson for the Isle of France Dec. 1812; left that island March 15, 1813; returned to U. S. Sept. 1813; was for twelve years 1814-1826 agent of the Baptist Gen. Missionary Convention, formed May 18, 1814 by his exertions ; had an important agency in the establishment of Columbian Coll., D.C.; was treasurer of said Coll.; and died Edgefield, District, S. C. Oct. 25, 1836, age 53). Never married.

MISSION TO THE MAHRATTAS

Commenced by Messrs Hall and Nott Feb. 11, 1813. Mr. Newell joined them in 1814.

MISSIONARIES

Gordon Hall, born Tolland, Mass, then the West Parish in Granville, April 8, 1784; grad. Williams Coll. 1808; Andover Sem. 1810;(prof. rel. 1806); attended medical lectures in Philadelphia 1811; ord. Salem, Mass. Feb. 6, 1812; sailed from Philadelphia in the ship Harmony Feb. 18, 1812; ar. Calcutta, Aug. 8, 1812; reached Bombay Feb. 11, 1813; conducted with great ability a correspondence with the government there; conducted the affairs of the mission with signal ability and success; died on a preaching tour, at Dhoorlee Dhapoor, about 70 miles from Bombay, of cholera, March 20, 1826.

Mrs. Hall (Margaret Lewis) born in the county of Pembroke, Wales, July 20, 1783; mar. at Bombay Dec. 19, 1816; arr. in U. S. July 30, 1825; died at the house of her son, Rev. Gordon Hall, Northampton, Mass. Jan. 25, 1868.

Samuel Newell, Roxbury, Mass.; born Durham, Me. July 24, 1784; prof. rel. Oct. 14, 1804; grad. Harvard Coll. 1807; Andover Sem. 1810; attended medical lectures in Philadelphia 1811; ord. Salem Feb. 6, 1812; sailed with Mr.Judson in the Caravan from Salem, Feb. 19, 1812; ar. Calcutta June 17; sailed for Isle of France Aug. 4, 1812; arr. there Oct. 31, 1812; emb. for Ceylon, Feb. 24, 1813; spent a year in that island; joined his bretheren Hall and Nott at Bombay, Mar. 7, 1814; died there of cholera May 30, 1821, age 37.

Mrs. Newell (Harriet Atwood) born Haverhill, Mass. Oct. 10, 1793; prof. rel. Aug. 6, 1809; mar. Feb. 9, 1812; emb. Feb. 19; died at Port Louis in the Isle of France (Mauritius) Nov. 30, 1812. See Memoir.

The nomenclature was changed in 1833 from "Bombay Mission" to "Mahratta Mission".

Mrs. Newell (Philomela Thurston) Bedford, N. H.; born Rowley, Mass. April 11, 1795; prof. rel. Dunbarton, N. H. Nov. 1810; emb. Charlestown, Mass. Oct. 5, 1817; ar. Bombay Feb. 23, 1818; mar. Rev. Samuel Newell, March 26, 1818; after his death mar. James Garrett, missionary printer at Bombay ,(infra) March 26, 1822; returned to U. S. March 1832; died Sept. 16, 1849.

Samuel Nott, son of Rev. Samuel Nott, D.D. of Franklin, Ct.; born there Sept. 11, 1788; prof. rel. May 1805; grad. Union Coll. 1808; Andover Sem. 1810; ord. Salem, Mass. Feb. 6, 1812; sailed with Messrs Hall and Rice from Philadelphia Feb. 18; ar. Calcutta Aug. 8, 1812; emb. for Bombay Nov. 20, 1812; reached Bombay Feb. 11, 1813. Left the mission from ill health Sept. 7, 1815; arrived in U. S. Aug. 14, 1816; released Sept. 20, 1816. (Afterwards, he was a teacher in New York, 1816-1823; pastor Galway, N. Y. 1823-1829; pastor Wareham, Mass. 1829-1849; teacher Wareham 1849-1866.) Lived in Wareham till 1868 or 1869, then removed to the family of his son in Hartford, Ct. where he died June 1, 1869, age 81.

Mrs. Nott (Roxana Peck) Norwich, Ct., born Jan. 21, 1785, Franklin, Ct.; mar. Feb. 6, 1812. Died Hartford, Conn., Dec. 11, 1876.

Horatio Bardwell, D.D., Goshen, Mass.; born Belchertown, Mass., Nov. 3, 1788; prof. rel. Feb. 1808; studied under private teachers; three years at Andover Sem. 1814; ord. Newburyport, June 21, 1815; emb. Newburyport Oct. 23, 1815; ar. Colombo, Ceylon March 22, 1816; ar. Bombay Nov. 1, 1816; returned to U.S. Jan. 22, 1821; released 1822. (Afterwards, pastor at Holden, Mass. from Oct. 1823 to Feb. 20, 1832; agent for A.B.C.F.M. 1832-1836; pastor Oxford, Mass. 1836 to 1864; died at Oxford, May 5, 1866, age 77.)

Mrs. Bardwell (Rachel Furbush) born Andover, Mass. Nov. 6, 1786; mar. July 11, 1815.
Died Oxford, Mass. Dec. 22, 1876.

John Nichols, born Antrim, N. H. June 20, 1790; prof. rel. Sept. 1811; grad. Dart. Coll. 1813; Andover Sem. 1816; ord. in Park Street Church, Boston with Sereno E. Dwight and others, Sept. 3, 1817; emb. Charlestown, Mass. Oct. 5, 1817; ar. Bombay Feb. 23, 1818; stationed at Tannah, on the island of Salsette 25 miles from Bombay Nov. 1818; died of fever at Bombay Dec. 9, 1824, age 34.

Mrs. Nichols (Elisabeth Shaw) Beverly, Mass. born
mar. Sept. 30, 1817. After the death of Mr. Nichols she married Oct. 19, 1826, Rev. Joseph Knight, church missionary of Nellore, Ceylon; and was released.

Allen Graves, born Rupert, Vt., April 8, 1792; prof. rel. July 1804; grad. Midd. Coll. 1812; Andover Sem. 1815; ord. Park Street Church, Boston, with S. E. Dwight, Levi Parsons and others, Sept. 3, 1817; emb. Charlestown, with Mr. Nichols (above) Oct. 5, 1817; ar. Bombay Feb. 23, 1818; stationed at Mahim, on the northern part of the island of Bombay; after the death of Mr. Hall, 1826, stationed at Bombay; removed to the new station at Ahmednuggur, Dec. 20, 1831; left Bombay to visit U. S. Aug. 7, 1832; ar. Boston Jan. 11, 1833; re-emb. Boston May 21, 1834; ar. Bombay Sept. 10, 1834; stationed for health's sake at Malcolm Peth 1836; engaged in translations; died there Dec. 30, 1843, age 51.

Mrs. Graves (Mary Lee) Rupert, Vt., born Lebanon, N. Y. Nov. 26, 1787; prof. rel. Rupert 1805; mar. Dec. 7, 1816; ar. Bombay Feb. 23, 1818; emb. Bombay for U. S. July 4, 1822; ar. Liverpool, Nov. 1822; ar. New York   ; re-emb. Boston Sept. 27, 1823; ar. Bombay June 28, 1824; vis. U. S. again as above, 1833; re-emb. May 21, 1834; after the death of her husband she continued in the mission till her own death at Malcolm Peth, March 23, 1866; age 79. She had been connected with this mission more than 48 years.

Edmund Frost, born Brattleboro, Vt. Nov. 16, 1791; prof. rel. spring of 1815; grad. Midd. Coll. 1820; Andover Sem. 1823; ord. Salem, Mass. Sept. 25, 1823;

emb. Boston Sept. 27, 1823; ar. Calcutta, March 1824; ar. Bombay June 28, 1824; died there of quick consumption Oct. 18, 1825.

Mrs. Frost (Clarissa Emerson, sister of Rev. John S. Emerson, missionary of the Board to the Sandwich Islands, 1831-1867,; born Chester, N. H. Nov. 13, 1798; mar. Sept. 23, 1823. After the death of Mr. Frost she mar. Oct. 12, 1826, Rev. Henry Woodward, missionary of the Board in Ceylon and after his death mar. Dec. 22, 1836, Rev..William Todd, missionary of the Board in Madura. She died there June 1, 1837.

David Oliver Allen, (brother of Nathan Allen, M.D. of Lowell,) Princeton, Mass.; born Barre, Mass. 1800; prof. rel. Feb. 1823; entered Williams Coll. was there 1 1/2 years; went with President Moore to Amherst and grad. Amh. Coll. 1823; Andover Sem. 1827; ord. Westminster, Mass. May 21, 1827; emb. Boston, June 5, 1827; ar. Calcutta Sept. 21; ar. Bombay Nov. 27, 1827; left Bombay on a visit to U. S. Dec. 7, 1832; ar. Boston April 20, 1833; re-emb. Boston July 1, 1833; ar. Bombay Jan. 7, 1834; spent much of his time in 1834-1835-1836 in itinerating; afterwards stationed at Bombay and devoting his time chiefly to the revision and printing of the Mahratta Bible. Returned to U. S. in feeble health 1853; released Nov. 4, 1853. (Afterwards, acting pastor at Westford, Mass. 1857-1858, and at Wenham, Mass. Died of congestion of the lungs, Lowell, Mass. July 19, 1863. In 1856, he published an elaborate work on "India", Ancient and Modern, Geographical, Historical, Political, Social, and Religious", etc. Boston, pp.618)

Mrs. Allen (Myra Wood) born Westminster, Mass. Dec. 7, 1800; mar. May 28, 1827; emb. Boston, June 5, 1827; died Bombay Feb. 5, 1831. See Memoir of Mrs. Allen, by Rev. Cyrus Mann, Boston, 1834, pp. 256.

Mrs. Allen (Orpah Graves, sister of Rev. Allen Graves, missionary of the Board to the Mahrattas, 1818-1843,) born Rupert, Vt.; emb. with her brother, Boston, May 21, 1834; ar. Bombay Sept. 10, 1834;

teacher before her marriage; mar. Feb. 22, 1838; died Bombay June 5, 1842.

Mrs. Allen (Azubah Caroline Condit, sister of Mrs. Nevins (See Mission to Borneo) born Mount Freedom, N. J. Dec. 4, 1808; emb. New York June 8, 1836; with the company of missionaries then sent out to Java; ar. Batavia, Sept. 15, 1836; removed to Borneo June 17, 1839; removed to Bombay latter part of 1843; mar. to Mr. Allen, Dec. 12, 1843; died Bombay June 11, 1844. (See obituary Herald, vol. 40, pp. 373,374)

Cyrus Stone, born Marlborough, N. H. June 9, 1793; prof. rel. 1815; grad. Dart. Coll. 1822; Andover Sem. 1825; ord. Springfield, Mass. May 10, 1826; emb. with Rev. D. O. Allen (supra) Boston June 5, 1827; ar. Calcutta Sept. 21; ar. Bombay Dec. 29, 1827; stationed at Jalna 1837; withdrew from his connection with the Board, June 20, 1838; dismissed Aug. 22, 1839; returned to U. S. 1841; (Afterwards, pastor Bingham, Me. 1841-1844; Harwich, Mass. 1844-1848; publisher of "Mothers' Assistant" in Boston 1850-1862; acting pastor of a new church, Beechwood, Cohasset, Mass. 1863; died July 19, 1867, age 74.)

Mrs. Stone (Atossa Frost) born Marlboro, N. H. 1798; prof. rel. 1818; mar. Aug. 21, 1826; died Bombay Aug. 7, 1833.

Mrs. Stone (Abigail Holt Kimball) born Waterford, Me. 1812; emb. Boston, May 21, 1834, with Mr. and Mrs. Graves (supra) went out as a teacher; ar. Bombay Sept. 10, 1834; mar. Oct. 23, 1834. Died Jan. 8, 1875, at Andover, Mass. (See obituary notice of Mrs. Atossa F. Stone, Herald, vol. 30, pp.170-172)

William Hervey, Troy, N. Y.; born Kingsbury, Warren Co., N. Y. Jan. 22, 1799; prof. rel. Bennington, Vt. autumn of 1824; grad. Williams Coll. 1824; Princeton Sem. 1828; ord. Boston (Park St.) Sept. 24, 1829; emb. Boston, Aug. 2, 1830; ar. Bombay March 7, 1831; joined Mr. Graves (supra) at the new station at Ahmednuggur, Dec. 20, 1831; died of cholera at Ahmednuggur, May 13, 1832. (See obituary Herald, vol. 28, p. 389)

Mrs. Hervey (Elisabeth Hawley Smith, sister of the wife of Rev. John Dunbar, missionary to the Pawnees, 1834-1847, (See Mission to the Pawnees); born Hadley, Mass. Jan. 26, 1798; prof. rel. June 1818; mar. June 30, 1830; emb. Boston Aug. 1830; died at Bombay of dysentery, May 3, 1831. See a very interesting account of her in Herald, vol. 27, pp. 378-380 and vol. 28, pp. 169-173. Also see notice of Mr. Hervey, Herald, vol. 28, pp.389-391.

William Ramsey, Philadelphia; born Thompsontown, Mifflin Co., Pa. Feb. 11, 1803; prof. rel. Sept. 1820; grad. N. Jersey Coll., Princeton, 1821; Princeton Sem. 1826; ord. in Sinking Valley, Pa. Oct. 11, 1827; emb. with William Hervey, Hollis Read, etc. Boston Aug. 2, 1830; arr. Bombay March 7, 1831; embarked to U. S. July 5, 1834; released June 6, 1837; pastor Southwark, Philadelphia. Died 1857.

Mrs. Ramsey (Mary Wire) born Philadelphia Dec. 9, 1804; prof. rel. July 1828; mar. Philad. July 12, 1830; emb. Boston Aug. 2, 1830; died of cholera at Bombay June 11, 1834.

Hollis Read, born Newfane, Vt. Aug. 26, 1802; prof. rel. in college Dec. 1825; grad. Williams Coll. 1826; Princeton Sem. 1829; appointed Dec. 24, 1828; ord. Boston Sept. 24, 1829; emb. Boston, with Hervey etc. Aug. 2, 1830; ar. Bombay March 7, 1831; joined Mr. Graves and Mr. Hervey at Ahmednuggur Dec. 20, 1831; emb. Bombay on his return to U. S. March 18, 1835; arr. New York Nov. 14, 1835; released July 25, 1837; 1877 at Elizabeth, N. J.; died in Somerville, N. J. April 7, 1887. (Rev. Edward G. Read of Somerville, N. J. is a son.)

Mrs. Read (Caroline Hubbell) born Bennington, Vt. Feb. 21, 1803; prof. rel. 1827; mar. Bennington June 24, 1830. Died in Elisabeth, N. J. Feb. 19th 1883. Illness brief, about one month. Burried in Bennington, Vt. Feb. 23, 1883.

George Washington Boggs, born York Co., South Carolina, June 20, 1796, grad.
Amherst Coll. 1827; Princeton Sem. 1831; ord. Charleston, S.C. March 14, 1832;
emb. Salem, Mass. May 28, 1832; ar. Bombay Sept. 14, 1832; joined Mr. Read at
Ahmednuggur Dec. 20, 1832; returned to U.S. Dec. 29, 1838; released Sept. 15,
1840. Died at Pickens, S.C. Aug. 14, 1871, aged 75.

Mrs. Boggs (Mrs. Isabella W. Adger) Winnsboro, S.C.

Sendol Barnes Munger, Shoreham, Vt.; born Fairhaven, Vt. Oct. 5, 1802; prof. rel.
Shoreham 1821; grad. Midd. Coll. 1828; Andover Sem. 1833; ord. Bristol, Vt.
Feb. 12, 1834; emb. Boston May 21, 1834; ar. Bombay Sept. 10, 1834; stationed
at Jalna 1837; vis. U.S. and ar. Salem, June 9, 1842; re-emb. Boston Jan. 3,
1846; stationed Ahmednuggur 1846; at Dhingar Oct. 1848; vis. U.S. 1853; re-emb.
N.Y. Sept. 6, 1854; ar. Ahmednuggur with the Deputation, Dr. Anderson and
Mr. Thompson, Nov. 17, 1854; stationed at Satara, 1855; revisited U.S. Aug. 28,
1860; re-emb. Boston October 29, 1862; ar. Bombay March 3, 1863; at Satara again
till 1866; then at Bombay; died at Bombay July 23, 1868. (See obituary notice
of this laborious and excellent missionary, Herald, vol. 64, p. 306-8)

Mrs. Munger (Maria L. Andrews) Bristol, Vt.; mar. 1834; emb. Boston May 21, 1834;
vis. U.S. June 9, 1842; re-emb. Jan. 3, 1846; died on the passage out, March 12,
1846.

Mrs. Munger (Mary E. Ely) Chicago, Ill.
mar. 1854; emb. New York Sept. 6, 1854; died June 3, 1856.

Mrs. Munger (Mrs. Sarah Spring Cushman Paul, a widow) of Boston; born Wiscasset,
Me. June 8, 1813; prof. rel. 1835; mar. 1862; emb. Boston Oct. 29, 1862; returned to U.S. Sept. 24, 1868. Died at Dorchester, Mass. Feb. 23, 1892, where
she had been for some time in City Missionary Work.

Amos Abbott, born Wilton, N.H. June 2, 1812; prof. rel.   ; studied at
Phillips Academy, Andover and one year in Andover Sem.; emb. with Mr. Graves
and Mr. Munger (supra) at Boston May 21, 1834; went out as a superintendent
of schools and tract distributor; ar. Ahmednuggur Oct. 15, 1834; continued

at that station till 1847; returned to U. S. July 23, 1847; released Oct. 26, 1847. He was licensed to preach in Ahmednuggur 1843. After his return to U. S. he was five years, 1852-1857, a City Missionary at Portsmouth, N. H.; ord. Portsmouth June 5, 1857; embarked Boston June 12, 1857; ar. Bombay Sept. 15, 1857; stationed at Rahoore till 1866; then at Satara; returned to U. S. 1869 (about March 1869); released 1870; 1878 at Fairfield, Neb.; 1887 Steele City, Neb.; 1888 Isle of Wight. Died in Isle of Wight April 24, 1889. (See notice in Herald, June 1889, p. 256)

Mrs. Abbott (Anstrice Wilson) Wilton, N. H.; born Danvers, Mass. Feb. 3, 1812; prof. rel. Nashua, N. H. 1832; mar. Wilton, May 12, 1834; emb. Boston May 21, 1834; returned to U. S. July 1847; re-emb. June 12, 1857; released 1870. Died at Isle of Wight, July 30, 1889. (See Herald, Sept. 1889, pp.381)

Henry Ballantine, Marion, Ohio; born Schodack, Rensselaer Co., N. Y. March 5, 1813; prof. rel. Lancaster, O. July 1831; grad. Ohio Univ., Athens, O. 1829; Princeton, Union, and Andover Seminaries finishing at Andover 1834; ord. Columbus, Ohio April 6, 1835; emb. Boston, May 16, 1835; ar. Bombay Oct. 11, 1835; stationed Ahmednuggur 1836; vis. U. S. arr. New York May 18, 1850; re-emb. Boston July 10, 1852; ar. Ahmednuggur, Dec. 31, 1852; continued to labor there as before, till 1865; emb. Bombay for the U. States Sept. 4, 1865, by way of Suez and Liverpool; was detained in the Red Sea four weeks; died on the passage and was buried in the ocean, off Cape St. Vincent, Coast of Portugal. Died Nov. 9, 1865, buried Nov. 10. (See obituary sketch, Herald, Vol. 62, pp. 37-41)

Mrs. Ballantine (Elizabeth Darling) born Henniker, N. H. Jan. 5, 1812; prof. rel. Feb. 1832; mar. May 5, 1835; emb. Boston May 16, 1835; vis. U. S. May 1850; re-emb. July 1852; returned to U. S. Dec. 1, 1865; and has since resided in Amherst, Mass. Died Amherst, Mass. May 8, 1874.

Ebenezer Burgess, born Grafton, Vt. June 26, 1805; prof. rel. in Coll. 1831; grad. Amherst Coll. 1831; tutor in that coll. 1833-1835; Andover Sem. 1837; teacher of Hebrew and Greek, Union Theol. Sem., New York 1837-1838; ordained March 19, 1839; emb. Salem, Mass. April 1, 1839; arr. Bombay Aug. 10, 1839; stationed at Ahmednuggur 1839; and so continued; vis. U. S. 1845; re-emb. Boston, Sept. 26, 1846; ar. Bombay Feb. 27, 1847; re-occupied his station at Ahmednuggur; transferred to Satara 1851; returned to U. S. 1854; released Sept. 25, 1855. (Afterwards, acting pastor at Centerville, Mass. 1857-1859; at Lanesville, Mass. 1861-1863; at South Franklin, Mass. 1864-1867. He delivered a course of lectures at Lowell Institute, Boston, in 1865 and again in 1867.) He died at Newton Centre, Mass. Jan. 1, 1870.

Mrs. Burgess (Mary Grant, niece of Mrs. Zilpah (Grant) Banister) born Colebrook, Ct. Aug. 18, 1811; prof. rel. July 1830; studied at Ipswich Fem. Sem.; mar. March 11, 1839; emb. Salem April 1, 1839; died of cholera at Ahmednuggur June 24, 1842. (See obituary notice Herald, vol. 38, pp.481-483)

Mrs. Burgess (Abigail Moore) South Hadley, Mass.; born New Marlboro, Mar. 2, 1813; grad. Mt. Holyoke Coll.; mar. Sept. 1846; emb. Sept. 1846; died Mahabalishwar Satara April 26, 1853.

Ozro French, Ashford, N. Y.; born Dummerston, Vt. June 8, 1807; prof. rel. Sept. 1827; grad. Williams Coll. 1834; Andover Sem. 1837; ord. Brattleboro, Vt. Nov. 7, 1838; emb. with Mr. Burgess and Mr. Hume, Salem, April 1, 1839; ar. Bombay Aug. 10, 1839; stationed at Ahmednuggur 1839; at Leroor, May 1841; returned to U. S. July 19, 1849; released April 15, 1851. (Afterwards, home missionary, Bentonsport, Iowa till 1856; Knoxville, Iowa 1856-1863; also Franklin, Iowa. Died Blairstown, Iowa Sept. 28, 1865, age 58.)

Mrs. French (Jane Hotchkiss) born Harpersfield, N. Y. Nov. 13, 1813; prof. rel. July 1831; mar. Harpersfield, March 11, 1839; emb. April 1, 1839; returned to U. S. July 19, 1849. Died in Blairstown, Iowa Dec. 27, 1900.

Robert Wilson Hume, born Stamford, Delaware,Co., N. Y. Nov. 8, 1809; prof. rel. in coll. 1833; grad. Union Coll. 1834; Princeton Sem. 1837; ord. Delhi, N. Y. March,18, 1839; emb. with Messrs Burgess and French at Salem April 1, 1839; ar. Bombay Aug. 10, 1839; labored at that station with great assiduity more than fifteen years, chiefly in connection with the press; edited for ten years, 1844-1854, the Dnyanodaya, or Rise of Knowledge, issued sem-monthly in the native language, which had an extensive circulation, the only christian journal in any native language in Western India. His health failing, he embarked with his family for the U. S. Sept. 20, 1854; but died on the passage Nov. 26, 1854, on the coast of Africa, a little east of the Cape of Good Hope, and was buried in the ocean. (See Herald vol. 51, pp. 175-178).

Mrs. Hume (Hannah Derby Sackett) born West Springfield, Mass. June 8, 1816; prof. rel. Babylon, Long Island, April 1838; mar. West Springfield, March 24, 1839; emb. April 1, 1839; returned to U. S. April 12, 1855; 1878, residing in New Haven; ditto 1888. Died New Haven April 18, 1903. (See June 1903 Herald, p. 247)

Royal Gould Wilder, Malone, N. Y.; born Bridgeport, Vt. Oct. 27, 1816; grad. Midd. Coll. 1840; Andover Sem. 1845; ord. Oct. 22, 1845, Malone; emb. Boston May 28, 1846; ar. Bombay Sept. 20, 1846; ar. at Ahmednuggur Oct. 27, 1846; removed to Kolapoor, Nov. 1852; returned to U. S. in the summer of 1857. The mission at Kolapoor was discontinued by vote of the Prudential Committee Oct. 5, 1858; and Mr. Wilder's name omitted thenceforth from the list of missionaries. (Afterwards, Mr. Wilder returned to India, and has continued, under some other arrangement, to conduct missionary operations at Kolapoor.) 1878, at Princeton, N. J. Died in New York City Oct. 10, 1887.

Mrs. Wilder (Eliza Jane Smith) West Rutland, Vt.; born there April 9, 1822, dau. of Silas and Chloe (Chatterton) Smith; emb. Boston May 28, 1846; grad. Mt. Holyoke Sem.; returned to U. S. 1857; married Mar. 25, 1846. Died

1910 at Islampus, Bombay Presidency.

Samuel Bacon Fairbank, D.D., Jacksonville, Ill.; born Stamford, Ct. Dec. 14, 1822; prof. rel, Jacksonville, 1838; grad. Illinois Coll. 1842; Andover Sem. 1845; ord. Jacksonville 1845; emb. Boston May 28, 1846; ar. Bombay Sept. 20, 1846; at Ahmednuggur Oct. 27, 1846; removed to Bombay and took charge of the printing establishment 1850; vis. U. S. Oct. 19, 1855; re-emb. Boston Aug. 18, 1856; ar. Bombay Jan. 12, 1857; stationed at Wadale 1857; still there 1868; visited U. S. 1869; sailed from Boston by steamer for Liverpool, with wife, June 6, 1871; arr. Bombay Aug. 23, 1871; Jan. 1878, still in India. Station, Ahmednuggur; vis. U. S. arr. N. Y. Nov. 15, 1887; re-emb. Nov. 17, 1888; arr. Bombay Jan. 14, 1889; died May 31, 1898. (See Herald Aug. 1898, p.300)

Mrs. Fairbank (Abbie Allen) Oakham, Mass.; born May 30, 1825; grad. Mt. Holyoke Sem.; mar. March 26, 1846; emb. Boston May 28, 1846; ar. Bombay Sept. 20, 1846; within six months from that time her "health became a wreck"; died Bombay Aug. 21, 1852. (See Herald vol. 49, p. 23)

Mrs. Fairbank (Mary Ballantine, daughter of Rev. Henry Ballantine, missionary to the Mahrattas; born at Bombay, India Sept. 10, 1836; prof. rel. Roxbury, Mass. Sept.1852; grad. Mt. Holyoke Sem.; mar. Roxbury July 31, 1856; emb. Boston, Aug. 18, 1856; ar. Bombay Jan. 12, 1857; vis. U. S. 1869; sailed as above; ar. Bombay Aug. 23, 1871. Died Jan. 15, 1878. (See Obit. Miss. Herald April 1878.)

Allen Hazen, D.D., son of Rev. Austin Hazen of Hartford, and Berlin, Vt.; born Hartford, Vt. Nov. 30, 1822; prof. rel. Berlin, Vt. March 1838; grad. Dart. Coll. 1842; Andover Sem. 1845; ord. Berlin, Vt. July 1, 1846; emb. Boston Sept. 26, 1846; ar. Bombay Feb. 27, 1847; Ahmednuggur March 30, 1847; removed

toSeroor, Sept. 5, 1847; transferred to Ahmednuggur 1852; removed to Bombay Jan. 1855; vis. U. S. March 22, 1858; re-emb. Boston Jan. 9, 1864; ar. Bombay May 19, 1864; again stationed at Ahmednuggur; vis. U. S. 1872; 1878 at Pomfret, Vt.; May 1878 S.S. Norwich, Vt.; 1886 at Deerfield, Mass.; returned to India accompanied by his daughter in 1891 and for three years they labored at their own charges in the mission; returned to U. S. arr. N. Y. April 3, 1894. Died in Washington, D. C. May 12, 1898. (See July 1898 Herald, p.254)

Mrs. Hazen (Martha Ramsey Chapin) sister of Rev. William W. Chapin, missionary to the Mahrattas; born Somers, Ct. April 9, 1822; prof. rel. autumn of 1841; studied at Mt. Holyoke Sem.; mar. Somers, Sept. 18, 1846; emb. Sept. 26, 1846; vis. U. S. 1872; May 1878, Norwich, Vt. Died at Deerfield, Mass. Jan. 20, 1884.

William Wood, born Henniker, N. H. Dec. 2, 1818; prof. rel. Nov. 1831; grad. Dart. Coll. 1842; was a teacher two years; Union Theol. Sem., New York City 1847; ord. Henniker, July 8, 1847; emb. with Mr. Bowen at Boston July 31, 1847; ar. Bombay Jan. 19, 1848; commenced a new station at Satara June 1, 1849; visited U. S. June 23, 1855; re-emb. Boston Aug. 18, 1856; ar. Bombay Jan. 12, 1857; again stationed at Satara; revisited U. S. July 26, 1862; re-emb. Boston May. 4,, 1865; ar. Bombay Aug. 3, 1865; stationed at Ahmednuggur; vis. U. S. 1872; released 1874; 1878, N. Branford, Ct. Died at Hartford, Conn. Feb. 22, 1887. (See obit. notice Herald Apr. 1887, p. 129)

Mrs. Wood (Lucy Maria Lawrence) born Groton, Mass. March 8, 1825; prof. rel. Sept. 1844; mar. Groton July 11, 1847; emb. Boston July 31, 1847; died at Satara Aug. 13, 1851.

Mrs. Wood (Eliza Maria Howard) Pittsfield, Mass.; born Dalton, Mass. May 26, 1825; prof. rel. Pittsfield 1836; mar. July 24, 1856; emb. Aug. 18, 1856; died of cholera at Satara Nov. 18, 1859.

Mrs. Wood (Elizabeth Woodhull Penney) Greenport, Long Island; born Southampton, Suffolk Co., Long I., May 7, 1831; prof. rel. Greenport, Nov. 1843; studied

Mr. Holyoke Fem. Sem.; mar. April 10, 1865; emb. Boston May 4, 1865; via. U. S. 1872; rel. 1874. Died at Madison, Ct. Aug. 13, 1890.

George Bowen, New York City; born Middlebury, Vt. April 30, 1816; prof. rel. New York June 1844; grad. Union Theol. Sem. N. York 1847; ord. New York July 4, 1847; emb. with Mr. Wood, above, July 31, 1847; ar. Bombay Jan. 19, 1848; stationed at Bombay 1848; released Oct. 30, 1855; not married. Now editor of the "Bombay Guardian". Died at Bombay Feb. 3, 1888.

Lemuel Bissell, D.D., Milan, Erie Co., Ohio; born South Windsor, Conn. Dec. 12, 1822; prof. rel. Milan April 1836; grad. Western Reserve Coll., Hudson, O. 1845; Sem. at Hudson 1848; ord. Milan April 9, 1851; emb. Boston May 8, 1851; ar. Bombay Aug. 27, 1851; at Seroor Oct. 6, 1851; transferred to Ahmednuggur 1861; vis. U. S. April 4, 1864; re-emb. Boston Aug. 15, 1866; ar. Bombay Oct. 11, 1866; again at Ahmednugger 1867; vis. U. S. 1876; sailed New York Oct. 20, 1877; station Ahmednuggur; vis. U. S. arr. N. Y. April 22, 1886; re-emb. Oct. 10; arr. Bombay Dec. 4, 1886. Died Mahableshwar, May 28, 1891. (See Herald Aug. 1891)

Mrs. Bissell (Mary Elizabeth Beaumont) Cleveland, Ohio; born Rochester, N. Y. April 19, 1827; prof. rel. Springville, N.Y. March 1844; mar. April 3, 1851; emb. Boston May 8, 1851; vis. U. S. 1876; sailed as above; ar. Bombay Dec. 22. Station Ahmednuggur; vis. U. S. arr. N. Y. May 15; 1894; re-emb. Sept. 21, 1895. Died at Panchgain, India April 21, 1906. (See July 1906 Herald, page 314)

William Pratt Barker, New York City; born South Wales, Erie Co., N. Y. Feb. 18, 1822; grad. New York University 1848; Union Sem., N. York 1851; ord. New York May 4, 1853; emb. Boston July 26, 1853; ar. Bombay Dec. 15, 1853; reached Ahmednuggur Jan. 9, 1854; removed to Khoker Dec. 1855; continued there till 1865; returned to U. S. Aug. 14, 1865; released 1869; Kolapoor Mission Pres. Board 1872-6; May 1878, in Seneca Mission, Pres. Bd.; app. October 1877; station, upper Cattaraugus. Died Ogden, Utah, Jan. 16, 1882.

Mrs. Barker (Lucelia N. Thompson) born Avon, Ct. Dec. 21, 1829; prof. rel. New Haven, Ct. April 1850; mar. May 8, 1853; emb. Boston July 26, 1853; died at Pimplus, India, 48 miles N.N.W. of Ahmednuggur, Jan. 27, 1864. (See Herald, vol. 60, pp.164-166)

Samuel Chase Dean. born Oakham, Mass. March 28, 1823; prof. rel. July 1842; grad. Amherst Coll. 1853; Andover Sem. 1856; ord. Reading, Mass. Aug. 13, 1856; emb. Boston Aug. 18, 1856; ar. Bombay Jan. 12, 1857; at Ahmednuggur 1857; at Satara 1861-1867; visited U. S. Aug. 22, 1867; released 1868; 1878, at Steele City, Neb.; 1885 at So. Bend, Nev.; 1888 ditto. Died South Bend, Neb. Sept. 9, 1890.

Mrs. Dean (Elizabeth Augusta Abbott, dau. of Rev. Amos Abbott, missionary to the Mahrattas) Andover, Mass.; born Ahmednuggur, April 8, 1835; grad. Mt. Holyoke Sem.; prof. rel. Ahmednuggur, Jan. 1846; mar. Andover Aug. 9, 1856; emb. Aug. 18, 1856. Died Feb. 12, 1916 at Minneapolis, Minn. (See Miss. Herald April 1916, page 192)

Charles Harding,Conway, Mass.; born Whately, Mass. Nov. 21, 1826; prof. rel. Sunderland, Mass. July 1843; grad. Yale Coll. 1853; Union Theol. Sem. N.York 1856; ord. Sunderland, Mass. July 3, 1856; emb. Boston Aug. 18, 1856; ar. Bombay Jan. 12, 1857; remained there till 1862; afterwards at Sholapur; vis. U. S. May 23, 1868; sailed from New York for Liverpool on the way to India, Oct. 16, 1869; ar. Bombay Dec. 21, 1869; Jan. 1878, still in India; station, Sholapur; vis. U. S. in 1881; re-emb. N. Y. May 14, 1882; arr. Bombay July 3; Dec. 1885 at Sholapur; vis. U. S. arr. May 22, 1891; re-emb. Boston Sept. 24, 1892; arr. Bombay Nov. 13. Died at Sholapur Sept. 29, 1899. (See Dec. 1899 Herald, p. 525)

Mrs. Harding (Julia M. Terry) born Plymouth, Ct. Nov. 17, 1833; prof. rel. March 1850; mar. June 25, 1856; emb. Aug. 18, 1856; died at Sholapur Feb.11, 1867. (See Herald, vol. 63, p. 175)

Mrs. Harding (Elizabeth Darling Ballantine) daughter of Henry Ballantine;
born Ahmednuggur, India Jan. 2, 1838; prof. rel. Portsmouth, N. H. summer
1852; studied Mt. Holyoke Fem. Sem.; a teacher in this country; mar. Amherst,
Mass. Aug. 19, 1869; ar. Bombay Dec. 21, 1869; Jan. 1878, still in India;
station, Sholapur; vis. U. S. in 1881 as above; vis. U. S. arr. N. Y. May 22,
1891; re-emb. Boston Sept. 24, 1892; arr. Bombay Nov. 13; vis. U. S. arr.
Boston June 13, 1903; re-emb. Boston Oct. 6, 1906; died at Ahmednuggur,
India Jan. 9, 1912. (See Herald Feb. 1912, p. 69)

Henry James Bruce, Springfield, Mass.; born Hardwick, Mass. Feb. 5, 1835;
prof. rel. Springfield, March 1852; grad. Amherst Coll. 1859; studied
theology one year at Bangor, two years at Andover, 1862; ord. Springfield,
Mass. Sept. 11, 1862; emb. Boston Oct. 29, 1862; arr. Bombay March 3, 1863;
stationed at Khokar; vis. U. S. 1872; returning ar. Ahmednuggur Oct. 20, 1875;
Jan. 1878 in India; station, Satara; vis. U. S. arr. N. Y. May 11, 1888; re-
emb. New York Oct. 19, 1889; arr. Bombay Dec. 13, 1889; vis. U. S. arr. San
Francisco May 20, 1899; re-emb. N. Y. Aug. 25, 1900; arr. Bombay Oct, 7, 1900.
Died at Panchgam, May 4, 1909. (See July 1909 Herald, p. 282)

Mrs. Bruce (Hepsibeth Perses Goodnow) born Sudbury, Mass. Jan. 16, 1844;
prof. rel. Dec. 1858; mar. Sudbury Oct. 7, 1862; ret. U. S. 1872; ar. Ahmednuggur Oct. 20, 1875; Jan. 1878 in India; station Satara; vis. U. S. arr. U.
S. May 11, 1888; re-emb. N. Y. Oct. 19, 1889; arr. Bombay Dec. 13, 1889; vis.
U. S. arr. N. Y. May 31, 1897; re-emb. Boston Nov. 27, 1901; retired and
placed on Honor Roll in 1925. Died Sept. 24, 1932 at Ahmednugger, India.

Henry Watkins Ballantine, son of Rev. Elisha Ballantine of Bloomington,
Indiana; born Prince Edward Co., Va. Nov. 6, 1838; prof. rel. Bloomington Jan.
1855; grad. Indiana Univ. 1856; Union Theol. Sem., N. York 1860; ord. Salem,
Ind. Jan. 10, 1861; emb. Boston Oct. 29, 1862; ar. Bombay March 3, 1863;
stationed at Bombay; returned to U. S. April 30, 1865; released May 23, 1865.
Jan. 1878, pastor 1st Pres. Ch. Bloomfield, N. J.; ditto 1887.

Mrs. Ballantine (Mary Elizabeth Loomis) born Suffield, Ct. Aug. 7, 1842; prof. rel. July 1856; mar. May 6, 1862; emb. Boston Oct. 29, 1862; returned to U. S. April 30, 1865; Jan. 1878 at Bloomfield, N. J.; ditto 1887.

William Wilberforce Chapin, brother of Mrs. Hazen; born Somers, Ct. Dec. 2, 1836; prof. rel. Nov. 1854; grad. Williams Coll. 1860; Andover Sem. 1863; ord. Somers, Sept. 24, 1863; emb. Boston Jan. 9, 1864; ar. Bombay May 19, 1864; died at Ahmednuggur March 22, 1865.

Mrs. Chapin (Catharine Isabella Hayes) Derry, N. H.; born Irasburgh, Orleans Co., Vt. April 17, 1845; prof. rel. July 1861; mar. Sept. 26, 1863; emb. Boston Jan. 9, 1864; returned to U. S. Dec. 1, 1865; m. Rev. S. J. Barrows (Unitarian) of Dorchester.

William Henry Atkinson, Brookfield, Missouri; born in Bradford, Yorkshire, England, May 29, 1838; prof. rel. Bloomington, Illinois, Nov. 1858; grad. Illinois Coll. 1864; Chicago Theol. Sem. 1867; ord. with four other foreign missionaries, Chicago, April 18, 1867; emb. Boston Aug. 13, 1867; ar. Bombay Dec. 18, 1867; vis. U. S. 1876; Jan. 1878, (at home) Orchard, Iowa; 1888, Green Mountain Iowa. Died in Soquel, Cal. Dec. 28, 1907.

Mrs. Atkinson (Calista Hatch) born Lisle, Illinois March 26, 1839; prof. rel. Aug. 1851; mar. July 8, 1867; vis. U. S. 1876; Jan. 1878 at home; 1888 Green Mountain, Iowa.

Spencer Rexford Wells, Delavan, Wis.; born Albany, N. Y. Aug. 25, 1838; prof. rel. 1861; grad. Beloit Coll. 1859; Chicago Theol. Sem. 1867; ord. with four other foreign missionaries, Chicago, April 18, 1867; sailed from Boston to Bombay July 10, 1869; arrived at Bombay Nov. 13, 1869. He was in the U. S. service as an enlisted man four years in the War of the Rebellion, and lost his right arm at the siege of Vicksburg, under General Grant; Jan. 1878, still

* For their names see Ceylon Mission

in India; station Panchgani; came to America 1881; arr. May 8; released Aug. 22, 1882. Died at Eagle Grove, Iowa Oct. 7, 1896.

Mrs. Wells (Mary Loeper) Atlanta, Logan Co., Illinois; born Princeton, Bureau Co., Ill. Aug. 31, 1839; prof. rel. Granville, Ill. 1854; studied at the Normal School, Bloomington, Ill.; mar. April 6, 1869; sailed as above; ar. Bombay Nov. 13, 1869; Jan. 1878 still in India; came to Am. 1881; released Aug. 22, 1882; station Panchgani.

Richard Winsor, of Oberlin, Ohio; born in England, Sept. 17, 1835; prof. rel. 1852; prepared for college in Wilbraham, Mass.; educated at Oberlin Coll.; grad. 1867; Oberlin Sem. grad. 1870; ord. at Medway, Mass. Sept. 7, 1870; sailed from New York for Liverpool, on the way to join this mission Oct. 19, 1870; arr. Bombay Jan. 22, 1871; Jan. 1878, still in India; station, Satara; vis. U. S. arr. June 3, 1883; re-emb. Boston Nov. 1, 1884; arr. Bombay Dec. 25; Dec. 1885 at Sirur; vis. U. S. arr. N. Y. June 10, 1890; re-emb. Boston Mar. 28, 1891; arr. Bombay May 25, 1891; vis. U. S. arr. Boston Aug. 5, 1898; re-emb. N. Y. May 19, 1900; arr. Bombay June 25. Died at Poona March 3, 1905. (See May 1905 Herald, page 223)

Mrs. Winsor (Mary Codman Sanford) of Medway, Mass., daughter of Rev. David Sanford of Medway; married Sept. 7, 1870; sailed as above; ar. Bombay Jan. 22, 1871; Jan. 1878, still in India; station, Satara; (Born Sept. 4, 1841, Medway, Mass.; prof. rel. 1857; educated at Wheaton Fem. Sem.; Teacher.) Vis. U. S. in 1883 as above; vis. U. S. arr. N. Y. June 10, 1890; re-emb. N. Y. Mar. 12, 1892; vis. U. S. arr. Boston Aug. 5, 1898; re-emb. N. Y. May 19, 1900; arr. Bombay June 25; ar. home Aug. 11, 1915; sailed Aug. 2, 1917. Died Mar. 31, 1929 at Pompano, Fla. See Mis. Rev. June 1929, p. 256.

Charles Ware Park, son of Rev. Calvin Park of West Boxford, Mass.; born Sept. 8, 1845; N. Andover, Mass.; prof. rel. Sept. 1863, Amherst, Mass.; grad. Amh. Coll 1867; passed his theological course, one year at Bangor, and two years at

Andover, grad. Andover 1870; ord. Amherst June 15, 1870; sailed from
New York by steamer for Liverpool, on the way to this mission Aug. 3, 1870;
ar. Bombay Sept. 16, 1870; Jan. 1878, still in India; station, Bombay;
returned to U. S. arr. May 30, 1881; released Oct. 24, 1882; 1886 Birmingham
Ct. Died in Pittsfield, Mass. Nov. 24, 1895, where he was pastor of the
Unitarian Church.

Mrs. Park (Anna Maria Ballantine) daughter of Rev. Henry Ballantine of this
mission; born Ahmednuggur, India, Dec. 16, 1844; prof. rel. June 1858;
educated at Mt. Holyoke, Sem; Teacher; mar. June 16, 1870, Amherst, Mass.;
sailed as above; ar. Bombay Sept. 16, 1870; Jan. 1878, still in India;
station, Bombay; returned to U. S. arr. May 30, 1881; released Oct. 24, 1882;
1886 Birmingham, Ct. Died Jan. 2, 1918, Brookline, Mass.

Robert Allen Hume, D.D., son of Rev. Robert W. Hume, (supra) born Bombay,
India, March 18, 1847; prof. rel. 1864; prepared at Williston Sem., East-
hampton, Mass.; grad. Yale Coll. 1868; two years at Yale Sem. and one at
Andover Sem.; grad. A. 1873; taught two years; sailed Aug. 11, 1874; ar. Oct.
29, 1874; ord. New Haven, May 10, 1874; Jan. 1878 in India; station,
Ahmednuggur; vis. U. S. arr. N. Y. Oct. 10, 1885; re-emb. June 30, 1887; arr.
Ahmednagar Sept. 10, 1887; vis. U.S. arr. N. Y. May 19, 1893; re-emb. N.Y.
Oct. 31, 1894; arr. Bombay Dec. 8, 1894; vis. U. S. arr. N. Y. Apr. 30,
1902; re-emb. Boston July 16, 1902; vis. U. S. arr. N. Y. May 5, 1904; re-emb.
N. Y. July 27, 1905; vis. U. S. arr. N. Y. July 3, 1910; sailed July 5, 1911;
arr. home June 3, 1919; sailed July 26, 1920; arr. home June 7, 1926; retired
June 6, 1927. Died June 24, 1929, Brookline, Mass. (See Herald Aug. 1929, page
316 and Herald Sept. 1929, pages 331-358)

Mrs. Hume (Abbie Lyon Burgess) dau. of Rev. Ebenezer Burgess (supra) born in
India, Sept. 9, 1849; is a grand niece of Mary Lyon; educated at Mt. Holyoke
and taught there nearly four years; mar. July 1874; sailed as above;

ar. Oct. 20, 1874; Jan. 1878 in India; station Ahmednuggur. Died at Panchgani July 25, 1881.

p. 137

Mrs. Hume (Katie Fairbank) (infra) mar. Ahmednagar Sept. 7, 1887; vis. U.S. arr. N. Y. May 19, 1893; re-emb. N. Y. Oct. 31, 1894; arr. Bombay Dec. 8; vis. U. S. in 1904; re-emb. N. Y. July 27, 1905; arr. home July 3, 1910; sailed July 3, 1912; arr. home June 3, 1919; sailed July 26, 1920; arr. home June 7, 1923; sailed Sept. 22, 1929; retired 1927. Died at Wai, India, April 1932.

Edward Sackett Hume, son of Rev. Robert W. Hume (supra); born Bombay, India June 4, 1848; prof. rel. June 1863; uniting with 3d Cong. Ch., New Haven, Ct. educated at Hopkins Grammar Sch., N. Haven, Ct.; grad. Yale Coll. 1870; grad. Hartford Sem., 1875; taught in Millbury, Mass. and Hartford, Conn.; ord. New Haven, Ct. June 2, 1875; sailed Aug. 11, 1875; ar. Ahmednuggur Oct. 20, 1875; Jan. 1878, in India; station, Bombay; vis. U. S. arr. N. Y. June 2, 1891; re-emb. N. Y. Nov. 18, 1893; arr. Bombay Dec. 30, 1893; vis. U. S. arr. N.Y. May 28, 1900; re-emb. New York Nov. 21, 1900; ar. Bombay Dec. 14; visi U. S. arr. N. Y. Sept. 20, 1903; released May 14, 1907. Died N. Y. Jan. 10, 1908.

Mrs. Hume (Charlotte Elizabeth Chandler, dau. of Rev. John E. Chandler, Madura Mission) born Madura, So. India, Sept. 3, 1847; prof. rel. 1860, in India; educated at Mt. Oburn Fem. Sem., Ohio, and Grove Hall, New Haven, Ct.; teache mar. July 21, 1875 at New Haven, Ct.; sailed as above; ar. Ahmednuggur Oct. 2 1875; Jan. 1878, in India; station Bombay; vis. U. S. arr. N. Y. June 2, 1891 re-emb. N. Y. Nov. 18,   ; arr. Bombay Dec. 30, 1893; vis. U. S. arr. N. Sept. 20, 1903; released May 14, 1907. Died at Clifton Springs, N. Y. Aug. 6 1920. (See Miss. Herald 1920, page 476)

Lorin Samuel Gates, born Hartland, Conn., Sept. 1, 1845; prof. rel. summer of 1863, Hartland, Conn.; prepared at Williston Sem., Easthampton, Mass.; grad. Williams Coll. 1871; grad. Yale Sem. 1875; ord. Cambridge, Vt. July 7, 1875;

U.S. arr. N.Y. April 22, 1886; re-emb. Nov. 26, 1887; vis. U.S. arr. N.Y. May 10, 1895; re-emb. Sept. 18, 1897; arr. Bombay Oct. 30, 1897; vis. U.S. in 1904; re-emb. N.Y. Oct. 15, 1904; vis. U.S. arr. N.Y. Feb. 17, 1908; re-emb. N.Y. June 5, 1909; arr. home June 7, 1920; sailed Oct. 21, 1921. Died in Bijapur, India Sept. 7, 1922. (Miss Herald 1922, page 413)

Mrs. Gates (Frances Ann Hazen) dau. of Rev. Allen Hazen, D.D.; born Seroor, India July 3, 1852; prof. rel. Jan. 7, 1865 in India; educated at Mt.Holyoke Sem.; mar. Oct. 20, 1875, Springfield,Mass.; sailed as above; Jan. 1878 in India, station Sholapur; vis. U.S. arr. N.Y. April 22, 1886; re-emb. Nov. 26, 1887 etc. as above; Sept. 18, 1897; Oct. 15, 1904; June 5, 1909; arr. home June 1920; sailed Oct. 21, 1921; arr. home May 11, 1923. Died May 20, 1946 at Hartford, Conn.

James Smith, born Hampton, Durham Co., Ont. July 13, 1851; prof. rel. Enfield, Ont.; grad. Victoria Coll. 1876; Knox Coll. Theol. Sem. 1879; ord. St. Mary's Ont. Sept. 29, 1879; emb. Dec. 13, 1879; Dec. 1885 at Ahmednager; vis. U.S. arr. Toronto, Can. Sept. 11, 1889; re-emb. June 25, 1890; arr. Ahmednagar Aug. 6, 1890; vis. U.S. arr. N.Y. May 30, 1896; re-emb. N.Y. Dec. 9, 1896; arr. Ahmednagar Jan. 16, 1897; vis. U.S. arr. Boston Dec. 15, 1899; re-emb. N.Y. Feb. 2, 1901; vis. U.S.Arr. Boston Dec. 28, 1905; re-emb. Boston April 3, 1906. Died June 23, 1929 at Loonoor, India. See Mar. 1930 Mis' Her. p. 127.

Mrs. Smith (Maud Nugent) born Township Ops. Co., Victoria, Ontario, Can. Oct. 22, 1852; prof. rel. Jan. 1875; studied Lindsay High and Toronto Normal Sch.; Mar. April 30, 1879; emb. Dec. 13, 1879; vis. U.S. 1883; re-emb. Boston Nov. 1, 1884; arr. Bombay Dec. 25.; Dec. 1885 at Ahmednagar; vis. U.S. arr. Toronto, Can. Sept. 11, 1889; re-emb. June 25, 1890; arr. Ahmednagar, Aug. 6, 1890; vis. the U.S. arr. N.Y. May 30, 1896; re-emb. Dec. 9, 1896; arr. Ahmednagar Jan. 16, 1897; vis. Am. arr. Toronto, Can. Jan. 17, 1899; re-emb. N.Y. Feb. 2, 1901. Died in England, Dec 28, 1935.

Justin Edwards Abbott, (son of Rev. Amos Abbott of this mission formerly); born Portsmouth, Rockingham Co., N.H. Dec. 25, 1853; prof. rel. Rahuri, India 1865;

grad. Dartmouth College 1876, Union Theol. Ser. 1879; ord. Nashua, N. H. emb. N. Y. Oct. 15, 1881; arr. Bombay Dec. 31. Dec. 1885 at Bombay; vis. U. S. arr. N. Y. May 8, 1893; re-emb. N. Y. Oct. 4, 1893; arr. Bombay Nov. 19, 1893; vis. U. S. arr. San Francisco May 20, 1899; re-emb. Boston Aug. 4, 1900; arrived Bombay Sept. 17, 1900; vis. U. S. arr. N. Y. Oct. 10, 1907; re-emb.   ; arr. field Oct. 16, 1908; left field Apr. 1, 1910; married Camilla L. Clarke. Died June 18, 1932 at Summit, N. J. (D.D. 1900)

Arthur Dart Bissell, son of Lemuel Bissell, D.D. of this mission; born Sirur, India, Oct. 25, 1858; prof. rel. 1872; grad. Amherst Coll. 1879, New Haven Theol. Sem. 1882; ord.   ; emb. N. Y. May 17, 1884; arr. Ahmednagar Aug.   ; returned to U. S. on account of Mrs. Bissell's health in 1885; released May 10, 1886; 1888 Honolulu, Sand. Is. Died May 24, 1925, Claremont, Calif. (See Miss'y Herald 1925, page 397)

Mrs. Bissell (Ellen A. Gower) born Haiku, Maui, Hawaiian Islands, Qt. 27, 1861; prof. rel. March 1877; studied public schools; mar.   ; emb. N.Y. May 17, 1884; arr. Ahmednagar Aug.   ; returned on account of health in 1885; released May 10, 1886; 1888 Honolulu, Sand. Is.

Mrs. Abbott (Camilla C.) Arrived field 1902; arrived home 1907; arr. field 1908; left Apr. 1, 1910. Died June 26, 1921 at Miraj, India, while on a visit there with her husband.

ASSISTANT MISSIONARIES

James Garrett, Utica, N. Y.; born July 16, 1797; emb. Boston April 6, 1820; ar. in Ceylon, Aug. 2, 1820, but was by Sir Edward Barnes, Liut. Gov. not permitted to remain; at Bombay May 9, 1821; went out unmarried and was ten years the printer in the Mahratta mission; married as below; died of dysentery at Bombay on his birthday, July 16, 1831, age 34. Active and faithful and a severe loss to the mission.

Mrs. Garrett, (Philomela Thurston, widow of Rev. Samuel Newell, one of the first band of missionaries (supra); mar. Mr. Garrett, Bombay, March 26, 1822; left Bombay on her return to U. S. Oct. 29, 1831; ar. at Salem, March 9, 1832. She died Sept. 16, 1849. (See her letter to Rev. Rufus Anderson, dated Aug. 12, 1838.

William Cummings Sampson, New York City; born Kingston, Canada West, July 7, 1806; prof. rel. Utica, N. Y. Jan. 1831; embarked Boston Dec. 22, 1832; ar. Bombay Nov. 22, 1833; died of pulmonary consumption at Alleppie, on the Malabar coast, about 120 miles north of Cape Comorin, on his way to Ceylon, Dec. 22, 1835. He was the printer in the Mahratta mission.

Mrs. Sampson (Mary Lavanche Barker) Augusta, N. Y.; born Clinton, N. Y. Aug. 7, 1809; prof. rel. Utica, N. Y. 1826; mar. Utica, July 1831; returned to U. S. June 1836.

George W. Hubbard, born Hanover, N. H. Dec. 25, 1809; emb. with Messrs Graves, Munger and Abbott at Boston May 21, 1834; ar. Bombay Sept. 10, 1834; was superintendent of native schools; recalled June 20, 1837; returned and ar. U. States Feb. 20, 1839; dismissed from service of the Board March 12, 1839.

Mrs. Hubbard (Emma Burge) born Hollis, N. H. Nov. 5, 1809.

Elijah Ashley Webster, Utica, N. Y.; born New Hartford, Oneida Co. Feb. 20, 1813; prof. rel. Rochester, N. Y. Dec. 1830; emb. with Mr. Ballentine, Boston, May 16, 1835; ar. Bombay Oct. 11, 1835; was the printer in the Mahratta mission; recalled 1842; dismissed.

Mrs. Webster (Mariette Rawson) Victor, Ontario Co., N. Y.; born West Stockbridge, Mass. Oct. 12, 1811; prof. rel. Rochester, N. Y. Sept. 1831; mar. Victor, April 4, 1835; emb. and returned as above.

The New York copies of Vinton Books say: "no page 137, no page 145." It appears that the pages were mis-numbered in the course of their being typed (from the manuscript). This statement is on the authority of the Rev. Dr. David M. Stowe, former Executive Vice President of the United Church Board for World Ministries and now Board Archivist. Letter of June 23, 1999, to Librarian Harold F. Worthley of the Congregational Library, Boston, Massachusetts.

Cynthia Farrar, born Marlborough, N. H. April 20, 1795; prof. rel. Aug. 1815; studied at Union Academy, Plainfield, N. H.; was a teacher before leaving the country; emb. with Messrs Allen and Stone (supra) at Boston, June 5, 1827; ar. Calcutta Sept. 21, 1827; ar. Bombay Dec. 29, 1827; vis. U. S. Jan. 1837; re-emb. Salem, April 1, 1839; ar. Bombay Aug. 10, 1839; was a teacher in the service of the Board at Bombay and Ahmednuggur thirty-four years; died Ahmednuggur Jan. 25, 1862, age 67.

Harriet Sturtevant Ashley, of Milan, Ohio; born there Sept. 13, 1840; prof. rel. Milan, O. May 1856; educated at Western Fem. Sem., Oxford, O. Teacher. Sailed from New York, for Liverpool, on the way to this mission, Oct. 18, 1871; arr. at Bombay Dec. 14, 1871. Returned U. S. 1877; released 1877.

Sarah Frances Norris, M.D., born Plymouth, N. H. Dec. 8, 1833; prof. rel. April 1864, Northampton, Mass.; received Med. education at N. E. Med. Coll. for Women, Boston. Practices Medicine for some time. Sailed, New York, Sept. 13, 1873; ar. Bombay Dec. 8, 1873; stationed at Bombay; Jan. 1878, still in Bombay; returned to U. S. arr. May 8, 1881; released Nov. 22, 1881.

Martha A. Anderson, dau. of Rev. Joseph Anderson; born Shelburne, Franklin Co., Mass. June 7, 1843; prof. rel. Nov. 1864; educated at Mt. Holyoke Sem. Teacher. Sailed, Sept. 19, 1874; ar. Ahmednuggur, Nov. 27, 1874; returned to U. S. 1877; released 1877; 1888, 30 Isabella St., Boston.

William Osborn Ballantine, M.D., born Ahmednuggur, India, Feb. 9, 1849; (son of Rev. Henry and Eliz. D. Ballantine (supra), prof. rel. 1864, at Ahmednuggur; grad. Amherst Coll. 1869; grad. M.D., Medical Dept., University of New York, practiced medicine one year in Columbus, Ohio. Sailed, New York Jan. 23, 1875; ar.   Jan. 1878, stationed at Rahuri. Vis. U. S. in the spring of 1884; ordained Dorchester July 8, 1885; re-emb. N. Y. Oct. 24, 1885; arr. Bombay Dec. 14, 1885; vis. U. S. arr. N. Y. Apr. 9, 1893; re-emb. N. Y. Nov. 18, 1893; arr. Bombay Dec. 25, 1893; vis. U. S. arr. San Francisco May 31, 1903; re-emb.

Boston July 5, 1904; ret. to U. S. July 8, 1912; sailed Aug. 30 1913; arr. field Oct. 17, 1913; ret. U. S. Nov. 25, 1922. In 1925 Dr. and Mrs. Ballantine were put on the Honor Roll of Missionaries after 47 years of active service in India. Died May 3, 1929, Pasadena, Calif. at 80 years. (See Aug. Herald p. 319)

Mrs. Ballantine (Alice C. Parsons) born Easthampton, Mass. June 22, 1851; prof. rel. 1856, at Easthampton; educated at Mt. Holyoke Sem. Teacher. Mar. Jan. 6, 1875, at Easthampton, Mass.; sailed as above; ar.   Jan. 1878, in India, station Rahuri. Died 1878, Sept. 9. (See Herald Dec. 1878)

Mrs. Ballantine (Josephine L. Perkins) born Royalston, Mass. Jan. 22, 1856; prof. rel. 1875; studied Fitchburg High Sch. and Mass. State Normal Art. Sch.; taught four years in Cape Colony, So. Africa; mar. Aug. 26, 1885; emb. N. Y. Oct. 24, 1885; arr. Bombay Dec. 14, 1885; vis. U. S. arr. N. Y. Apr. 3, 1893; re-emb. N. Y. Nov. 18, 1893; arr. Bombay Dec. 25, 1893; vis. U. S. arr. N. Y. May 27, 1899; re-emb. Boston, Nov. 1, 1905; arr. home June 14, 1911; sailed Aug. 30, 1913; arr. home Nov. 25, 1922. Died Nov. 15, 1940, at Fitchburg, Mass.

Emma Katharine Ogden, M.D., born Pittsburg, Penna., Feb. 21, 1840; prof. rel. 1854; educated at Pittsburg; grad. M.D., 1875, Woman's Med. Coll., Philadelphia; practiced medicine in Pittsburg, Pa. 1 year; sailed New York Nov. 4, 1876; went out to join the Madura Mission, but was trans. to the Mahratta Mission and was stationed at Sholapur. Jan. 1878 at Sholapur; ret. to U. S. 1879.

Katie Fairbank, dau. of Rev. Samuel B. Fairbank of this mission; born Ahmednagar, India, May 8, 1859; prof. rel. March 1871; studied Mt. Holyoke Sem. and Bradford Acad.; emb. N. Y. May 14, 1882; arr. Bombay July 3. Dec. 1885 at Ahmednagar; mar. Rev. R. A. Hume, Sept. 7, 1887 (supra) Died at Wai, in April 1932.

Ruby Elizabeth Harding, dau. of Rev. Chas. Harding of this mission; born Bombay, India, Oct. 23, 1860; prof. rel. Auburndale March 1873; studied Poughkeepsie Fem. Acad. & Wellesley Coll.; emb. N. Y. May 14, 1882; arr. Bombay, July 3. Dec. 1885 at Ahmednager; married Rev. Henry Fairbank of same mission Sept. 16, 1886. (See p. 83, vol. II) Died at Ahmednagar Dec. 24, 1906. (See Miss. Herald Feb. 1907, p. 54)

MISSION IN CEYLON

Commenced 1816.

This mission is established in the district of Jaffna, in the northern extremity of the island of Ceylon. It was begun by Messrs. Richards, Warren, Meigs, and Poor, who together were ordained in the Presbyterian Church in Newburyport, June 21, 1815; the largest house of worship then in this commonwealth being filled with worshippers, whom that interesting occasion had drawn together. The four bretheren embarked at that port in the brig Dryad, Oct. 23, 1815, which vessel left them at Colombo, the principal port in Ceylon, March 22, 1816. Mr. Bardwell (see Mahratta Mission) was ordained with them, and was a companion in this voyage, but after their arrival in Ceylon, thought it best to join the mission at Bombay. Messrs. Spaulding, Woodward, Winslow, and Scudder, joined the Ceylon mission in 1819. Fourteen years more elapsed before this mission was again reinforced.

MISSIONARIES

James Richards, brother of Rev. William Richards, missionary at the Sandwich Islands, Plainfield, Mass.; born Abington, Mass. Feb. 23, 1784; prof. rel. 1803; was a classmate of Samuel John Mills in Williams College; to him and to Gordon Hall, Mills first communicated his missionary impulses; grad. Williams Coll. 1809; Andover Sem. 1812; Medical School at Philadelphia 1814; ord. (see above) June 21, 1815; emb. Newburyport, Oct. 23, 1815; ar. Colombo, Ceylon, March 22, 1816; at Batticotta Feb. 7, 1817; at Tillipally June 25, 1821; died of pulmonary disease, at Tillipally, Aug. 3, 1822. (See obituary notices Herald, vol. 19, pp. 145, 241-247, also vol. 20. pp. 233-236. Also "Memoirs of Am. Missionaries".) Buried in an enclosure on the campus of Union College, Tellipallai.

Mrs. Richards (Sarah Bardwell, sister of Rev. Horatio Bardwell (See Mahratta Mission), Goshen, Mass.; born Belchertown, Mass. Feb. 22, 1791; mar. May 1815;

emb. as above. Mar. for second husband Rev. Joseph Knight, English missionary, Nellore, So. India Sept. 17, 1823, and died Nellore April 26, 1825.

Edward Warren, Middlebury, Vt.; born Marlborough, Mass. Aug. 4, 1786; prof. rel. 1810; grad. Middlebury Coll. 1808; read law in Middlebury, after graduating till the winter of 1809-1810, when he experienced the great change; entered Andover Sem. and finished his course of study there in 1812; attended medical lectures the winter following as did Mr. Richards, at Philadelphia; ord. ut supra, Newburyport, June 21, 1815; emb. Newburyport, in brig Dryad, Oct. 23, 1815; ar. Colombo, Ceylon, March 22, 1816; at Tillipally, Ot. 15, 1816; compelled by hemorrhage from the lungs to leave the mission, Aug. 13, 1817; removed to Jaffnapatam, and in Oct. 1817 to Colombo, for the benefit of his health; and continued to languish and decline, till his death at Cape Town, South Africa, Aug. 11, 1818, age 32. (See Herald vol. 15, pp. 152-154. Also see "Memoirs of Am. Missionaries".) Never married.

Benjamin Clark Meigs, born Bethlehem, Ct. Aug. 9, 1789; prof. rel. in a revival in Yale Coll. and united with the College church 1809; grad. Yale Coll. 1809; taught school till May 1811; then entered Andover Sem. where he remained 2 1/2 years, ending Sept. 1813; ord. with Richards, Warren, and others Newburyport, June 21, 1815; emb. with them Newburyport Oct. 23, 1815; ar. Colombo, Ceylon, Mar. 22, 1816; reached Jaffna Oct. 2, 1816; after an absence from his native land of nearly 25 years, he emb. at Madras Jan. 16 and ar. Philadelphia with his family, May 9, 1840; sailed again from Boston Oct. 14, 1841, leaving wife and children in the U. States, where they ever after remained. He ar. at Colombo, Ceylon, March 15, 1842, and in Jaffna April 1. Stationed Batticotta, Tillipally, Manopy and other places; left Manopy in Oct. 1857; ret. to U. S. in 1858, and died in New York City May 12, 1862. He labored more than forty years in connection with this mission, of which he was one of the founders; and was for many years the oldest ordained missionary of the Board. (See Herald vol. 58; pp. 205,206)

Mrs. Meigs (Sarah Maria Poet) born Bethlehem, Ct. March 27, 1787; prof. rel. 1805; mar. Aug. 14, 1815; emb. as above; returned to U. S. May 3, 1840; and never went back to Ceylon.

Daniel Poor, born Danvers, Mass. June 27, 1789; prof. rel. Sept. 8, 1805; commenced study with a view to missionary labors; studied Phillips Acad., Andover; grad. Dartmouth Coll. 1811; Andover Sem. 1814; ord. Newburyport with Richards and others, ut supra, June 21, 1815; sailed with them in the Dryad, Oct. 23, 1815; ar. Colombo, Ceylon, March 22, 1816; at Tillipally, Oct. 15, 1816; Batticotta, July 1, 1823; at Batticotta, he founded a Missionary Seminary for native youth of which he was many years the principal; removed to Madura, March 16, 1836, to strengthen the new mission there, begun by Messrs. Todd and Hoisington, July 1834. He went to Tillipally, and rejoined the Ceylon mission in Oct. 1841; left for England and the U. States Feb. 1848; landed in New York Sept. 1848; preached often in this country, and by his eloquent appeals, did much to arouse a missionary spirit; re-emb. Boston Nov. 6, 1850; ar. Calcutta, March 12, 1851; at Colombo May 1851; returned to the mission May 17, 1851. From that time till his death, he resided at Tillipally. He died there of cholera, Feb. 3, 1855, only 24 hours after the first attack. He was a man of eminent ability and learning; a laborious and faithful missionary. (See Herald, vol. 51, pp. 168,169.) Buried in an enclosure on the campus of Union College, Tillipallai.

Mrs. Poor (Susan Bulfinch) born Boston, on Bulfinch St., Dec. 1, 1789; mar. Danvers, Oct. 9, 1815; emb. ut supra; died at Tillipally May 7, 1821. See a very interesting account of her last hours, Herald, vol. 18, pp. 94-96 and 121-127. (Bulfinch Street named for her father.)

Mrs. Poor (Ann Knight, sister of Rev. Joseph Knight of the church Missionary Society, Nellore, Ceylon, and of Rev. Charles Knight, Church Missionary in Sierra Leone, who died there in 1825) born in the county of Gloucester, Eng. Sept. 10, 1790; prof. rel. 1806; left England for Ceylon to assist her brother

in the mission, 1821; mar. Jan. 21, 1823; visited U. S. with her husband, Sept. 1848; re-emb. Nov. 6, 1850; after his death returned to England, 1856.

Miron Winslow was a member of this mission from 1819 till 1836, when he became connected with the Madras Mission.

Levi Spaulding, born Jaffrey, N. H. Aug. 22, 1791; prof. rel. Jaffrey Sept. 1815, having experienced conversion in the remarkable revival of that year in Dartmouth College; grad. Dart. Coll. 1815; Andover Theol. Sem. 1818; ord. with Messrs Fisk, Winslow and Woodward, at Salem, Nov. 4, 1818; emb. Boston, June 8, 1819; ar. Calcutta Oct. 19; reached Ceylon Dec. 1, 1819; Jaffnapatam Feb. 18, 1820; Oodooville, June 15, 1820; Manepy Aug. 25, 1821; Tillipally Aug. 25, 1828; Oodooville again March 8, 1833. He has spent half a century, nearly, of his life in Ceylon, with the exception of a visit to U. S. 1844-1846, and is now, 1869, the oldest living missionary of the Board. He vis. U. S. 1844; re-emb. Boston Nov. 15, 1846; ar. Ceylon March 1847. Died June 18, 1873, at Oodooville. (Obit. Miss. Herald Oct. 1873.)

Mrs. Spaulding (Mary Christie) born Antrim, N. H. Oct. 24, 1795; prof. rel. 1815; studied Bradford Academy, Mass.; mar. Antrim Dec. 10, 1818. Died Oct. 28, 1874, at Batticotta.

Henry Woodward, son of Prof. Bezaleel and Mary (Wheelock) Woodward, and grandson of Dr. Eleazar Wheelock, the founder and first President of Dartmouth College; born at Hanover, N. H. Feb. 3, 1797; prof. rel. Hanover, May 1815, one of the fruits of the revival of that spring; grad. Dart. Coll. 1815; Princeton Sem. 1818; (there only 2 years); ord. Salem, with Messrs. Fisk, Spaulding, and others, Nov. 4, 1818; emb. Boston June 8, 1819; ar. Calcutta, Oct. 19; ar. Batticotta in Ceylon Feb. 3, 1820; Tillipally June 30, 1823; moved to Manepy April 3, 1829; Batticotta again March 8, 1833; went to NeilgherryHills on the continent in pursuit of health, which had been impaired for a year or two; left the Hills, proposing to visit the new station at Madura, but died at Coimbatoor, on the way, Aug. 3, 1834.

The New York copies of Vinton Books say: "no page 137, no page 145." It appears that the pages were mis-numbered in the course of their being typed (from the manuscript). This statement is on the authority of the Rev. Dr. David M. Stowe, former Executive Vice President of the United Church Board for World Ministries and now Board Archivist. Letter of June 23, 1999, to Librarian Harold F. Worthley of the Congregational Library, Boston, Massachusetts.

Mrs. Woodward (Lydia Middleton) born Crosswicks, N. J. Aug. 3, 1795; prof. rel. Trenton, 1816; mar. Trenton, Nov. 18, 1818; died Tillipally, Ceylon, Nov. 24, 1825.

Mrs. Woodward (Clarissa (Emerson) Frost, widow of Rev. Edmund Frost of the Mahratta Mission, and sister of Rev. John S. Emerson, missionary to Sandwich Islands); born Chester, N. H. Nov.13, 1798; mar. Mr. Woodward Oct. 12, 1826. After his death she mar. Dec..22, 1830, Rev. William Todd, of the Madura Mission. She died June 1, 1837.

John Scudder, M.D. was a member of this mission from 1819 till 1836, when, along with Mr. Winslow, he founded the Madras mission.

No more missionaries were sent by the Board to Ceylon till 1833.

George Henry Apthorp, born Quincy, Mass. May 31, 1798; prof. rel. Yale College, July 1827, converted in a revival there; grad. Yale Coll. 1829 ; Princeton Sem. 1832; appt. Feb. 13, 1832; ord. Norfolk, Va. June 16, 1832; emb. with Messrs. Hoisington, Todd, Hutchings, and Dr. Ward, Boston, July 1, 1833; Madras, Oct. 12, 1833; at Jaffna Oct. 26, 1833; stationed successively at Panditeripo 1834, Varany 1836; and died at Valverty, Ceylon June 8, 1844.

Mrs. Apthorp (Mary Robertson) born Albemarle Co., Virginia March 10, 1808; prof. rel. April 1825; mar. Amelia Co., Va. June 10, 1833 . Died at Panditeripo Sept. 3, 1843. (See obituary, Herald vol. 46, p. 76)

William Todd (See Madura Mission)

Henry Richard Hoisington, Aurora, Cayuga Co., N. Y.; born Vergennes, Vt. Aug. 23, 1801; grad. Williams Coll. 1828; Auburn Sem. 1831; ord. Pastor Aurora, Aug. 1831; pastor there nearly two years.; appt. Feb. 13, 1833; emb. with Messrs Apthorp, Hutchings and others, at Boston, July 1, 1833; ar. in Ceylon, Oct. 26, 1833; stayed there till July 1834. Messrs Hoisington and Todd, in-

troduced by Mr. Spaulding (supra) who had previously examined the territory, commenced the Madura mission, July 31, 1834. Shortly after, Feb. 1835, Mr. Hoisington returned to Batticotta, Ceylon, and succeeded Mr. Poor as principal of the Seminary. He visited the U. S. June 3, 1842; re-emb. Boston May 6, 1844; ar. Madras, Sept. 5, 1844; resumed his former duties at Batticotta; returned to U. States, March 5, 1850; released Jan. 31, 1854. Died May 16, 1858, Saybrook, Conn.

Mrs. Hoisington (Nancy Lyman) Aurora, N. Y.; born Chester, Mass. April 12, 1804; prof. rel. Sept. 1819; mar. Chester, Sept. 21, 1831; emb. July 1, 1833; vis. U. S. 1842; re-emb. May 1844; returned to U. S. March 5, 1850. Died Cleveland, Ohio, March 29, 1878. (See Herald, June 1878) (A son, Rev. Henry R. Hoisington is (1878) a Pr. pastor in Cleveland.)

Samuel Hutchings, born New York City, Sept. 15, 1806; prof. rel. there April 1822; grad. Williams Coll. 1828; Princeton Sem. 1831; ord. Elyria, O. Nov. 8, 1831; appt. Dec. 18, 1832; emb. with Messrs Hoisington and others at Boston, July 1, 1833; ar. in Ceylon, Oct. 28, 1833; at Oodooville 1834; Varany 1835; Chavagachery 1837; Manepy 1840; at Madras two years, 1842-1844; returned U.S. 1844; released 1847; 1877 at Newark, N. J., engaged in teaching; 1888 Orange, N. J. Died in East Orange Sept. 1, 1895.

Mrs. Hutchings (Elizabeth Coit Lathrop, dau. of Charles and Joanna Lathrop, and sister of the first Mrs. Winslow (see Madras Mission), Mrs. Perry (infra), and Mrs. Cherry see Madura Mission), New York City; born New London, Ct. April 16, 1813; prof. rel. Norwich, Ct. 1828; mar. New Haven, Ct. Sept. 18, 1831.

Nathan Ward, M.D., Durham, N. H.; born Plymouth, N. H. Nov. 21, 1804; prof. rel. Brownington, Vt. 1821; studied medicine at Hanover, N. H. and Brunswick, Me.; had degree of M.D. from Bowdoin Coll. 1832; emb. with Apthorp, Hoisington,

and others, at Boston, July 1, 1833; ar. Ceylon Oct. 29, 1833; stationed at Batticotta, and one of the instructors of the Seminary there; returned to U. S. 1847; released 1848; re-appointed Nov. 15, 1859; emb. Boston for Madras Nov. 1, 1860; died very suddenly on the passage, Nov. 25, 1860, and buried in the ocean.

Mrs. Ward (Hannah Woodward Clark, sister of Rev. Ephraim W. Clark, missionary at Sandwich Islands) born Peacham, Vt. 1804: prof. rel. 1818; mar. Greenboro, Vt. Jan. 6, 1833; emb. Boston July 1, 1833; returned U. S. 1847; released 1848; re-app. Nov. 15, 1859; re-emb. Nov. 1, 1860; ar. Madras, March 11, 1861; ar. Jaffna April 21, 1861; returned to U. S. July 24, 1865. Died at Richmond, Ill. Feb. 3, 1884.

James René Eckard, born Philadelphia, Pa. Nov. 22, 1805; prof. rel. Sept. 1829; grad. University of Pennsylvania 1823; studied at Princeton Sem. and with Rev. Dr. Skinner, then of Phila.; ord. Philad. July 21, 1833; emb. Salem, Oct. 29, 1833; stationed at Batticotta, March 5, 1834; transferred to Madura Feb. 9, 1835; returned to Ceylon 1837, and located at Pamiiteripo; teacher in the Seminary at Batticotta 1839; left the island Sept. 1843; returned to U.S. Nov. 6, 1843; released Nov. 12, 1844; 1858-1873, prof. in Lafayette Coll, Easton, Penn. 1877 in Germantown, Penn.

Mrs. Eckard (Margaret Esther Bayard) Savannah, Ga.; born Cumberland Island, Ga. Oct. 18, 1810; prof. rel. Philadelphia June 1828; mar. Savannah May 26, 1833.

John MacStrong Perry, son of Rev. David Lord Perry of Sharon, Ct. and grandson of Rev. David Perry of Harwinton, Ct. and Richmond, Mass. and of Rev. Nathan Strong of Hartford, Ct., Mendon, Mass.; born Sharon, Ct. Sept. 7, 1806; prof. rel. Sept. 1825; grad. Yale Coll. 1827; New Haven Sem. 1831; ord. pastor, Mendon, Nov. 9, 1831; pastor 3 1/2 years; appt'd. Nov. 4, 1834; embarked Boston May 16, 1835; ar. in Jaffna Sept. 24, 1835; stationed at Batticotta 1836; died of cholera March 10, 1837.

Mrs. Perry (Harriet Joanna Lathrop, sister of Mrs. Hutchings (supra), of the first Mrs. Winslow (see Madras Mission) and of Mrs. Cherry (see Madura Mission), Menlon, Mo.; born Norwich, Ct. Sept. 3, 1816; prof. rel. Norwich 1827, only eleven years old; mar. Aug. 11, 1833. Died at Batticotta, Ceylon of cholera March 13, 1837, three days after her husband.

Samuel Goodrich Whittlesey, son of Rev. Samuel Whittlesey; New York City; born New Preston, Ct. Nov. 8, 1809; prof. rel. Boston May 1827; grad. Yale Coll. 1834; tutor there 1836-1838; New Haven Sem. 1840; ord. New Haven, Ct. Feb. 10, 1841; emb. Boston with Mr. Meigs (supra) and others, Oct. 14, 1841; ar. at Colombo, March 15, 1842; in Jaffna April 1, 1842; stationed at Manepy April 1842; at Chavagacherry Jan. 17, 1843; took charge of the Female Boarding School, Oodooville, early in 1844; died of inflammatory fever, at Dindegul, on the neighboring continent, March 10, 1847.

Mrs. Whittlesey (Anna Cook Mills) born Morristown, N. J. Feb. 10, 1820; prof. rel. June 1832; mar. Sept. 29, 1841; emb. as above; returned to U. S. 1848.

Edward Cope, Louisville, N. Y.; born New Lisbon, Otsego Co., N. Y. May 25, 1806; prof. rel. Cooperstown, N. Y. 1827; studied 3 years in Centre Coll., Ky.; Auburn Sem. 1836; ord. Clinton, N. Y. June 7, 1836; emb. Boston Nov. 23, 1836; ar. Madura, May 10, 1837; three years a member of the Madura Mission; transferred to Ceylon Mission Jan. 1840; returned to U. S. April 30, 1843; released 1850; 1860, Gilbertsville, N. Y.; 1877 ditto.
Mrs. Cope (Emily Kilbourn) Marshall, N.Y. Mar. Oct. 29, 1836.

John Curtis Smith, brother of Rev. Asa B. Smith, missionary to the Indians in Oregon and Sandwich Islands; born Williamstown, Vt. Sept. 24, 1812; prof. rel. Nov. 1831; grad. Middlebury Coll. 1838; Andover Sem. 1841; ord. Sept. 29, 1841; emb. with Messrs Meigs, Whittlesey and Wyman, Boston, Oct. 14, 1841; ar. Colombo March 15, and at Jaffna April 1, 1842; stationed at Manepy May 1842; Varany, March 1844; Panditeripo May 1845; continued there till his visit to U.S.

1857; re-emb. with Dr. Ward, (supra) and others, Boston, Oct. 30, 1860; ar. Madras March 11, 1861; reached Jaffna April 21, 1861; stationed at Oodoopitty, 1861; was there 1868; vis. U. S. July 1872; released 1874; 1878, at Winchester, N. H. Died at Hartford, Conn. March 21, 1884.

Mrs. Smith (Eunice Taft Morse) born Paxton, Mass. April 15, 1815; prof. rel. Holden April 1831; mar. Oct. 7, 1841; emb. Oct. 14, 1841; died of a decline, at Batticotta, May 9, 1842.

Mrs. Smith (the widow of Dr. John Steele of the Madura Mission, originally Mary Snell) born Plainfield, Mass. Sept. 21, 1814; mar. Mr. Smith Oct. 13, 1843. She died of pneumonia at Rocky Hill, Ct. May 14, 1873. (Obit. Miss. Herald August 1873)

Robert Wyman, Cumberland, Me.; born North Yarmouth, Me. Aug. 31, 1814; prof. rel. Cumberland, 1830; grad. Bowdoin Coll. 1838; Bangor Sem. 1841; ord. Bangor Aug. 26, 1841; emb. with Mr. Meigs and others, ut supra, Boston, Oct. 14, 1841; ar. Colombo March 15, 1842; ar. Jaffna April 1, 1842; stationed at Batticotta as instructor in the Seminary; emb. at Madras for the U. S. for the benefit of his health, Dec. 27, 1844. Died on the passage, Jan. 13, 1845, and was buried in the deep. (See Obituary, Herald, vol. 41, p. 240) (He was born in that part of North Yarmouth, which is now Cumberland.)

Mrs. Wyman (Martha Emmons Weston, dau. of Rev. Isaac Weston of Cumberland, Me.) North Edgecomb, Me.; born Portland, Me. Dec. 8, 1813; prof. rel. Cumberland 1830; mar. Sept. 22, 1841; emb. Boston Oct. 14, 1841; returned to U. S. May 4, 1845.

Adin Haywood Fletcher, Quincy, Illinois; born Littleton, Mass. April 9, 1816; prof. rel. Boxborough, Mass. 1836; grad. Mission Institute near Quincy, Ill. 1845; ord. Boxboro, Mass. Oct. 15, 1845; emb. Boston with Mr. Howland (infra) and others, Nov. 12, 1845; ar. Madras March 28, 1846; ar. Jaffna, June 1, 1846; stationed at Chavacherry 1846; at Manepy 1847; at Tillipally 1848; returned to U. S. 1850; released Oct. 29, 1850; Since 1864, pastor at Pontiac, Michigan.

1878 at Portland, Mich. Died at Armada, Mich. Feb. 8, 1880.

Mrs. Fletcher (Elizabeth Winslow Safford) Quincy, Ill.; born New Ipswich, N. H. May 9,.1819; prof. rel. 1831; mar. Quincy, May 13, 1845; emb. and returned as above. Died in Armada, Mich. Aug. 29, 1881.

William Ware Howland, Worcester, Mass.; born West Brookfield, Mass.Feb. 25, 1817; prof. rel. Heath, Mass. 1832; grad. Amherst Coll. 1841; Union Theol. Sem. N. York 1845; ord. South Hadley, Mass. Oct. 14, 1845; emb. with Mr. Fletcher and others, ut supra, Nov. 12, 1845; ar. Madras March 28, 1846; ar. Jaffna May 1846; stationed at Batticotta from 1846 to his visit to U. S. in 1857; re-emb. Boston May 26, 1862; ar. Madras Sept. 26, 1862; resumed his station at Batticotta soon after; removed thence to Tillipally 1868; there 1873. Jan. 1878, still in Ceylon; Station Tillipally. Died in Jaffna, Aug. 26, 1892. (See Miss. Herald for Nov. 1892, p. 435)

Mrs. Howland (Susan Reed) born Heath, Mass. Oct. 2, 1813; prof. rel. July 1837; studied Mt. Holyoke Fem. Sem.; mar. South Hadley Oct. 14, 1845; emb. Nov. 12, 1845; vis. U. S. 1857; re-emb. May 26, 1862. Jan. 1878, still in Ceylon. Station, Tillipally. Died at Oodooville, July 23, 1887. (See notice in Sept. 1887 Herald, p. 349)

William Waterbury Scudder was a member of the Ceylon Mission from 1846 to 1853, when he was transferred to Arcot. His first wife died while in connection with the mission to Ceylon. 1873, present time (May 1878) p. at Glastonbury, Conn. Died Glastonbury Mar. 4, 1895.

Mrs. Scudder (Catharine Eunice Hastings) (See Arcot Mission) Died March 11, 1849.

Eurotas Parmelee Hastings, born Clinton, N. Y. April 17, 1821; prof. rel. autumn of 1838, after a revival; grad. Hamilton Coll. 1842; Union Sem., N.Y. 1846; ord. Clinton, Oct. 6, 1846; emb. with Mr. Spaulding (supra) Dr.Scudder (see Madras Mission) and others, at Boston, Nov. 18, 1846; went out unmarried; ar. Madras March 17, 1847; at Batticotta from 1847 to 1850, when he removed to Manepy; visited U. States, March 12, 1852; re-emb. with Mrs. Hastings, June 2, 1853; ar. Madras Sept. 17, and Batticotta, Oct. 16, 1853; removed to Chavagacherry 1855; to Manepy 1858; still there 1868; visited U. S. 1869; sailed with wife from Boston for Liverpool, on the way to Ceylon Oct. 31, 1871; ar. Ceylon Jan. 10, 1872; Jan. 1878, still in Ceylon; station Batticotta; vis. U. S. arr. June 17, 1881; re-emb. N. Y. Aug. 10, 1882; arr. Jaffna Oct. 13. Dec. 1885 at Batticotta. Died at Manepy July 31, 1890. (See Nov. Herald 1890, p. 442)

Mrs. Hastings (Anna Cleveland, dau. of Rev. Richard F. Cleveland of Fayetteville, N. Y.) Clinton, N. Y.; born Windham, Ct. July 9, 1830; mar. Clinton, March 9, 1853; emb. June 2, 1853; vis. U. S. 1869; ret. as above. Jan. 1878, in India. Station Batticotta. Vis. U. S. arr. June 17, 1881; re-emb. N. Y. Aug. 10, 1882; arr. Jaffna Oct. 13. Dec. 1885 at Batticotta. Returned to U. S. arr. N. Y. May 27, 1891; released Oct. 2, 1891. Died Hartford, Ct. June 23, 1909. (See Oct. 1909 Herald, p. 413)

Joseph Thomas Noyes and Mrs. Noyes, were members of the Ceylon Mission from 1849 till 1853, when they were transferred to the Madura Mission (infra).

Cyrus Taggart Mills and Mrs. Mills were members of the Ceylon Mission from 1849 to 1854. More recently they were connected with the mission to the Sandwich Islands, (infra). 1877, in Brooklyn, Cal. Died at Oakland, Cal. April 1884.

Marshall Danforth Sanders, born Williamstown, Mass. July 3, 1823; prof. rel. there 1840; grad. Williams Coll. 1846; Auburn Sem. 1851; ord. Williamstown

July 17, 1851; emb. Boston Oct. 31, 1851; ar. Madras, Feb. 21, 1852; reached Ceylon March 12, 1852; stationed Chavagacherry, 1852; Tillipally 1856; Batticotta 1857; continued there till his visit to U. States; ar. in U. S. July 24, 1865; re-emb. Boston for Ceylon by way of England Oct. 9, 1867; reached Batticotta Dec. 18, 1867; visited U. S. 1869; sailed with second wife from New York for Liverpool by steamer May 10, 1871; arr. Batticotta July 4. Died there of apoplexey Aug. 23, 1871. (Spent several months of labor in U. S. 1870-1 in raising funds for a college in Ceylon.) (See Obituary notice in Miss. Herald for Dec. 1871.)

Mrs. Sanders (Georgiana Knight, daughter of Rev. Joseph Knight) Peru, Mass.; born West Stafford, Ct. June 15, 1825; prof. rel. Peru Sept. 1846; mar. Peru Sept. 4, 1851; emb. Boston Oct. 31, 1851; visited U. S. July 1865; re-emb. Boston Oct. 9, 1867; reached Batticotta Dec. 18, 1867; died Nov. 2, 1868.

Mrs. Sanders (Caroline Z. Webb) of Adams, N. Y.; born there Feb. 18, 1840; mar. April 6, 1870; sailed from New York for Liverpool on the way to Ceylon May 10, 1871; returned to U. S. a few weeks after the death of her husband, 1868 at Auburndale, Mass.

Nathan Lynde Lord, M.D., Hudson, O.; born Norwich, Ct. Dec. 8, 1821; prof. rel. Ellsworth, O. Jan. 1843; grad. Western Reserve Coll. Hudson, 1845; studied divinity one year and seven months at the Seminary in that place; after which he was agent and financial secretary of the college. Licensed to preach Mar. 6, 1849; ord. Hudson Oct. 12, 1852; emb. Boston Dec. 13. 1852; ar. Jaffna June 9, 1853; stationed at Oodoopitty; remained there till 1858. Prostrate in health, he went to Madras May 1858; and with his family embarked at that port Sept. 27, 1859, by the overland route to England; and reached New York Dec. 8, 1859; After his return, he attended medical lectures in Cleveland, Ohio, where he received the degree of M.D.; afterwards, in Brooklyn and New York. He re-emb. Boston, July 1, 1863, with a view to join the Madura mission; the voyage was long and

very injurious to his health; ar. Madras Dec. 7, 1863. Sailed from Madras, March 29, 1867; reached England, May 3 and New York June 20. Spent some months in New York and died there Jan. 24, 1868.

Mrs. Lord (Laura Weld Delano) Hudson, O.; born Stowe, Vt. Dec. 11, 1827; prof. rel. Hudson, May 1848; a teacher before marriage; mar. Stowe, Vt. Aug. 11, 1850; emb. as above; returned to U. S. June 26, 1867; released Jan. 26, 1869. 1886 at Hudson, O. Died May 20, 1915 at Hudson, O. (See Miss. Herald July 1915, p. 345)

Milan Hubbard Hitchcock, North Bergen, Genesee Co., N. Y.; born Marshall, Oneida Co., N. Y. Jan. 27, 1831; prof. rel. Brockport, N. Y. Dec. 1849; grad. Amherst Coll. 1854; Bangor Sem. 1857; ord. North Bergen Aug. 25, 1857; emb. Boston, Nov. 23, 1857; with Mr. Quick, infra; ar. Madras March 15, 1858; reached Jaffna April 28, 1858. Took charge of Tillipally Jan. 1859. Returned to U. S. Jan. 17, 1861; released . (Afterwards, he was pastor in Westminster, Mass. 1862-1867; dismissed Feb. 20, 1867; then acting pastor at Winchendon, Mass. 1867-1869.) Re-appointed, and designated to Western Turkey Mission Jan. 26, 1869. At Hubbardston, Mass. 1903. Died Jan. 28, 1910 at Winchendon, Mass.

Mrs. Hitchcock (Lucy Ann Rice, dau. of Rev. Benjamin Rice, of New Gloucester, Me. and Winchendon, Mass.) Winchendon, Mass.; born South Deerfield, Mass. Sept. 26, 1827; prof. rel. Westminster, Mass. 1851; mar. Winchendon Sept. 24, 1857; emb. Boston Nov. 23, 1857; suffered greatly from ill health in Ceylon; returned U. S. Jan. 1861. Re-app. Jan. 26, 1869. Died Nov. 3, 1912 at Winchendon, Mass.

James Quick, Birmingham, Mich.; born Royal Oak, Oakland Co., Mich. Aug. 26, 1823; prof. rel. March 1847; grad. Univ. of Michigan 1854; studied theology two years Union Theol. Sem., N. Y.; ord. Washington, Tazewell Co., Illinois April 1857;

emb. with Mr. Hitchcock (supra) Boston, Nov. 23, 1857; ar Madras March 15, 1858; reached Jaffna April 30, 1858; removed to Batticotta March 1, 1859; Panilterippo 186 - 70; returned to U. S. Nov. 27, 1868. Released 1870. 1877, Bryan, Ohio. 1888 Birmingham, Mich.; died June 16, 1889 at Pomona, Cal. (See Herald Sept. 1889, p.380)

Mrs. Quick (Maria Elizabeth Thacher) Birmingham, Mich.; born Kendall, Orleans Co., N. Y. Nov. 16, 1833; prof. rel. 1846; studied Ohio Female Coll.; mar. College Hill, Ohio, July 2, 1857; emb. Boston Nov. 23, 1857; returned to U. S. Nov. 27, 1868. Released 1870.

James Atwood Bates, Son of Rev. James and Emily (Atwood) Bates of Newton and Granby, Mass. and nephew of Harriet Newell (see Mission to Mahratta); born Newton, Mass, May 2, 1832; prof. rel. Granby Sept. 1848; grad. Amherst Coll. 1856; Andover Sem. 1860; ord. Granby Sept. 13, 1860; emb. Boston Nov. 1, 1860; ar. Madras March 11, 1861; ar. Jaffna April 21, 1861; stationed at Chavagacherry. Left the field Oct. 1863. Returned to U. S. Dec. 21, 1863; released July 25, 1865. (Afterwards, active pastor, Huntington, Mass. 1866; and Belpre, O. 1867.) 1878, at Wolcott, Vt. 1887 Williston, Vt. 1902 So. Royalston, Mass. Died Sept. 3, 1916 at South Royalston, Mass.

Mrs. Bates (Sarah Adams Tobey, dau. of Rev. Alvan Tobey of Durham, N. H.); born Charlestown, Mass. Aug. 20, 1836; prof. rel. Durham Sept. 1857; studied at Bradford Academy; mar. Durham, Oct. 25, 1860; emb. Boston, Nov. 1, 1860; returned U. S. Dec. 21, 1863; released July 25, 1865; 1887 Williston, Vt.

William Edward DeRiemer, Berlin, Wis.; born Springfield, Ill. May 5, 1839; prof. rel. Berlin, summer of 1856; studied Lawrence Univ., Appleton, Wis.; grad. Amherst Coll. 1862; Chicago Theol. Sem. 1867; appt. March 13, 1867; ord. with four other foreign missionaries, whose names were Carrie C. Thayer (Central Turkey Mission), Spencer R. Wells (Mahratta Mission). William H. Atkinson (Mahratta Mission), Samuel E. Evans, in Chicago April 18, 1867; emb. Boston Oct. 28, 1868; ar. Batticotta March 16, 1869; Jan. 1878, still in Ceylon, Station, Oodoopitty.

Returned to U. S. May 29, 1878. Formally released Jan. 13, 1879. 1887, Miles, Iowa.

Mrs. DeRiemer (Emily Frances True, daughter of Rev. Charles K. True of the Methodist connection) Newton, Mass.; born Boston, Mass. July 7, 1842; prof. rel. July 4, 1857; studied Abbot Fem. Sem., Andover, and Mansfield Fem. Sem., Middletown, Ct.; mar. Newton Upper Falls, Mass. Sept. 1, 1868; emb. ut supra. Jan. 1878, still in Ceylon. Station, Oodoopitty..
1887 Miles, Iowa.

Thomas Snell Smith, son of Rev. John C. Smith of this mission (supra); born in Ceylon (Varany, Jaffna) Jan. 24, 1845; prof. rel. Jan. 1859; prepared at Monson Acad., Mass.; grad. Amh. Coll. 1866; studied theology at Bangor and Andover seminaries; grad. Andover 1869; preached at Charlemont, Mass. some months, 1869-1870; ord. Concord, Ill. March 21, 1871; sailed from New York with Rev. M. D. Sanders(supra) by steamer for Liverlpool, on the way to Ceylon, May 10, 1871; ar. Batticotta July 4, 1871; Jan. 1878, still in Ceylon. Station, Manepy. Vis. U.S. ar. N. Y. Apr. 22, 1886; re-emb. N. Y. Oct. 22, 1887; arr. Tillipally Jan. 12, 1888. Vis. U. S. arr. June 20, 1898. Died at Easthampton, Mass. Dec. 16, 1900. (See Herald Feb. 1901)

Mrs. Smith (Emily Maria Fairbank) daughter of Rev. S. B. Fairbank of the Mahratta Mission; born Ahmednuggur, India, Nov. 21, 1846; prof. rel. Concord, Ill. 1860; educated at Rockvill Fem. Sem. and Wisconsin Fem. Coll. Teacher. Mar. March 21, 1871 at Concord, Ill. Sailed as above. Jan. 1878, still in Ceylon, Station Manepy. Vis. U. S. arr. N. Y. Apr. 22, 1886; re-emb. N. Y. Oct. 22, 1887; arr. Tillipally Jan. 12, 1888; vis. U. S. arr. June 20, 1898. Died in Waban, Mass. 1935.

Samuel Whittlesey Howland, son of Rev. W. W. Howland (supra); born Batticotta, Ceylon, March 4, 1848; prof. rel. Conway, Mass. Sept. 1864; grad. Amherst Coll. 1870; grad. Union Sem. 1873; ordl 1873, May 7. Sailed New York May 10, 1873; ar. Ceylon Aug. 1873; Jan. 1878 in Ceylon, Station Oodooville. Vis. U. S. arr. N.Y.

Feb. 21, 1885; re-emb. New York April 10, 1886; temporarily transferred to Madura, Nov. 20, 1888; vis. U. S. arr. N. Y., Apr. 22, 1895; re-emb. N. Y. Sept. 5, 1896; arr. Jaffna Oct. 15, 1896; vis. U. S. arr. N. Y. Oct. 23, 1897; released Dec. 28, 1897. Went to professorship Talladega Coll., Alabama 1901-2. 1903 went to Atlanta Theol. Sem. as professor. Died at Atlanta, Ga. April 6, 1912. (See Miss. Herald June 1912, p. 265)

Mrs. Howland (Mary E. K. Richardson) born N. Y. C.
prof. rel.   ; educated   ; mar. April 29, 1873.
Engaged in City Mission work in New York, eight years. Sailed as above. Ar. Ceylon, August 1873; Jan. 1878 at Oodooville. Vis. U. S. arr. N. Y. Feb. 21, 1885; re-emb. N. Y. April 10, 1886; temporarily transferred to Madura, Nov. 20, 1888; vis. U. S. Arr. N. Y. April 22, 1895; re-emb. N. Y. Sept. 5, 1896; arr. Jaffna Oct. 15, 1896; vis. U. S. arr. N. Y. Oct. 23, 1897; released Dec. 28, 1897. Died Atlanta, Ga. Nov. 17, 1903. (See Jan. 1904 Herald, p. 6)

Mrs. Howland (Ella Deane) Married Brockton, Mass. September 5, 1906..

Richard Cleveland Hastings, son of Rev. Eurotas P. Hastings of this mission; born Batticotta, Jaffna, March 27, 1854; prof. rel. Cincinnati Oct. 7, 1866; grad. Hamilton College 1875, Auburn Theol. Sem. 1878; ord. Clinton, N. Y. April 9, 1878; emb. N. Y. Oct. 26, 1878; arr. Jaffna Jan. 22, 1879; Dec. 1885 at Oodoopitty. Vis. U. S. arr. N. Y. May 27, 1891; re-emb. N. Y. Aug. 12, 1893; arr. Udupitty Oct. 6.; vis. U. S. arr. Boston July 9, 1904. Released Aug. 14, 1905. Appt'd Pres. of Straight Univ. and assumed the office Oct. 1st 1905. May 1912 at New Windsor, Maryland. Died at New Windsor, Md. on Jan. 18, 1922. (See Miss. Herald 1922, p. 121))

Mrs. Hastings (Minnie Blanchard Trunx) born Cincinnati, O., Feb. 22, 1855; prof. rel. Madison, Ind. Feb. 1873; studied common and private schools; emb. Aug. 10, 1882; arr. Jaffna Oct. 13; mar. Batticotta Aug. 10, 1883; Dec. 1885 at Oodoopitty. Vis. U. S. arr. N. Y. May 27, 1891; re-emb. N. Y. Aug. 12, 1893; arr. Udupitty

Oct. 6, 1893; vis. U. S. arr. N. Y. June 21, 1900; re-emb. N. Y. Nov. 3, 1900; vis. U. S. arr. Boston July 9, 1904; released Aug. 14, 1906. Died at New Windsor, . March 2, 1921. (See Miss. Herald 1921, page 152)

Missionary Physician

Samuel Fiske Green, M.D., born Worcester, Mass. Oct. 10, 1822; prof. rel. N.Y. April 1841; for a time a practicing physician in Worcester; emb. Boston April 20, 1847; ar. Madras Sept. 1, 1847; ar. Ceylon Oct. 1847; stationed at Batticotta; went out unmarried. Visited U. S. July 21, 1858; emb. with wife, Boston, May 26, 1862; ar. Madras Sept. 26, 1862; at Ceylon soon after. Station Manepy. Returned U. S. 1873. Released 1877. Died at Worcester, Mass. May 28, 1884. (See Herald July 1884, p. 284)

Mrs. Green (Margaret Phelps Williams) Worcester, Mass.; born Pomfret, Ct. July 16, 1836; prof. rel. Worcester Jan. 1855; teacher in Worcester; mar. Worcester, May 22, 1862; emb. ut supra. Ret. U. S. 1873. Released 1877. 1888 at Worcester, Mass. Died March 20, 1927. (See Herald July 1927, page 213)

ASSISTANT MISSIONARIES

Eastman Strong Minor, printer, New Haven, Ct.; born Milford, Ct. July 6, 1809; prof. rel. New Haven, July 1828; acquired the printer's art at New Haven, with Dea. Nathan Whiting, office of the Religious Intelligencer; emb. with Mr. Eckard, (supra) Salem, Oct. 29, 1833; ar. Ceylon, March 5, 1834; station, Manepy till 1850; after that Batticotta; returned to U. S. July 8, 1851; released Feb. 17, 1852; Seventeen years printer to the mission.

Mrs. Minor (Lucy Bailey) Boston; born New Ipswich, N. H. July 18, 1809; prof. rel. Essex St. Church, Boston 1831; mar. Boston Aug. 27, 1833; emb. Oct. 29, 1833; died of consumption Manepy June 23, 1837.

Mrs. Minor (Judith M. Taylor) born Madison, N. Y. Nov. 2, 1815; emb. unmarried with Messrs Caswell, Benham, and others, to join the mission to Siam; Boston

July 6, 1839; mar. at Singapore Dec. 18, 1839; returned to U. S. July 8, 1851. Returned to India 1873 (See Madura Mission) 1888 Andover, Mass.

Eliza Agnew, born New York City Feb. 2, 1807; prof. rel. in Dr. McCartee's church, N. York Jan. 1824; emb. with Mr. Hunt of the Madras Mission, Boston, July 30, 1839; ar. Colombo Dec. 31, 1839; ar. Jaffna, Jan. 27, 1840. Now and for many years, the faithful teacher of the Female Boarding School at Oodooville. Jan. 1878, still at Oodooville. Died at Oodooville June 14, 1883. (See Miss. Herald p. 329, Sept. 1883)

Sarah Freeman Brown, Newark, N.J.; born Woodbridge, N. J. Oct. 5, 1805; prof. rel. Rahway, N. J. July 1825; emb. Boston with Miss Agnew and others, July 30, 1839; ar. Colombo Dec. 31, 1839; ar. Jaffna Jan. 27, 1840; returned to U. S. Aug. 9, 1841; released 1841.

Jane Eleanor Lathrop, of Bozrah, Ct. went out unmarried in the same vessel, the Black Warrior, from Boston, July 30, 1839; and mar. Rev. Henry Cherry 1840 of the Madura Mission. Died Jan. 19, 1844.

Mary Ann Capell, of Jersey, O. went out unmarried and was a teacher in the Female Boarding School at Oodooville 1846-1847; mar. Rev. Clarendon F. Muzzey of the Madura Mission Feb. 1, 1848.

Thomas Scott Burnell and Mrs. Burnell, were members of the Ceylon Mission from 1849-1855, and then transferred to Madura Mission.

Harriet Eliza Townsend, Tabor, Fremont County, Iowa; born Avon, Lorain Co., Ohio Dec. 13, 1841; prof. rel. Tabor April 1856; emb. with Mr. Sanders (supra) Boston Oct. 9, 1867, by way of England and the overland route; ar. Batticotta Dec. 18, 1867; Ret. U. S. 1877; returned to Ceylon Oct. 19, 1878. Died at Oodoopitty, Jaffna, Aug. 15, 1882.

Maggie Webster, Binghamton, N. Y.; born Hamilton, Canada West, Oct. 26, 1846; prof.

rel. Rochester, N. Y. June 1860; for some time teacher of Freedmen at
Petersburg, Va.; emb. with Mr. DeRiemer and other, Boston, Oct. 28, 1868; ar.
Batticotta, March 16, 1869; mar. to an English missionary 1869.

Hester A. Hillis of Magnolia, Iowa; born Parkersburgh, Ind. Oct. 1, 1841; prof.
rel. Dec. 1857; educated at Iowa Coll. Teacher. Emb. with Rev. John Rendall of
the Madura Mission, Boston, Jan. 22, 1870; arr. Madras April 28. Jan. 1878,
still in Ceylon; station Panditeripo. Released.
Joined Bishop Taylor's mission at Secenderabad, India and died at Singarenni
Aug. /6?, 1887.

Susan Reed Howland, dau. Rev. W. W. Howland (supra); born Batticotta, Ceylon,
Nov. 15, 1849; prof. rel. May 1862; Conway, Mass.; grad. Mt. Holyoke Sem. 1870.
Teacher two years. Sailed, New York, Sept. 13, 1873; ar. Jaffna Dec. 2, 1873;
Jan. 1878, stationed at Tillipelly; vis. U. S. arr. N. Y. Feb. 21, 1885; re-emb.
N. Y. Apr. 10, 1886; vis. U. S. arr. N. Y. Apr. 22, 1895; re-emb. N. Y. Sept. 5,
1896; arr. Jaffna Oct. 15. Vis. N. Y. arr. May 14, 1904; arr. field Nov. 1905;
arr. home May 13, 1913; sailed May 2, 1914; arr. home 1921. Retired in 1925.
Died July 25, 1934 at Claremont, California.

George Washington Leitch, born Danville, Caledonia Co., Vt. Jan. 25, 1843;
prof. rel. 1858; studied McIndoes Falls Acad.; emb. N. Y. Oct. 11, 1879; arr.
Jaffna, Jan. 14; returned to U. S. arr. Jan. 14, 1883; released Dec. 18, 1883.
Died October 18, 1925, Claremont, California.

Mary Leitch, born Danville, Vt. Nov. 25, 1851; prof. rel. 1865; studied McIndoes
Falls and St. Johnsbury academies; emb. N. Y. Oct. 11, 1879; arr. Jaffna Jan. 14.
Dec. 1885 at Manepy. Vis. England in 1887; vis. U. S. arr. New York Aug. 10,
1888; released July 22, 1890.

Margaret Hinning Leitch, born Ryegate, Vt. Mar. 25, 1857; prof. rel. Ryegate 1872; studied McIndoes Falls Acad., Peacham Acad., St. Johnsbury Acad., and Oberlin Coll.; emb. N. Y. Oct. 11, 1879; arr. Jaffna Jan. 14. Dec. 1885 at Manepy. Vis. Eng. in 1887; vis. U. S. arr. New York Aug. 10, 1888; released July 22, 1890. Died February 2, 1926, Claremont, Cal.

Katherine E. Hastings, dau. of Eurotas P. Hastings, D.D. of this mission; born Jaffna, Ceylon, April 10, 1858; prof. rel. 1876; studied Cincinnati High and private schools; emb. Aug. 10, 1882; arr. Jaffna Oct. 13. Dec. 1885 at Batticotta. Returned to U. S. arr. N. Y. May 27, 1891; released June 9, 1891.

MADURA MISSION

Commenced 1834.

This is an outgrowth from the Ceylon Mission, the people in both vicinities speaking the same language. After a tour of exploration by Mr. Spaulding (Ceylon Mission) in Jan. and Feb. 1834, Messrs. William Todd and Henry R. Hoisington (Ceylon Mission) accompanied by Mr. Spaulding, left Jaffna, July 21, in that year, and reached Madura July 31, and forthwith commenced missionary operations in that place. Mr. Hoisington soon returned to Jaffna, and his place was supplied by Mr. Eckard (Ceylon Mission) who also returned to Ceylon 1837..

MISSIONARIES

William Todd, born Marcellus, N. Y. March 8, 1801; prof. rel. 1817; grad. Hamilton Coll. 1821; Auburn Sem. 1824; ord. Ira, N. Y. 1827; pastor three years in Benton, N. Y. and three years in West Dresden, N. Y.; embarked with Messrs. Apthorp, Hoisington, Hutchings, and Dr. Ward, at Boston, July 1, 1833; ar. Madras Oct. 12, 1833; in Ceylon Oct. 28, 1833; at Panditeripo till July 21, 1834; then removed to Madura; removed to Shevagunga Jan. 1839; left the mission in poor health, Feb. 23, 1839; ar. in his native country with his three children June 19, 1839; released July 16, 1839. Died in Kansas, Aug. 10, 1874.

Mrs. Todd (Lucy Brownell) born Ledyard, Cayuga Co., N. Y. Sept. 20, 1800; prof. rel. Penn-yan, N. Y. Sept. 1825; mar. Dec. 12, 1828; emb. Boston July 1, 1833; died at Davapatam, on the sea-coast, 80 miles from Madura, to which she was carried two days previous, Sept. 11, 1835.

Mrs. Todd (originally Clarissa Emerson) born Chester, N. H. Nov. 13, 1798; went out as the wife of Rev. Edmund Frost (Mahratta Mission); after his death was the wife of Rev. Henry Woodward (Ceylon Mission); when again a widow married Mr. Todd at Batticotta, Dec. 22, 1836; and died at Madura June 1, 1837. See a notice of Her, Herald, vol. 33, pp. 487, 488..

Henry R. Hoisington, was one of the founders of this mission; but remained in connection with it only a few months, from July 31, 1834 to Feb. 1835. (... Ceylon Mission). Died May 16, 1858.

James Reed Eckard, was a member of this mission, 1835 to 1837. In 1837, he returned to Ceylon.

Alanson C. Hall, Rochester, N. Y.; born Catskill, N.Y. May 29, 1808; studied theology at Auburn Sem.; appt. to India; emb. Boston, Nov. 4, 1834; ar. Calcutta Feb. 25, 1835; ar. Madura, Oct. 18, 1835; left the mission Sept. 1836; ar. New York April 1837; released Aug. 29, 1837.

Mrs. Hall (Frances A. Willard) Cayuga, N. Y.
Died at Madura Jan. 2, 1836; (Mar. Aug. 21, 1834.)

John Jay Lawrence, New York City; born Geneseo, N. Y. July 12, 1807; prof. rel. .. Canandaigua, N. Y. 1826; grad. Union Coll. 1829; Andover Sem. 1834; ord. Newcastle Del. Feb. 24, 1835; emb. Boston with Mr. Perry (Ceylon Mission), May 16, 1835; ar. Colombo Sept. 9.; Jaffna Sept. 24; Madura, Oct. 18, 1835; removed to Dindigul 1838; died of dysentery at Tranquebar on his way to Madras Dec. 20, 1846.

Mrs. Lawrence (Mary Hulin) Troy, N. Y.; born Malta, Saratoga Co., N. Y. Dec. 3, 1809; prof. rel. Jan. 1826; a teacher in Troy Female Seminary; mar. Troy, April 6, 1835; emb. Boston May 16, 1835; returned to U. S. 1847. 1858 at Ballston, Saratoga Co., N. Y.

Daniel Poor of the Ceylon Mission, came to Madura in Oct. 1835, with Mr. Lawrence and spent three months there in active missionary labor. He removed with his family to Madura, March 16, 1836; and rejoined the Ceylon Mission in Oct. 1841. Died Feb. 3, 1855.

Mrs. Poor (Ann Knight) See Ceylon Mission).

Robert Ogden Dwight, Northampton, Mass.; born Stockbridge Oct. 31, 1902; grad. Andover Sem. 1834; ord. at Northampton Aug. 29, 1835; emb. Philadelphia Nov. 16, 1835; ar. Madras March 22, 1836; at Madura April 22, 1836; at Dindigul near the close of 1936; removed to Madura 1842; died of cholera at Madura Jan. 8, 1844.

Mrs. Dwight (Mary Billings) Conway, Mass., dau. of Dea. Elisha and Mary(Storrs); born Mar. 8, 1808; mar. Sept. 21, 1835; emb. Nov. 16, 1835; after the death of Mr. Dwight, she mar. Rev. Miron Winslow of the Madras Mission, died at Madras April 20, 1852.

Henry Cherry, New York City; born Pompey, Onondaga Co., N. Y. March 30, 1808; grad. Auburn Theol. Sem. 1836; ord. Rochester, N. Y. Aug. 31, 1836; emb. Boston Nov. 23, 1836; ar. Madura Mar. 21, 1837; stationed at Sevagunga; removed to Madura 1844; to Periacolum 1847; to Madura 1849; returned to U.S. 1850; released Dec. 17, 1850; deposed from ministry; lived in Norwich, Conn. Died in Rockford, Ill. Sept. 20, 1891. (Rochester, N. Y. 1851-53)

Mrs. Cherry (Charlotte Huntington Lathrop, daughter of Charles and Joanna Lathrop, and sister of the first Mrs. Winslow (Madras Mission) of Mrs. Hutchings (Ceylon Mission) and of Mrs. Perry (Ceylon Mission) Norwich, Ct.; born New London, Ct. May 13, 1811; prof. rel. May 1827; mar. Plainfield, Mass. Aug. 3, 1836; died of pulmonary disease Nov. 4, 1837.

Mrs. Cherry (Jane Eleanor Lathrop, daughter of Ezra and Rebecca Lathrop) Bozrah, Ct.; born Norwich, Ct. Dec. 17, 1811; prof. rel. Bozrah, May 1830; emb. Boston, July 30, 1839; went out unmarried as a teacher; ar. Colombo, Ceylon Dec. 31, 1839; ar. Jaffna Jan. 27, 1840; joined the Ceylon Mission; mar. Mr. Cherry 1840, and joined the Madura Mission at Sevagunga; died of cholera, Madura Jan. 10, 1844.

Mrs. Cherry (Henrietta Ebele, grand-daughter of a former English missionary in Jaffna, Ceylon; mar. Madura Nov. 3, 1844.

Edward Copes, Lewisville, N. Y.; born New Lisbon, N. Y. May 25, 1806; was a member of the Madura Mission from 1837 to 1840; and then transferred to the Mission at Ceylon. 1861, Gilbertsville, N. Y.; 1877, same address.

Nathaniel Marcus Crane, born West Bloomfield, Essex Co., N. J. Dec. 12, 1805; prof. rel. Newark, N. J. Aug. 1825; studied at Williams College and Washington, Pa. graduating at Washington Coll. 1833; Theology at Western Theol. Sem. Pittsburg, and Auburn Sem. 1836; ord. Auburn, July 6, 1836; emb. Boston in a company of seven missionaries and their wives, Nov. 23, 1836; ar. Madura May 10, 1837; at Tirupuvanum till 1842, then at Dindigul; returned to U. S. May 1845; released March 30, 1847; 1861 at Iowa. Died

Mrs. Crane (Julia Ann Jerusha Ostrander) born Pompey, Onondaga Co., N. Y. Oct. 7, 1809; prof. rel. Dec. 1826; mar. Nov. 7, 1836; emb. Nov. 23, 1836; returned to U. S. May 1845.

Clarendon Fay Muzzy, Athens, Pa.; born Dublin, N. H. Nov. 20, 1804; grad. Middlebury Coll. 1833; Andover Sem. 1836; ord.   emb. Boston Nov. 23, 1836; ar. Madura May 10, 1837; station, Tirumangalum; removed to Tirupuvanum, March 1842; to Madura 1844; to Malur 1855; returned to U. S. May 1857; released March 1, 1864. Died Amherst, Mass. Jan. 4, 1878.

Mrs. Muzzy (Semantha Bowen Robbins) born Wardsboro, Vt. Nov. 2, 1808; prof. rel. Middlebury, Vt. Sept. 1831; mar. Hardwick, Mass. Sept. 27, 1836; emb. Boston Nov. 23, 1836; died Madura Dec. 3, 1846.

Mrs. Muzzy (Mary Ann Capell) Jersey, Licking Co., Ohio; born Newstead, Erie Co., N. Y. March 7, 1820; prof. rel. Jersey, O. 1837; emb. with Messrs Herrick, Webb, and Rendall and their wives, Boston, Nov. 12, 1845; went out unmarried; joined the Ceylon mission and was a teacher at Oodooville, 1846 to 1847; mar. Mr. Muzzy Feb. 1, 1848; returned to U. S. May 31, 1857; released March 1, 1864; 1878 in Boston, 1898. 100 East 57th St., New York City, N. Y. Died New York Dec. 5, 1898.

William Tracy, born Norwich, Ct. June 2, 1807; prof. rel. Philadelphia Feb. 1827; studied for a time at Williams Coll.; grad. Princeton Sem. 1835; ord. Philadelphia April 12, 1836; emb. Boston Nov. 23, 1836; ar. Madras March 1837; reached Madura after spending some months at Madras Oct. 3, 1837; stationed at Tirumungalum 1838; removed to Pasumalie 1845; in charge of the seminary there; visited U.S. 1851; re-emb. Boston, Oct. 28, 1853; ar. Madras March 19, 1854; again at Pasumalie 1854-67; again visited U. S. ar. in New York Aug. 9, 1867; sailed with wife from New York for Liverpool on the way to India April 2, 1870; still in the field, 1873. Died Nov. 28, 1877. (Obit, Herald, March 1878.)

Mrs. Tracy (Emily Frances Travilli, sister of Rev. Joseph S. Travilli, of the Singapore Mission); born Philadelphia Feb. 20 1811; mar. Nov. 5, 1836; emb. as above; still in the good work. Jan. 1878, still in India; station Tirupuvanam. Died at Tirupuvanam, April 17, 1879. (See Herald July 1879.)

Ferdinand DeWilton Ward, Rochester, N. Y.; born Bergen, Genesee Co., N. Y. July 3, 1812; grad. Union Coll. 1831; Princeton Sem. 1834; ord. Rochester, Sept. 21, 1836; emb. Boston with the five preceding missionaries and Dr. John Steele, Nov. 23, 1836; stationed at Madura Oct. 3, 1837; removed to Madras early in 1843; returned to U. S. 1846; released 1850; 1877 in Geneseo, N. Y. Pastor there since 1866. Ditto 1887. Died at Clarens, Switzerland, Aug. 11, 1891.

Mrs. Ward (Jane Shaw) born New York City, Dec. 26, 1811; mar. Sept. 21, 1836; emb. Nov. 23, 1836; returned to U. S. 1846; 1887 Geneseo, N. Y.

Horace Sedgwick Taylor, Claridon, Geauga Co., Ohio; born West Hartland, Ct. Oct. 31, 1814; prof. rel. Claridon 1831; grad. Western Reserve Coll. 1840; studied in the Theol. Dept. of that Coll. 1840-1843; ord. Milan, Erie Co., O. April 17, 1844; emb. Boston May 6, 1844; ar. Madura Oct. 10, 1844; stationed Tirupuvanam; removed to Mandapasalie May 1850; continued there till his death; vis. U. S. July 24, 1865; re-emb. Boston Aug. 10, 1867; ar. Madras Dec. 23, 1867; died at the Pulney, Nielgherry Hills, Feb. 3, 1871, age 56. (See obituary sketch, Herald

Mrs. Taylor (Martha Elizabeth Sturtevant) Milan, Erie Co., Ohio; born Ruggles, Huron Co., O. May 17, 1825; prof. rel. Milan 1837; mar. Milan April 17, 1844; eb. Boston May 6, 1844; vis. U. S. without her husband, May 16, 1857; re-emb. Dec. 8, 1858; ar. Madura May 1859; again vis. U. S. July 24, 1865; re-emb. Boston Aug. 10, 1867. Returned to U. S. 1875; 1883 Geneva, Ashtabula Co., O. Died Aug. 28, 1911 at Ruggles, Ohio. (See Miss. Herald Oct. 1911, page 471)

James Herrick, Dummerston, Vt.;.born Broome, Canada East, March 13, 1814; (his father was a native of Brattleboro, Vt.) prof. rel. West Brattleboro, Vt. May 1834; grad. Williams Coll. 1841; Andover Sem. 1845; ord. Brattleboro Oct. 10, 1845; emb. Boston Nov. 12, 1845; ar. Madras March 23, 1846; ar. Madura April 29, 1846; stationed at Tirumangalum; removed to Pasumalie and took charge of the seminary 1850; at Tirumangalum again 1854; vis. U. S. May 30, 1864; re-emb. Boston Nov. 7, 1866; ar. Madras April 27, 1867. Ar. Madura, May 6, 1867; Jan. 1878, in India. Station Tirumangalam. Returned to U. S. arr. April 22, 1883; ied W. Brattleboro, Vt. Nov. 30, 1891. (See Herald Jan. 1892, p. 10)

Mrs. Herrick (Elizabeth Hopkins Crosby) born West Brattleboro, Vt. Jan. 27, 1817; prof. rel. May 1834; mar. Nov. 2, 1845; emb. Boston Nov. 12, 1845; vis. U.S. May 1864; re-emb. Nov. 7, 1866; ar. Madura May 6, 1867; vis. U. S. 1875. Jan. 1878 in India. Station, Tirumangalam. Returned to U. S. arr. April 22, 1883. Died at West Brattleboro, Vt. Oct. 1900.

Edward Webb, born Lowestoft, county of Suffolk, England, Dec. 15, 1819; studied at Bury Saint Edmunds, and made prof. rel. there 1837; came to New England; grad. Andover Sem. 1845; ord. Ware, Mass. Oct. 23, 1845; emb. Boston with Messrs Herrick and Rendall Nov. 12, 1845; ar. Madras March 23, 1846; Madura April 29, 1846; station Sivaganga; removed to Dindigul 1850; vis. U. S. March 21, 1859; re-emb. Boston March 11, 1861; ar. Madras June 26, 1861; again at Dindigul till 1864; returned to U. S. July 12, 1864; released Jan. 3, 1865. Afterwards, acting pastor Darby, Pa. 1865; Glasgow, Del. 1866; 1875 Pastor at Oxford, Pa. 1878 at

Oxford. Ditto 1888. Died Apr. 6, 1833 at Oxford, Pa.

Mrs. Webb (Nancy Allyn Foote) Cayuga, Cayuga Co., N. Y.; born Portageville, Alleghany Co., N. Y. July 13, 1825; prof. rel. Nov. 1839; grad. Mt. Holyoke; mar. Cayuga Sept. 30, 1845; emb. Boston Nov. 12, 1845; vis.U. S. Mar. 1853; re-emb. Boston March 11, 1861; returned U. S. July 1864; released Jan. 1865. Did Oxford, Pa. Jan. 20, 1902.

John Rendall. Quincy, Illinois; born Halifax, Nova Scotia, Jan. 21, 1821; brought up from infancy in Utica, N. Y.; prof. rel. Utica 1831, at ten years of age; grad. Mission Institute, Quincy, Ill. 1842; pursued theological studies at the same Institute till 1845; ord. Boxboro, Mass. Oct. 15, 1845; emb. with Messrs Herrick, Webb, and others, Boston Nov. 12,1845; ar. Madras March 28, 1846; ar. Madura April 29, 1846; stationed at Dindigul; removed to Madura 1850; continued there till 1867; visited U. S. Oct. 1, 1867; sailed from Boston for Madras Jan. 22, 1870; arr. Madras April 28. Jan. 1878 in India. Station Madura. Died at Madura, June 13, 1883. (See obit. in Herald Aug. 1883, p. 295)

Mrs. Rendall (Jane Ballard) Quincy, Ill; born Athol, Mass. March 4, 1826; prof. rel. Athol April 1834; at eight years of age; mar. Quincy, Ill. Aug. 18, 1845; emb. Boston Nov. 12, 1845; visited U.S. May 1, 1858; re-emb. New York May 21, 1859; reached Madras Sept. 15, 1859; left Madura for U. S. July 16, 1867; but died at sea between Alexandria and Marseilles Sept. 4, 1867 and found a grave in the Mediterranean.

George Washington McMillan, Gettysburgh, Pa.; born Fountain Dale, Adams Co., Pa. Oct. 19, 1812; prof. rel. 1830; grad. Penn. Coll. 1842; studied Lane Sem., Ohio, two years; ord. Brattleboro, Vt. Oct. 8, 1845; emb. Boston March 17, 1846; ar. Madras July 27, 1846; stationed at Dindigul from 1846 to 1854; returned to U.S. Nov. 8, 1854; released 1859. Madison, N. J. w.e. 1880; 1888 Perrineville, N.J. Died at Perth Amboy, N. J. (Presb'n Ministers' Home) Sept. 15, 1885.

Mrs. McMillan (Rebecca Newman Brand) New York City; born Monmouth, N. J. Dec. 10, 1817; prof. rel. Dec. 1834; mar. N. York March 10, 1846;

John Eddy Chandler, born North Woodstock, Ct. June 12, 1817; prof. rel. Dec. 1831; studied three years at Yale but did not graduate; Lane Sem. 1846; ord. Cincinnati Sept. 14, 1846; emb. Boston Nov. 16, 1846; ar. Madras March 17, 1847; stationed at Madura; removed to Sivagunga 1850; to Dindigul 1854; to Battalagundu 1855; visited U. S. April 24, 1861; re-emb. Boston, Jan. 20, 1864; at Tirumangalum 1864; at Madura 1868; vis. U. S. 1874; sailed N. Y. Aug. 24, 1876; Jan. 1878 at Pulney; vis. U. S. arr. Boston, May 12, 1889; re-emb. N. Y. July 16, 1892; arr. Madura Sept. 12, 1892. Died Madura Jan. 10, 1894 of cholera. (See Herald March 1894, page 95, also April 1894, page 147)

Mrs. Chandler (Charlotte Maria Hopkins) Cincinnati; born LeRoy, Jefferson Co., N.Y. Nov. 16, 1821; prof. rel. 1832; mar. Cincinnati Sept. 10, 1846; emb. Boston, Nov. 16, 1846; vis. U. S. April 24, 1861; re-emb. Boston Jan. 20, 1864; vis. U.S. 1874; sailed as above. Jan. 1878 at Pulney; vis. U. S. arr. Boston May 12, 1889. Did Auburndale Sept. 25, 1891. (See Nov. 1891, Herald, page 448)

George Ford, Groton, Mass.; born Boston, Mass. Feb. 27, 1819; prof. rel. Groton 1831; grad. Harvard Coll. 1842; Andover Sem. 1845; ord. Groton, Oct. 7, 1846; emb. Boston Nov. 18, 1846; ar. Madras Mar. 15, 1847; stationed Periacolum 1847; at Tirumangalum 1851; returned to U. S. 1853; released March 11, 1856; (Afterwards, pastor E. Falmouth, Mass. 1856-62; Tolland, Mass. 1863-69.) Took charge of a station in the Seneca Mission May 1869 (See New York Indians). 1887 Elwood, Ill. Died at Kansas City, Mo. Feb. 2, 1901. A son, Rev. James T. Ford, is pastor of Pres. Ch., Warren, Ill. Feb. 1901.

Mrs. Ford (Ann Jeannette Tooker) Patchogue, Long Island; born Brookhaven, Long Island June 23, 1824; prof. rel. 1837; married Oct. 25, 1846; emb. Boston Nov. 18, 1846; returned U. S. 1853; released 1856. Died at Elk Point, Dak., March 21, 1882.

Charles Little, born Columbia, Ct. Sept. 26, 1813; prof. rel. in Yale Coll. April 1841; grad. Yale Coll. 1844; Auburn and New Haven Sem. 1847; ord. Columbia, Ct. Sept. 1, 1847; emb. Boston, Dec. 4, 1847; ar. Madras April 16, 1848; stationed Tirumangalum 1850; vis. U. S. Aug. 1852; re-emb. Boston Oct. 20, 1853; stationed Tirupuvanam 1854; returned to U. S. Feb. 25, 1859; released June 13, 1860; 1868 at Lincoln, Neb. and 1873 at Lewis and 1888 Clay, Iowa. Died in Lincoln, Neb. August 14, 1892.

Mrs. Little (Amelia Newton) born Sherburne, Chenango Co., N.Y. Feb. 7, 1823;/mar. prof. rel. 1836 Sherburn, Sept. 29, 1847; emb. Dec. 1847; died of dysentery at Madura July 4, 1848.

Mrs. Little (Susan Robbins) Brockport, N. Y.; born Camillus, N. Y. Dec. 18, 1825; prof. rel. 1850; mar. Sept. 15, 1853; emb. Boston Oct. 20, 1853; returned to U.S. Feb. 1859; released June 13, 1860. Died Aug. 31, 1873, at Lincoln, Nebraska.

Joseph Thomas Noyes, Bradford, Mass.; born Newburyport, Mass. March 4, 1818; prof. rel. March 1834; grad. Amherst Coll. 1845; Andover Sem. 1848; ord. Newburyport Sept. 20, 1848; emb. Boston Oct. 10, 1848; ar. Madras Feb. 20, 1849; ar. Jaffna March 6, 1849; at Panditeripo till July 21, 1849; when he removed to Chavagacherry; transferred to Madura mission 1853; stationed at Tirumangalum till Jan. 1854, then removed to Periacolum at which station he labored till 1862, when he removed to Kambam; still there in 1871; visited U. S. 1871; sailed again, N. Y. May 10, 1873; Jan. 1878 at Periakulam; vis. U. S. arr. Aug. 7, 1881; re-emb. N. Y. Nov. 13, 1881; arr. Madura Feb. 1882; vis. U. S. arr. N. Y. Oct. 23, 1886; re-emb. N. Y. July 30, 1887; arr. Madras Oct. 4, 1887. Died in Madras Aug. 3, 1892.

Mrs. Noyes (Elizabeth Achsah Smith) born Amherst, Mass. Sept. 19, 1822; prof. rel. May 1838; studied at Mount Holyoke Sem.; mar. Sept. 12, 1848; emb. Boston Oct. 10, 1848; visited U.S. May 7, 1856;; re-emb. Dec. 8, 1858; ar. Madura May 1859; visited U.S. 1871; sailed again New York Sept. 1, 1877; Jan. 1878 at Periakulan. Died Apr. 10, 1880.

Mrs. Noyes (Martha J. Hazleville) born   ; mar. Rowe May 30,
l851; arr. U. S. Aug. 7, 1881 re-emb. Nov. 19, 1881; arr. Madura Feb. 1882; vis.
U. S. arr. N. Y. Oct. 23, 1886; re-emb. N. Y. July 30, 1887; arr. Madras Oct. 4,
1887; vis. U. S. arr. N. Y. Sept. 10, 1894. Died Aug. 6, 1915, Pasadena, Calif.
(See Miss. Herald. Feb. 1916, p. 92)

Nathan Lynde Lord, M.D. was connected with this mission about three years, from the
end of 1863 to the beginning of 1867, but extreme ill health compelled his return
to U.S. (See Ceylon Mission). Died Jan. 24, 1868.

Thomas Scott Burnell, Worcester, Mass.; born Chesterfield, Mass. Feb. 3, 1823;
brought up to the printer's trade; emb. with Mr. Noyes and others, Boston, Oct.10,
1848; ar. Jaffna Feb. 27, 1849; printer at Manepy, Ceylon from 1849 to Sept. 1855;
then transferred to the Madura Mission; ord. Madura Sept. 10, 1856; visited U.S.
1869; spent about two years attending the "special course" of theological instruc-
tion at Andover; sailed with wife from San Francisco for Shanghai on the way to
India Sept. 30, 1871; ar. Melur Dec. 19, 1871; Jan. 1878, still at Melur; returned
to U.S. arr. Jan. 14, 1883; Died Northampton, Mass. Apr. 16, 1899. (See June 1899
Herald, p. 218)

Mrs. Burnell (Martha Sawyer) Worcester, Mass.; born Heath, Mass. April 3, 1820;
prof. rel. Northampton, Mass. July 1829; grad. Mt. Holyoke Sem.; mar. Westminster,
Vt. Feb. 4, 1847; vis. U. S . 1869; sailed as above; ar. Melur Dec. 19, 1871; Jan.
1878, still in Melur. Died at Belleville, Canada, Mar. 13, 1885. (See Herald
May 1885, p. 180)

William Banfield Capron, born Uxbridge, Mass. April 14, 1824; prof. rel. Sept. 1850;
grad. Yale Coll. 1846; Andover Sem. 1856; ord. Uxbridge Sept. 3, 1856; emb.
Boston, Nov. 24, 1856;; ar. Madura April 6, 1857; stationed at Patienur, Manu,
Magyr; still there 1868; vis. U. S. 1872; sailed again New York Sept. 12, 1874.
Died Oct. 6, 1876. (Obit. Herald Feb. 1877)

Mrs. Capron (Sarah Brown Hooker, daughter of Rev. Henry Brown Hooker, Sec. Mass. Home Miss. Soc.) Falmouth, Mass.; born Lanesborough, Mass. April 24, 1828; prof. rel. March 1843; mar. Falmouth Oct. 1, 1856; emb. Boston Nov. 24, 1856; vis. U.S. 1872; sailed New York Sept. 12, 1874; ar. Madras Dec. 2, 1874; January 1878, still in Madura. Returned to U.S. arr. Boston Sept. 10, 1886; released Jan. 25, 1889. Died in Poughkeepsie, N. Y. Dec. 15, 1918. (Miss. Herald 1919, p. 39)

Charles Taylor White, son of Rev. Samuel White, Dart. Coll. 1812; born Starkey, Yates Co., N. Y. April 12, 1829; prof. rel. in college March 1848; grad. Wabash Coll. 1851; Lane Sem. 1855; ord. Havanna, N. Y. Oct. 1, 1856; emb. Boston Nov. 24, 1856; ar. Madura April 4, 1857; station Pulney 1858-68; returned to U. S. 1869; released previously to Oct. 1870; 1887 Fowler, Ind. Died Apr. 8, 1916 at Rock Stream, N. Y. (See Miss. Herald June 1916, p. 292)

Mrs. White (Anna Maria Child) born Derby, Vt. April 11, 1834; prof. rel. Peacham, Vt. Dec. 1850; studied Mt. Holyoke Fem. Sem.; mar. Derby, Vt. Sept. 4, 1856; emb. Nov. 24, 1856; returned to U. S. 1869. Died Cambridge City, Ind. July 30, 1877. (Obit Herald Oct. 1877)

Edward Chester, M.D. born New York City July 12, 1828; prof. rel. New Haven, Ct. 1842; grad. Union Theol. Sem., N. Y. 1857; appt. June 3, 1858; ord. New York May 31, 1857; emb. Boston Dec. 8, 1858; ar. Madura May 1859; stationed at Tirupuvanum; removed to Madura 1864; Dindigul 1864-72; vis. U.S. 1873; sailed N.Y. Aug. 1873; Jan. 1878 at Dindigul; vis. U. S. arr. N. Y. Mar. 11, 1888; re-emb. N. Y. Oct. 13, 1888; arr. Dindigul Nov. 28; returned to U.S. on account of ill health, arr. N. Y. Mar. 2, 1890; re-emb. N. Y. May 3, 1890; arr. Dindigul July 1890 Died at Dindigul Mar. 26, 1902. (See May 1902 Herald, p. 195)

Mrs. Chester (Sophia Hoffman) born New York City Dec. 5, 1830; mar. Aug. 15, 1848; emb. Boston, Dec. 8, 1858; vis. U. S. 1873; sailed as above; Jan. 1878, still at Dindigul; vis. U.S. arr. N.Y. Mar. 11, 1888; re-emb. Oct. 13, 1888; arr. Dindigul Nov. 28; returned to U.S. arr. N. Y. Mar. 2, 1890; re-emb. N.Y. May 3, 1890; arr.

Dindigul July 1890. Died at Dindigul March 13, 1895. (See June 1895 Herald)

N. Chester (S.R.Kistler of Guntur India, formerly connected with the General Synod of the Evangelical Lutheran Ch.) born Histler, Penn. Oct. 25,1863; united with Even. Luth. Ch. 1877; studied Hartwick Sem., N. Y., Bloomfield Acad., and St. Joseph Sem.; emb. N.Y. Feb. 29, 1896; mar. Guntur, India April 9, 1896.; vis. U.S. arr. N.Y. Sept. 23, 1904.

George Thomas Washburn, born Lenox, Mass. Sept. 5, 1832; prof. rel. 1849; grad. Williams Coll. 1855; Andover Sem. 1858; ord. Lenox, March 24, 1859; emb. Boston Jan. 2, 1860; ar. Madura May 1, 1860; stationed Battalagundu 1860-68; at Pasumalie autumn 1870; visited U.S. 1872; sailed New York July 11, 1873; Jan. 1878 at Pasumalai; vis. U.S. arr. June 10, 1883; re-emb. N.Y. July 10, 1884; arr. Madura Sept. 27; Dec. 1885 at Pasumalai; vis. U.S. arr. N.Y. May 7, 1890; re-emb. N.Y. Oct. 11, 1890; arr. Madura Dec. 1890; vis. U.S. arr. N.Y. May 30, 1896; re-emb. N.Y. Aug. 4, 1897; arr. Madura Oct. 6, 1897; returned to U.S. arr. N.Y. May 9,1900. Died Apr. 30, 1927. (See June Herald 1927, page 241)

Mrs. Washburn (Eliza Ellen Case) Gloversville, Fulton Co., N.Y.; born Kingsborough, Fulton Co., N. Y. Sept. 27, 1833; prof. rel. May 1851; mar. Sept. 1, 1859; emb. Boston Jan. 2, 1860; vis. U.S. 1872; sailed as above; Jan. 1878 at Pasumalai; vis. U.S. in 1883-4 as above. Dec. 1885 at Pasumalai; vis. U.S. arr. N.Y. May 7, 1890; re-emb. N.Y. Oct. 11, 1890; arr. Madura Dec. 1890; vis. U.S. arr. N.Y. May 30, 1896; re-emb. N.Y. Aug. 4, 1897; arr. Madura Oct. 6, 1897; returned to U.S. May 7, 1900. Died July 23, 1914 at Meriden, Ct. (See Miss. Herald Sept. 1914, p. 301)

David Coit Scudder, son of Dea. Charles Scudder of Boston; born in Boston Oct. 27, 1835; prof. rel. Essex St. Ch. Boston Feb. 1852; grad. Williams Coll. 1855; Andover Sem. 1859; ord. Essex St. Boston Feb. 25, 1861; emb. Boston March 11, 1861; ar. Madras June 26, 1861; stationed at Periaculum; drowned in a river swollen with

heavy flood, Nov. 10, 1862. (See obituary of this zealous and promising
young missionary, Herald, vol. 59, pp. 65-67.)

Mrs. Scudder (Harriet Louisa Dutton) born in Boston Feb. 3, 1837; prof. rel.
Essex St. Ch. Boston, April 1851; studied Wheaton Seminary, Norton, Mass.;
mar. Feb. 27, 1861; emb. Boston March 11, 1861; returned to U.S. May 16, 1863.
Jan. 1873, residing in Boston. 1888, 250 Newbury St., Boston.

Thornton Bigelow Penfield, step-son of Rev. Henry Cowles of Oberlin, O.; born
Alden, Erie Co., N.Y. Oct. 2, 1834; converted at the age of eight years; prof.
rel. 1846;; studied two years in Union Theol. Sem., New York City and part of
one year at Oberlin Sem.; grad. Oberlin Coll. 1856; Oberlin Sem. 1858; a missionary;
7 years in Jamaica, where he was ordained 1859; emb. Boston Nov. 7, 1866;
ar. Madura, May 1867. He died at Pasumalie Aug. 10, 1871 of typhus fever. (See
obituary notice in Miss. Herald for December 1871)

Mrs. Penfield (Charlotte Elizabeth Hubbard) Montclair, N.J.; born New York City
Aug. 9, 1844; prof. rel. Newark, N.J. 1860; studied Mt. Holyoke and Oberlin; mar.
at Montclair, N.J. Oct. 23, 1866. Returned to U.S. 1872. Released 1873.
(Mr. Penfield's first wife was Sarah C. Ingraham, dau. of Rev. David S. Ingraham.)

Hervey Crosby Hazen, born Ithaca, Tompkins Co., N.Y. June 26, 1841; prof. rel.
1850; grad. Amherst Coll. 1862; Auburn Sem. 1865; ord. Ithica, July 10, 1867;
emb. Boston Aug. 10, 1867; ar. Madura Jan. 1868; returned to U.S. 1869; released
July, 1869; 1871, Liverpool, N.Y.; re-appointed Nov. 6, 1883; emb. May 17,
1884; arr. Madura July 16. Dec. 1885 at Madura; vis. U.S. arr. N.Y. Apr. 13,
1895; re-emb. N.Y. Dec. 21, 1895; arr. Madura Feb. 13, 1896; vis. U.S. arr. N.Y.
Apr. 10, 1904; re-emb. Boston May 13, 1905.; arr. home Apr. 24, 1912; sailed Apr.
1913. Died July 20, 1914 at Manamadura, India. (See Herald Sept. 15, p. 382)

Mrs. Hazen (Ida Julia Chapin) Ludlow, Vt.; born Windham, Vt. Feb. 20, 1843;
prof. rel. April 7, 1867; mar. July 2, 1867; sailed as above; ret. U.S. 1869;

released   1869   . Died at Holby, N.Y. Mar. 29, 1883.

Mrs. Haren (see page 199) vis. U.S. arr. Apr. 13, 1895; re-emb. N.Y. Dec. 21, 1895. Died Kodaikanal April 3, 1903. (See June 1903 Herald, page 234).

William Southworth Howland, born Batticotta, Ceylon July 8, 1846, son of Rev. W.W. Howland, p. 151 ; prof. rel. May 1862, Conway, Mass.; educated at Monson Academy, Amherst College (grad. 1870) and Andover Sem. (grad. in 1873); ord. Conway, Mass. May 7, 1873. Sailed New York Sept. 17, 1873. Ar. Madras Dec. 6, 1873. Jan. 1873 at Mandapasalai; vis. U.S. arr. New York June 17, 1886. Died at Auburndale, Mass. Mar. 7, 1887. (See obit. Miss. Herald Apr. 1887, pp. 126,131)

Mrs. Howland (Mary Louise Carpenter) born Monson, Mass. Feb. 3, 1846; prof. rel. Monson, July 1862; educated at Monson Acad. and Mt. Holyoke; grad. at latter 1870. Teacher. Mar. June 19, 1873, at Monson, Mass. Sailed as above; ar. M. Dec. 6, 1873; Jan. 1878 at Mandapasalai. Vis. U.S. arr. N.Y. June 17, 1886. Died at Auburndale, Mass. March 5, 1887. (See obituary Miss. Herald April 1887, pp.126,131)

John Scudder Chandler, born Madura, India, April 12, 1849, son of Rev. John E. Chandler; prof. rel. New Haven, Ct. 1865. Educated at Hopkins Grammar Sch., New Haven, Yale Coll. grad. 1870; Yale Sem., grad. 1873; ord. New Haven May 8, 1873. Sailed New York Sept. 17, 1873. Ar. Madras Dec. 6. Jan. 1878 at Battalagundu; vis. U.S. arr. May 31, 1885; re-emb. Sept. 8, 1887; arr. Battalagundu Nov. 23, 1887; vis. U.S. arr. N.Y. Sept. 15, 1896; re-emb. Boston Nov. 3, 1897; arr. Madura Jan. 7, 1898; vis. U.S. arr. Boston May 24, 1906; re-emb. San Francisco Apr. 14, 1908; arr. home June 1, 1915; re-emb. Feb. 5, 1916; arr. home May 23, 1923; D.D. Yale June 20, 1923; re-emb. May 10, 1924; arr. home May 26, 1930; sailed Oct. 20, 1932. Retired Jan. 1, 1928. Died June 18, 1934 at Neutral Saddle, near Madura, So. India.

Mrs. Chandler (Jane Elizabeth Minor) dau. of E. S. Minor (Ceylon Mission); born Panepy, Ceylon, June 8, 1849; prof. rel. New Haven Jan. 1861; educated at New Haven High Sch. Teacher. Mar. May 21, 1873, at New Haven. Sailed as above.

Ar. Madras Dec. 6, 1873. Jan. 1878 at Battalagundu; vis. U.S. arr. May 31, 1895. Died at Auburndale, Mass. Apr. 3, 188?.

Mrs. Chandler (Henrietta Shelton Rendall) Mar. July 11, 1887; re-emb. Sept. 8, 1887; arr. Battalagundu Nov. 23, 1887; vis. U.S. arr. N.Y. Sept. 15, 1896; re-emb. Boston Nov. 3, 1897; arr. Madura Jan. 7, 1898; vis. U.S. arr. Boston May 24, 1906; re-emb. San Francisco Apr. 14, 1908. Died July 9, 1932 at Mt. Rest, Goshen, Mass. (Re-emb. etc. as Dr. Chandler) Born Jan.16,1856,Madura. Taught Madura 1877-1884. Grad. Wellesley Coll.1886.

Marshall Reuben Peck, born Aug. 22, 1846, Brookfield, Vt.; united with Cong. Ch. Newbury, Vt. May 1866; educated at Randolph, Northfield and Newbury, Vt.; grad. Dartmouth Coll. 1870; at Chicago Sem. one year, and at Yale Sem. two years; grad. there 1875; ord. Brookfield, Vt. Sept. 2, 1875; sailed Ot. 2, 1875; ret. to U.S. June 24, 1876 and died Aug. 6, 1876 at Brookfield, Vt.

Mrs. Peck (Helen Maria Nelson) born Monroe, N. H. Jan. 10, 1840; united with Meth. Ch. 1855, in Newbury, Vt.; educated at Newbury Sem. and Monticello Sem., Ill. Taught somewhat. Mar. June 3, 1875, Godfrey, Ill. Sailed as above. Returned as above. Released

James Edward Tracy son of Rev. William Tracy; born Pasumalai, Madura July 4,1850; prof. rel. Norwich, Conn. May 1865; educated at Norwich Free Acad.; grad. Williams Coll. 1874 and Union Sem. 1877; ord. June 27, 1877, Williamstown, Mass. Sailed, N.Y. Sept. 1, 1877; ar. Nov. 8, 1877: vis. U.S. arr. N.Y. May 23, 1889; re-emb. N.Y. Oct. 3, 1891; arr. Madura Dec. 3, 1891; vis. U.S. arr. N.Y. May 18, 1902; re-emb. N. Y. Sept. 1, 1903. Took furlough in Kodaikanal 1914 to June 7, 1915. Died at Kodaikanal Aug. 4, 1923.

Mrs. Tracy (Fannie Sabin Woodcock) born Williamstown, Mass. Aug. 6, 1846; prof. rel. Dec. 1864; educated at South Williamstown and Pittsfield, Mass.; mar. Aug.1, 1877 at S. Williamstown; sailed as above; ar.   ; vis. U.S. arr. N.Y. May 23, 1889; re-emb. N.Y. Oct. 3, 1891; arr. Madura Dec. 3, 1891; vis. U.S. arr. N.Y.

May 15, 1902; re-emb. N.Y. Sept. 1, 1903. Took furlough at Kodaikanal 1914 to June 7, 1915. Retired May 1, 1927. Died Dec. 29, 1927.

George Herbert Gutterson born Andover, Mass. May 12, 1847; prof. rel. March 3, 1872; studied Phillips Acad. and Punchard Free School, Andover; grad. Andover Theol. Sem. 1878; ord. Old South Church, Andover, Dec. 3, 1878; emb. Dec. 28, 1878; Dec. 1885 at Melur; vis. U.S. arr. Boston, Mar. 18, 1889; released April 18, 1893. Dist. Sec. Am. Miss'y Assoc., Boston. Died in 80th year, Clifton Springs, Oct. 13, 1926.

Mrs. Gutterson (Emma Sampson Wilder) dau. of Rev. H. A. Wilder for 28 years in the Zulu mission; born Umtwalumi, Natal, April 24, 1853; prof. rel. 1868; studied Abbott Academy, Andover; mar. Sept. 18, 1878; emb. Dec. 7, 1878. Dec. 1885 at Melur; vis. U.S. arr. Boston, Mar. 18, 1889; released April 18, 1893. Died in Calif. May 21, 1927. (See Sept. Herald 1927, page 347)

John Peter Jones, D.D., born Wrexham, Denbighshire, Wales, Sept. 4, 1847; prof. rel. Shenandoah City, Pa.; grad. Western Reserve Coll. 1875; Andover Theol. Sem. 1878; ord. Hudson, O., Aug. 20, 1878; emb. N.Y. Sept. 7, 1878. Dec. 1885 at Madura. Vis. U.S. arr. N.Y. Sept. 20, 1890; re-emb. Boston Nov. 7, 1891; vis. U.S. arr. Boston Apr. 20, 1901; re-emb. Boston Nov. 29, 1902; vis. U.S. arr. Boston Dec. 11, 1908; re-emb. San Francisco Nov. 8, 1910; March 11-Sept. 2 1913 in Europe for health reasons. Retired Sept. 1914, when he became a Prof. in the Kennedy Sch. of Missions, Hartford, arr. home Apr. 14, 1914. Died Oct. 3, 1916 at Hartford, Conn. (Miss. Herald 1916, p. 488) (D.D. 1895)

Mrs. Jones (Sarah Amy Hosford) born Sunderland, Franklin Co., Mass. Aug. 8, 1851; prof. rel. Jan. 1867; studied Lake Erie Sem., Painesville, O.; mar. Aug. 13, 1878; emb. N.Y. Sept. 7, 1878. Dec. 1885 at Madura; vis. U.S. arr. N.Y. Sept. 20, 1890; re-emb. Boston Nov. 7, 1891; vis. U.S. arr. Oberlin May 16, 1899; re-emb. Boston Nov. 29, 1902; vis. U.S. arr. Boston Dec. 11, 1908; re-emb. San Francisco Nov. 8, 1910; arr. home Apr. 14, 1914.

Alfred Hastings Burnell, son of Rev. T. S. Burnell of this mission; born Manepy, Ceylon, Aug. 13, 1852; prof. rel. April 26, 1867; grad. Williams Coll. 1878; Auburn Theol. Sem. 1881; ord. W. Westminster, Vt. June 30, 1881; emb. N.Y. Nov.13, 1881; arr. Madura Feb. 1882. Dec. 1885 at Mana-Madura. Returned to U.S. arr. N.Y. Feb. 19, 1887. Released June 29, 1888. Died Nordhoff, So. Cal., Nov.2,1891.

Mrs. Burnell (Abbie J. Snell) born Rushford, Filmore Co., Minn., Sept. 22, 1858; prof. rel. 1872; studied Carleton Coll.; mar. Aug. 11, 1881; emb. N.Y. Nov. 13, 1881; arr. Madura Feb. 1882. Dec. 1885 at Mana-Madura. Returned to U.S. arr. N.Y. Feb. 19, 1887. Released June 29, 1888. Died March 13, 1935.

MISSIONARY PHYSICIANS

John Steele, M.D. Auburn, N.Y.; born Hebron, N.Y. Aug. 19, 1804; embarked at Boston Nov. 23, 1836; ar. Madura May 10, 1837; died of pulmonary consumption at Madura Oct. 6, 1842.

Mrs. Steele (Mary Snell) born Plainfield, Mass. Sept. 21, 1814; mar. Nov. 11, 1836. After the death of Dr. Steele, she mar. Rev. John C. Smith, of the Ceylon Mission Oct. 1843. She died May 15, 1873.

Charles Smith Shelton, M.D., Brooklyn, N.Y.; born Huntington, Ct. Aug. 28, 1819; prof. rel. Yale Coll. Jan. 1837; grad. Yale Coll. 1840; studied at New Haven Medical School, where he received M.D. in 1844; practiced medicine some time in Brooklyn, N.Y.; emb. Boston Oct. 10, 1848; arr. Madura March 23, 1849; returned to U.S. May 7, 1856; released Sept. 30, 1856. Died in Jersey City, N.J. May 21, 1879. (See Herald July 1879)

Mrs. Shelton (Henrietta Mills Hyde) Brooklyn, N. Y.; born New York City, Nov.20, 1826; prof. rel. Steubenville, O. 1837; mar. July 6, 1848; emb. Boston Ot. 10, 1848; returned U.S. May 1856; released Sept. 30, 1856. Died in Montclair, N.J. Dec. 4, 1908.

Henry Knox Palmer, M.D., Litchfield, Ill.; born Madison Co., Ill. July 28, 1837; prof. rel. Carlinville, Ill. Dec. 1856; grad. Rush Medical College, Chicago, Ill.; spent some time in the practice of medicine at Litchfield; emb. Boston Oct. 28, 1868; ar. Madura March 5, 1869. Returned to U.S. 1874, through ill health. Released 1876.

Mrs. Palmer (Flora Day, daughter of Rev. James Day) born New Athens, Harrison Co., Ohio, May 22, 1844; prof. rel. 1856; mar. Memphis, Tenn. April 26, 1866. Ret. U.S. 1874. Rel. 1876.

Mrs. Hazen (Hattie Adell Cook) born Elba, Genesee Co., N.Y. Nov. 17, 1859; prof. rel. Holley, N.Y. Feb. 1875; studied Holley Acad. and Brockport Normal School; mar. Apr. 15, 1884; emb. May 17, 1884; arr. Madura July 16. Dec. 1885 at Madura; vis. U.S. arr. N.Y. Oct. 26, 1888; re-emb. N.Y. Oct. 13, 1889; arr. Bombay Dec. 13, 1889; vis. U.S. arr. Apr. 10, 1904; re-emb. Boston Oct. 27, 1906.

James Coffin Perkins, born Sacramento, Cal., April 30, 1853; prof. rel. San Fran. Feb. 1881; grad. Univ. of Cal. 1874; Princeton Theol. Sem. 1885; ord. Jersey City, N.J. May 29, 1885; emb. N.Y. July 7, 1885; arr. Madura Oct. 14; vis. U.S. arr. N.Y. May 28, 1896; re-emb. N.Y. Aug. 23, 1897; vis. U.S. arr. N.Y. Aug. 28, 1900; re-emb. Boston Oct. 15, 1902; vis. U.S. arr. Boston Mar. 23, 1910; released Dec. 6, 1910; re-appointed October 24, 1911; sailed for India Jan. 13, 1912 from Boston. Came to U.S. Apr. 14, 1914 because of son James' health. Accepted a call to churches at Scroon Lake, N.Y.

Mrs. Perkins (Charlotte Jane Taylor) born Baltimore, Md. Dec. 21, 1860; prof. rel. 1875; studied High School, Baltimore; mar. June 24, 1885; emb. N.Y. July 7, 1885; arr. Madura Oct. 14; vis. the U.S. arr. N.Y. May 28, 1896; re-emb. N.Y. Aug. 23, 1897; Died Tirumangalam Jan. 19, 1898. (See April 1898 Herald, p.133)

Mrs. Perkins (Lucy Elizabeth Crosswell) born Adrian, Mich. April 1, 1866; united with Episcopal Church, Pittsburg, Penn.; studied in Penn. College for Women and

Comments by Mrs. Isabel Palmer Wister, daughter of the late Dr. Henry Max Palmer, in her letter of September 16, 1950 written from 2018 Parker Street, Berkeley, Calif. to Mr. Belcher:

"Dr. Chandler's book mentioned my father often, but to my surprise, with scant attention to the fact that my father was a MEDICAL MISSIONARY and a graduate physician-- the first among the Madura Mission, so I have always understood.

"His interest in, and scholarly knowledge of the Bible accounted for his being called a minister many times, and, I noticed in your statement, he was so described. This caused him much secret amusement, because his medical profession was instrumental in his being more useful than had he been solely an evangelist, he thought.

"So please record him as an M.D., graduate of RUSH MEDICAL, and founder of what is now the great ALBERT VICTOR MEMORIAL HOSPITAL now in Madura, 'founded' on his little dispensary. I say 'founder' with pride, and have some letters which I am including in my book INDIA JOURNAL I am preparing as a gift to the Board in memory of my parents, with many pictures of that period, when I joined the family. . ."

Hildesheim, Germany; taught in Kodaikanal school for missionaries children; mar. Kodaikanal March 24, 1904; vis. U.S. arr. Boston March 23, 1910; released b. 6, 1910; re-appointed Oct. 24, 1911. Sailed from Boston Jan. 13, 1912. See above.

ASSISTANT MISSIONARIES

Alfred North, Boonville, Oneida Co., N.Y.; born Exeter, N.H. March 10, 1807; a printer by trade; which trade he learned at Utica, N.Y.; prof. rel. at St. George's Church, New York, 1833; emb. Boston, July 20, 1835; ar. at Singapore Feb. 6, 1836; was missionary printer at Singapore till the relinquishment of that mission in 1843; he then removed to Madura, where he was engaged in teaching and preaching; arrived in Madura Jan. 1, 1844; returned to U.S. 1847; released Aug. 22, 1848. (He died suddenly at Chilton, Wisconsin, March 3, 1869.)

Mrs. North (Minerva Bryan) Fairfield, Herkimer Co., N.Y.; born Saratoga, N.Y. ly 14, 1815; prof. rel. Aug. 1831; mar. June 7, 1835; emb. Boston, July 20, 1835; died of spasmodic cholera; at Madura, Jan. 13, 1844.

Sarah Wilbur Ashley, born Milan, Erie Co., Ohio June 21, 1839; prof. rel. May 1856; emb. with Mr. Chester and others at Boston Dec. 8, 1858; ar. Madras April 7, 1859; at Madura May 1859; teacher in the Female Boarding School at Madura; released March 15, 1864. Then became the wife of W. Yorke, Esq. of Tirumungalum, principal of the Training Institution of the Christian Vernacular Education Society. She died March 23, 1872. (See obituary notice in Herald, July 1872.)

Rosella Annette Smith, born Lyme, N.H. Oct. 24, 1842; prof. rel. Sept. 1862; studied at Glenwood Seminary, West Brattleboro, Vt.; a teacher in this country; emb. with Mr. Penfield at Boston Nov. 7, 1866; ar. Madura May 1867; visited U.S. 1872. Released 1873.

Martha Sturtevant Taylor, daughter of Rev. Horace S. Taylor, missionary at Mandapasalie; born at Madura, S. India, March 31, 1846; united with her father's church at Mandapasalie 1857; studied at Lake Erie Female Sem. in this country; a teacher here; emb. with her father and others Aug. 10, 1867; reached Madras Dec. 29, 1867. Jan. 1878 in India. Station, Mandapasalai. Returned to U.S. arr. May 24, 1882. Released March 11, 1884. 1888 Painesville, O. Died in Calif. Oct. 9, 1922. (Miss. Herald 1923 page 123)

Sarah Pollock, daughter of Robert Pollock, a Scotsman, but not the poet; Dane Co., Wisconsin, her father's residence; born in Greenock, Scotland, Dec. 9, 1839; prof. rel. Dec. 1856; emb. Boston Aug. 10, 1867; reached Madras Dec. 29, 1867; vis. U.S. 1872; released 1873; 1888 Chicago, Ill.

Carrie Hartley, Hyde Park, Luzerne Co., Pa.; born Glenwood, Susquehanna Co., Pa. Oct. 13, 1834; prof. rel. Scranton, Pa. May 1863; was engaged some years in teaching; emb. Boston Oct. 28, 1868; ar. Madura March 5, 1869. Ret. U.S. 1871.

Mary E. Rendall, daughter of Rev. John Rendall, of this mission; born Madura, So. India, April 18, 1851; prof'l rel. Quincy, Ill. 1861; educated at Quincy Acad. and Quincy College, Ill.; emb. Boston in the Winged Hunter for Madras accompanying her father on his return, Jan. 22, 1870; arr. Madras April 28, 1870; married Sept. 1877 to Rev. Hugh Horsley of the Church Missionary Society.

Elizabeth Sisson, New London, Ct.; born 1843; prof. rel. July 1863, 2nd Cong. Ch., New London; emb. New York for Liverpool to join this mission March 2, 1872; arr. Madras April 16, 1872; Jan. 1878 Stationed at Madura; 1878 withdrew from Mission; 1888 at Bagin, West Berar, Central India. Died Sept. 17, 1934, at New London, Conn.

Henrietta Susan Chandler, dau. of Rev. John E. Chandler; born Madura, So. India Dec. 3, 1855; prof. rel. Canaan, Ct. May 1871; educated at Canaan and Farmington, Ct. Teacher. Sailed New York Aug. 24, 1876; ar. ; Jan. 1878, stationed at Pulney. Died Jan. 26, 1879 at Madura. (See Herald April 1879.

Henrietta Shelton Rendall, dau. of Rev. John Rendall; born Madura 1856; came to U.S. 1865; prof. rel. in Illinois 1867; educated at Oxford, Penn. and at Wellesley Coll.; sailed N. Y. Sept. 1, 1877; vis. U.S. arr. May 18, 1884; mar. Rev. John S. Chandler, July 11, 1887.

Mrs. Judith M. Taylor Minor, widow of E. S. Minor. From 1839-1851, member of Ceylon Mission. Her daughter (Jane E. Minor) mar. John S. Chandler, May 21, 1873. Mrs. Minor returned to India with Mr. and Mrs. Chandler, Sept. 1873. In 1876 she resumed missionary labor under the Board. Station Battalagundu. Returned to U.S. arr. May 18, 1884. Released 1888 Andover, Mass.

Gertrude Abigail Chandler, dau. of Rev. J. E. Chandler of this mission; born Madura, South India, May 26, 1857; prof. rel. Union Church, Boston, Feb. 1871; studied public schools, Boston, and Wellesley College; emb. Oct. 11, 1879; Dec. 1885 at Battalagundu; vis. U.S. arr. Boston, May 12, 1889; mar. in the chapel at Wellesley Coll. June 22, 1892, Rev. J. H. Wyckoff of the Arcot mission; released July 12, 1892.

Mary Pauline Root, M.D., born Providence, R. I. May 22, 1859; prof. rel. 1885; studied Woman's Medical College of Penn. and grad. Mar. 1883; one year in Philadelphia Hospital; emb. N.Y. July 30; arr. Madura Oct. 14, 1885; Jan. 1886 in Madura. Returned to U.S. Released Oct. 13, 1895. Died July 10, 1944.

Eva M. Swift, born Huntsville, Ala. May 3, 1863; member of the First Cong. Ch. Dallas, Texas; studied No. Texas Fem. Coll. and Female Sem., Atlanta, Ga.; emb. May 17, 1884; arr. Madura July 16; Dec. 1885 at Madura; vis. the U.S. arr. N.Y. Sept. 20, 1890; re-emb. N.Y. July 10, 1892; arr. Madura Sept. 12, 1892; vis. U.S. arr. N.Y. Sept. 15, 1895; re-emb. N.Y. Nov. 6, 1895; vis. U. S. arr. Boston June 6, 1902; re-emb. N. Y. Mar. 7, 1903; vis. U.S. arr. Boston, July 25, 1910; sailed July 22, 1911; arr. home Jan. 9, 1922; sailed Jan. 13, 1923; arr. home Nov. 13, 1929; sailed Dec. 20, 1930; retired Oct. 1, 1931 at Bangalore, So.India. Died Nov. 4, 1943 at Bangalore, India.

MADRAS MISSION

Commenced by Messrs Winslow and Scudder of the Ceylon Mission, in the summer of 1836. Relinquished in 1866, after the death of Mr. Winslow, its last clerical member.

MISSIONARIES

Miron Winslow, born at Williston, Vermont, Dec. 11, 1789; prof. rel. Norwich, Ct. Jan. 5, 1811; he was then in business in that place as a merchant. Entered Junior Class, Middlebury Coll., Vt. 1813, and grad. there 1815; grad. Andover Sem. 1818; ord. with Levi Spaulding, Woodward, and Pliny Fisk, at Salem, Nov. 4, 1818; emb. with Spaulding, Woodward, and Scudder, at Boston June 8, 1819; arr. Calcutta Oct. 19, 1819; reached Jaffna, Ceylon, February 18, 1820; took up his residence at Oodooville July 4, 1820; labored there thirteen years. Mrs. Winslow having died, he left that place in Sept. 1833; ar. in the U.S. March 25, 1834; re-emb. with second wife at Philadelphia Nov. 16, 1835; and reached Madras, March 22, 1836. A new mission with special reference to a printing establishment was commenced at that place last named, by Mr. Winslow, Aug. 18, 1836. This was his station and his home, the remaining twenty-eight years of his life. He again visited U.S. March 4, 1856; and re-emb. with fifth wife, at Boston, in the steamer Europe, for Liverpool, Aug. 12, 1857; sailed from London for Madras Oct. 10, 1857, reaching that place early in 1858. He sailed from Madras accompanied by his wife, Aug. 29, 1864; reached Cape Town, South Africa, Oct. 20 and died there Oct. 22, 1864. He was distinguished as a scholar; his great work being the revision of the Tamil Scriptures, and a Tamil and English Dictionary. He received the degree of Doctor of Divinity from Harvard College in 1858. (See obituary notice in Herald, vol. 61, pp. 65-69.

Mrs. Winslow (Harriet Wadsworth Lathrop, daughter of Charles and Joanna Lathrop, see Mrs. Hutchings (Ceylon Mission); born Norwich, Ct. April 9, 1796; prof. rel.

Died at Oodooville Jan. 14, 1835. (See a Memoir of her, by her husband, published 1835)

Mrs. Winslow (Mrs. Carman; her maiden name was Catharine Waterbury, sister of the wife of Dr. John Scudder, below and also sister of Rev. Jard B. Waterbury, now of Brooklyn, N. Y.; born in New York City, Nov. 22, 1798; prof. rel. 1817; mar. April 22, 1835; emb. Philadelphia, Nov. 16, 1835; ar. Madras March 22, 1836; died there of cholera Sept..23, 1837. (See obituary in Herald, vol. 34, pp. 159-163).

Mrs. Winslow (Anne Spiers) her home was Hastings, England; born Cuddalore, in the Presidency of Madras, May 21, 1812; left England, Aug. 1836; mar. Sept. 13, 1838; died Madras June 20, 1843.

Mrs. Winslow (Mrs. Dwight, maiden name, Mary Billings, widow of Rev. Robert O. Dwight of the Madura Mission.) mar. Mr. Winslow March 12, 1845. In January 1846, she left India for the U.S. for the benefit of her health; re-emb. Boston, Oct. 10, 1848; ar. Madras Feb. 20, 1849; died Madras April 20, 1852. (See obituary in Journal of Missions Aug. 1852)

Mrs. Winslow (Ellen Augusta Reed) Boston, Mass.; born Charlestown, Mass. July 11, 1813; prof. rel. Boston, Sept. 1835; mar. Boston May 20, 1857; emb. Boston, Aug. 12, 1857; returned to U.S. 1864; released Feb. 21, 1865; Jan. 1878, residing in Boston. Ditto 1888. Ditto 1908. Died Boston Oct. 12, 1908. (See Dec. 1908 Herald, page 557)

John Scudder, M.D., New York City; born Freehold, N.J. Sept. 3, 1793; grad. Princeton Coll. 1811; prof. rel. Freehold 1810; studied medicine with Dr. Samuel Forman in New Jersey and Dr. David Hosack in New York; received the degree of M.D. in 1814; practiced medicine in New York; embarked with Messrs Spaulding, Woodward, and Winslow at Boston, June 8, 1819; ar. Calcutta Oct. 19, 1819; settled at Tillipally Dec. 17, 1819; at Panditeripo July 4, 1820; ordained

Jaffna May 1801; continued at Panditeripo till Jan. 2d, 1834, when he removed
o Chavagacherry; joined Mr. Winslow at Madras in the new mission there, Sept.
2., 1836; this was his home till the end of his mortal career. He visited U.S.
Aug. 1841; travelled and labored in this country extensively and to good effect;
re-emb. Boston Nov. 18, 1846; ar. Madras March 17, 1847; died of apoplexy at
the Cape of Good Hope, Jan. 13, 1855.

Mrs. Scudder (Harriet Waterbury, sister of the 2nd Mrs. Winslow; born N.Y.City
Aug. 14, 1795; prof. rel. N.Y. 1816; mar. N.Y. Jan. 15, 1816; emb.Boston June 8,
1819; died at Madras Nov. 10, 1849. Dr. and Mrs. Scudder labored in connection
with the Madura mission after their return from America in 1847, until relieved
by the arrival of Dr. Shelton in March 1849.

Samuel Hutchings of the Ceylon Mission labored in connection with the Madras
mission, two years. April 1842 to Dec. 1843 and returned hence to the U.S.1844.
? in Newark, N.J. Died in East Orange, N.J. Sept. 1, 1895.

Ferdinand DeWilton Ward, of the Madura Mission, joined the Madras Mission early
in 1843 and continued therein until his return to the U.S. in 1846. 1877 in
Geneseo, N.Y. Died at Clarens, Switzerland, Aug. 11, 1891. (The proper location
of Messrs Hutchings and Ward and their wives is in the Madras Mission, in
conformity with a rule announced in the Preliminary Remarks of this record.)

John Welsh Dulles, D.D., born Philadelphia, Pa. Nov. 4, 1823; prof. rel. Yale
Coll. 1843; grad. Yale Coll. 1844; Union Theol. Sem. 1847; ord. Philadelphia
Oct. 2, 1848; emb. Boston Oct. 10, 1848; ar. Madras Feb. 20, 1849; returned to U.S.
1853; released Nov. 4, 1853; received D.D. from Princeton Coll. 1871; 1878 in
Philadelphia; Edit. Sec'd Pres. Bd. of Publication. Died at Philadelphia
April 13, 1887.

Mrs. Dulles (Harriet Lathrop Winslow, daughter of Rev. Miron Winslow of this
mission, by his first wife) home Bloomingdale, N.Y.; born Oodooville, Ceylon,

April 10, 1829; mar. Sept. 20, 1848; emb. Oct. 10, 1848; returned 1853; released Nov. 4, 1853; 1888 Philadelphia, Pa.

Isaac Newton Hurd, Big Flat, Chenango Co., N.Y.; born Scipio, Cayuga Co., N.Y. June 9, 1821; prof. rel. Aurora, N.Y. April 1846; grad. Auburn Sem. 1848; ord. Big Flat Jan. 1850; appointed July 8, 1851; emb. Boston March 24, 1852; ar. Madras July 13, 1852; returned to U.S. Aug. 27, 1858; released June 21, 1859; 1371 Carson City, Nev.; 1877, Mento Park, Cal.; 1888 Fresno, Cal.

Mrs. Hurd (Mary Catharine Bassett) born Hector, Tompkins Co., N.Y. Feb. 29, 1828; prof. rel. Sept. 1842; mar. Feb. 4, 1852; emb. Boston, March 24, 1852; died of typhoid fever at Madras Jan. 30, 1854.

Henry Martyn Scudder, son of Dr. John Scudder, was a member of this mission from his arrival in 1844 till his removal to Arcot in 1851. See Arcot Mission. 1878 in Brooklyn, N.Y. Died Winchester, Mass. June 4, 1895.

ASSISTANT MISSIONARY

Phinehas Rice Hunt and Mrs. Hunt, were members of the Madras Mission, from 1840 to the abandonment of the mission in 1866. Since March 1868, they have been connected with the North China mission. Died May 30, 1878, in Peking, No. China, of typhus fever; He was the missionary printer at Madras twenty-seven years. The amount of printing at that establishment from July 1838 to Dec. 1864 was 446, 617, 620 pages, of which 223, 417, 013 were pages of scripture.

ARCOT MISSION

Commenced in 1851, by Henry M. Scudder, after an exploration by him and John W. Dulles in June 1849. It was originally a part of the Madras Mission, but was detached therefrom in 1853. It was carried on wholly by the Scudder family, consisting of five brothers and their wives, and one sister.

The connection between the American Board and the General Synod of the Reformed Dutch Church, established in 1832, having been dissolved by mutual consent in September 1857, the Arcot Mission and the Amoy Mission were forthwith transferred to the Board of Foreign Missions of said church, and the members of these two missions released from their relation to the A.B.C.F.M.

MISSIONARIES

Henry Martyn Scudder, M.D. (D.D.) son of Rev. John Scudder, M.D. missionary to the Ceylon and Madras missions; born Panditeripo in the district of Jaffna, Ceylon Feb. 5, 1822; came young to U.S.; prof. rel. in the Carmine St. Ch., New York, 1840; grad. Union Coll. 1840; Union Theol. Sem., N.Y. 1843; ord. N.Y. 1843; emb. Boston May 6, 1844; ar. Madras Sept. 5, 1844; removed to Arcot 1851; released Sept. 22, 1857; Jan. 1878, Cong. Pastor, Brooklyn, N.Y. Died in Winchester, Mass. June 4, 1895. (See July 1895 Herald, p. 266) It is belived that the case here recorded is the first instance in which the son of a missionary has been sent forth as a preacher to the heathen. (Herald vol. 41, p. 7)

Mrs. Scudder (Fanny Lewis) born Walpole, Mass. 1819; prof. rel. 1832; mar. April 18, 1844; emb. May 6, 1844; Jan. 1878 residing with Dr. S. in Brooklyn, N.Y. Died at Woburn, Mass. Nov. 30, 1900.

William Waterbury Scudder, D.D., son of Rev. John Scudder, and brother of the preceding; born at Panditeripo, Ceylon Sept. 17, 1823; left Ceylon when a child; prof. rel. Elizabeth, N.J. 1837; grad. coll. of New Jersey, Princeton, 1841; Theol. Sem. Princeton 1843; ord. Elizabeth, N.J. July 1846; emb. Boston, Nov. 19, 1846;

ar. Madras March 17, 1847; ar. Jaffna in Ceylon April 1847; stationed at Tavagacherry in Ceylon Jan. 1848; at Manepy 1850; visited U.S. 1852; re-emb. Boston Dec. 13, 1852; ar. Madras May 2, 1853; transferred to the Arcot Mission, now detached from the Madras mission 1853; visited U.S. May 16, 1857; released Sept. 22, 1857; Jan. 1878, pastor Cong. Ch., Glastonbury, Conn. India 1885. Died in Glastonbury, March 4, 1895.

Mrs. Scudder (Catharine Eunice Hastings, daughter of Thomas Hastings, the distinguished professor of Music) born Utica, N.Y. Aug. 22, 1825; mar. N.Y. City Sept. 24, 1846; emb. Boston Nov. 18, 1846; died of cholera on board of a small native vessel, after a visit to friends at Madura, and on the passage across the strait which separates Ceylon from the main land, March 11, 1849. (See obituary in Herald vol. 45, pp. 260-262.) She was a member of the Ceylon, but not of the Arcot mission.

Mrs. Scudder (Elizabeth Oliver Knight) Newark, N.J.; born Boston Sept. 15, 1830; prof. rel. Brooklyn, N.Y. June 1849; mar. Newark, Sept. 23, 1852; emb. Boston for Madras Dec. 15, 1852; ar. Madras May 2, 1853; died Madras Sept. 14, 1854.

Joseph Scudder, brother of the preceding; born Panditeripo, Ceylon, Jan. 14, 1826; came to this country when a child; prof. rel. New York July 1843; grad. Rutgers Coll., New Brunswick, N.J. 1848; Seminary of Ref. Dutch Ch., N. Brunswick, 1851; ord. New York March 1853; emb. June 2, 1853; ar. Madras Sept. 17, 1853; stationed at Arnee in the territory of Arcot; released Sept. 22, 1857; vis. U.S. 1860; 1875, at Upper Red Hook, N.Y. Died Nov. 1876.

Mrs. Scudder (Sarah Anna Chamberlain) Hudson, Ohio; born Sharon, Ct. June 1, 1830; prof. rel. July 1843; mar. April 4, 1853; emb. June 2, 1853; released Sept. 22, 1857. She died at Saratoga, N.Y. Feb. 12, 1870.

Ezekiel Carman Scudder, M.D., brother of the preceding; born Panditeripo, Ceylon (?O, 1823; came to the U.S. young; united with Congregational Church, Milan, Ohio 1846; grad. Western Reserve Coll., Hudson. O. 1850: Seminary of Ref. Dutch Ch., New Brunswick, N.J. 1855; ord. New York, Sept. 16, 1855; emb. Boston Oct. 13, 1855; ar. Madras March 3, 1856; stationed at Chittoor in the Arcot mission; released Sept. 22, 1857; vis. U.S. 1870; 1878 at Upper Red Hook, N.Y.; 1888 San Antonio, Tex. where he died Jan. 31, 1896.

Mrs. Scudder (Sarah Ruth Tracy, daughter of Rev. Miron Tracy, of Hudson, O. and niece of Ira Tracy, missionary at Singapore) born Claridon, Ohio May 20, 1832; prof. rel. May 1847; mar. Aug. 22, 1855; emb. Boston Oct. 13, 1855; released Sept. 22, 1857. 1873, at Upper Red Hook.

Jared Waterbury Scudder, M.D., brother of the preceding; born at the health station on the Neilgherry Hills, on the continent of India, Feb. 8, 1830; united with Presbyterian Ch., Hudson, Ohio in 1847; grad. Western Reserve Coll., Hudson, O. 1850; Sem. of Ref. Dutch Church, New Brunswick, N.J. 1855; ord. with his brother Ezekiel at New York Sept. 16, 1855; emb. with same brother, Boston, Oct. 13, 1855; ar. Madras March 3, 1856; stationed at Arnee, Arcot mission; released Sept. 22, 1857. 1875, returned to America. May 1878, returned to India.

Mrs. Scudder (Julia Clayton Goodwin) New Brunswick, N.J.; born Savannah, Georgia Dec. 10, 1821; prof. rel. June 1850; mar. N. Brunswick Aug. 23, 1855; emb. Oct. 13, 1855; released Sept. 22, 1857. May 1878, ret. to India.

ASSISTANT MISSIONARY

Louisa Scudder, dau. of Ref. John Scudder, and sister of the preceding missionaries born at Madras in South eastern India, April 26, 1837; came to this country early; united with a Presbyterian Ch., N. York City July 1853; emb. with her brother Ezekiel and Jared, Boston, Oct. 13, 1855; ar. Madras Mar. 3, 1856; released Sept. 22, 1857. Sept. 1861, married Col. Sweet of English army. 1878, in Stuttgart, Germany.

www.ingramcontent.com/pod-product-compliance
Lightning Source LLC
Chambersburg PA
CBHW022122290426
44112CB00008B/775